LIBRARY OF RELIGIOUS BIOGRAPHY

Edited by Mark A. Noll and Nathan O. Hatch

The LIBRARY OF RELIGIOUS BIOGRAPHY is a series of original biographies on important religious figures throughout American and British history.

The authors are well-known historians, each a recognized authority in the period of religious history in which his or her subject lived and worked. Grounded in solid research of both published and archival sources, these volumes link the lives of their subjects — not always thought of as "religious" persons — to the broader cultural contexts and religious issues that surrounded them. Each volume includes a bibliographical essay and an index to serve the needs of students, teachers, and researchers.

Marked by careful scholarship yet free of footnotes and academic jargon, the books in this series are well-written narratives meant to be *read* and *enjoyed* as well as studied.

LIBRARY OF RELIGIOUS BIOGRAPHY

available

Billy Sunday and the Redemption of Urban America
  by Lyle W. Dorsett

Liberty of Conscience: Roger Williams in America
  by Edwin S. Gaustad

The Divine Dramatist:
George Whitefield and the Rise of Modern Evangelicalism
  by Harry S. Stout

William Ewart Gladstone:
Faith and Politics in Victorian Britain
  by David Bebbington

forthcoming

Footlights, Flappers, and the Sawdust Trail:
The Life of Aimee Semple McPherson
  Edith L. Blumhofer

Thomas Jefferson
  Edwin S. Gaustad

Charles G. Finney and the Spirit of American Evangelicalism
  Charles Hambrick-Stowe

Emily Dickinson: The Fate of Theology in American Culture
  Roger Lundin

William Ewart Gladstone

Faith and Politics in Victorian Britain

David Bebbington

WILLIAM B. EERDMANS PUBLISHING COMPANY
GRAND RAPIDS, MICHIGAN

Library of Congress Cataloging in Publication Data

Bebbington, D. W. (David William), 1949-
    William Ewart Gladstone: faith and politics in Victorian Britain/
David Bebbington.
        p.   cm.   — (Library of religious biography)
    Includes bibliographical references and index.
    ISBN 0-8028-0152-8 (pbk.)
    1. Gladstone, W. E. (William Ewart), 1809-1898. 2. Gladstone,
W. E. (William Ewart), 1809-1898 — Religion. 3. Great Britain —
Politics and government — 1837-1901. 4. Prime ministers — Great
Britain — Biography. 5. Christian biography — Great Britain.
6. Christianity and politics. I. Title. II. Series.
DA563.4.B43   1993
941.081'092 — dc20
    [B]   93-9642
                                                            CIP

Contents

Foreword

William Gladstone, the eminent British Prime Minister and Christian statesman, embodied contrasting strengths that the modern world has largely divorced. He was both a genuine scholar and a consummate political operative, a thinker and an orator. He devoted his life to the rough-and-tumble world of parliamentary politics yet was acknowledged by friend and foe alike for his commitment to principle and to Christian ideals. He was a man of action and accomplishment, formulating many of the systems still at the heart of the British government, such as the Prime Minister's Question Time. Yet he continually restocked his mind with fresh reading. He was a serious student of Augustine, Homer, and Dante as well as a full range of Victorian intellectuals and poets. He was both the architect of the financial machinery of modern Britain and the author of serious theological reflection. This multifaceted statesman articulated a progressive philosophy of international affairs even as he negotiated the interests of Great Britain in the starkly realistic climate of European power politics.

David Bebbington's biography shows respect but does not idolize Gladstone. Drawing on a wealth of studies of the man and his time, Bebbington explains the course of Gladstone's life and career in a straightforward and judicious manner. Gladstone was no saint and combined in his person strong elements of the passionate, the combative, and the religious. He was also clearly a man of his times. Early in his career he espoused convictions that were predictable given the privileged world into which he had been born. Entering the House of Commons upon his graduation from Oxford in 1832, Gladstone defended a rigidly conservative position in matters religious and political. Over time, however, he hewed an independent and unexpected political course. He switched parties and by the 1860s led the Liberal Party in expanding the franchise, correcting abuses in the administration of Ireland, and establishing a system of elementary education open to all children.

Gladstone's religious convictions, which Bebbington suggests were the mainspring of his life, followed an equally significant evolution. Gladstone was a devoted son of the Anglican Church who also had deep sympathy with the nonconformists of England, Scotland, and Wales. As a youth, he was self-consciously evangelical. Over time, and in concert with the Oxford Movement, he came to support a higher view of the authority and sacramental power of the church, defending, for instance, Anglican teaching about baptismal regeneration. He became a broad churchman, open-minded and flexible in his theological commitments. He espoused the supremacy of the Bible but rejected theories of verbal inspiration. He defended orthodox Christianity from the attacks of the first self-professed "agnostic," T. H. Huxley, who believed that scientific knowledge made traditional religion untenable. At the same time, Gladstone saw no reason to depict Darwinian evolution and revelation at variance. His genius as Christian statesman and reformer may have been that he was a man of unflinching Christian commitment who rarely gave his entire allegiance to any one school of thought or to any one religious party. This biography provides a superb introduction to the interplay of faith and public life in the experience of the versatile William Gladstone.

Nathan O. Hatch

Preface

"I may indeed say," reflected William Ewart Gladstone in his diary at the end of 1883, "that my political or public life is the best part of my life: it is that part in which I am conscious of the greatest effort to do and to avoid as the Lord Christ would have me do and avoid." Gladstone, the subject of this book, was writing while he was Prime Minister to Queen Victoria, for he rose as high as the British political system would allow, but he was most aware of his responsibilities as a servant of Jesus Christ. A religious sense of duty was the mainspring of his public life. He was convinced that, though he was a layman, he must allow his faith to penetrate his daily work. His career is therefore a fascinating case study in the complex relationship of Christianity and politics. Unlike Islam, which offers direct guidance on many political matters, Christianity stands back a little from the public arena, prescribing no structures for the state and laying down moral principles rather than binding rules for the statesman. There is in fact a high degree of tension between Christian faith and political activity. Whereas Christianity is about trust, love, holiness, and forgiveness, politics is about power, legislation, manipulation, and, in the last resort, force. It is no wonder that many have found it difficult or impossible to bring them together. Some have kept the two in different compartments, others have intruded political methods into the religious sphere, and yet others have abandoned in despair either Christian discipleship or public responsibility. Gladstone took none of these paths but instead pursued a long career as a politician while trying to avoid the pitfalls of his vocation. He did not always succeed, but his constant efforts brought him, even in his own day, the aura of a great man.

Gladstone was perhaps the most eminent of eminent Victorians. A master alike of parliamentary debate and public oratory, he governed Britain at a time when the country stood at the apex of world affairs. His decisions, for good or ill, affected the welfare of millions at home and abroad. To an astonishing extent, Britain is still ruled according to the maxims and devices that he introduced: government finance is subject to treasury control; there is a permanent and apolitical civil service entered by competitive examination; there is still a Prime Minister's Question Time in the House of Commons. Gladstone's principles for the conduct of international affairs underlay the structures of the twentieth-century League of Nations and still underlie, though to a lesser extent, those of the United Nations. He probably left a greater political legacy than any of his contemporaries. Nevertheless, as comparison with some contemporary Christians in politics reveals, his achievement was in certain respects limited. Lord Shaftesbury, the evangelical peer who campaigned on behalf of exploited factory workers, refused office in Conservative administrations so that he could devote himself to philanthropic causes. Gladstone, by contrast, was a career politician whose frequent periods in government prevented him from identifying himself with such pressure groups as Shaftesbury championed. Lord Salisbury, the Conservative statesman who alternated with

Gladstone as Prime Minister in his closing years, was an equally devout High Church member of the Church of England who had a sounder grasp of the realities of diplomacy in an epoch of intense international competition. John Bright, the Quaker champion of free trade who served in Gladstone's administrations, surpassed him in two of his areas of strength: Bright was more skillful in bringing his public speeches to a resounding climax and was more devoted to the principle of peace. These men illustrate that there were other formulae than Gladstone's for playing a Christian part in public life. Yet Gladstone came to be seen as the greatest Christian statesman of his day. Over the four decades during which he was at the center of power he insisted that earthly authority must bow before the Almighty. He was unusually explicit in setting political affairs in a Christian perspective.

Gladstone's public avowals of faith created problems of their own. His more cynical opponents saw his religion as little more than a cloak for ambition. Like most politicians, he was assailed for putting expediency before principle, the interests of his party before the welfare of the nation, but Gladstone was particularly criticized for inconsistency, hypocrisy, and humbug. He seemed to blend partisan policies with grand moral claims even when he had recently changed his mind, as his detractors were not slow to point out. On one such occasion, in 1868, Gladstone replied in *A Chapter of Autobiography* that he had adopted a new policy because of altered circumstances rather than altered convictions. His underlying moral premises were consistent, he asserted, even though his views had necessarily changed over time. It was a fair response, and one that a close examination of his career tends to vindicate. Gladstone is remarkable for working out in his early years a political outlook that was conditioned by the Christian faith and then, while maintaining its Christian flavor, for modifying it gradually in the light of experience. Consequently he was transformed in practice from a traditionalist Conservative into a progressive Liberal. He gradually came to urge the centrality of liberty among political values, but all along he continued to relate his views to Christian orthodoxy. Gladstone was struggling to apply his faith to the public life of Victorian Britain.

It will be plain that this book is written by an admirer of Gladstone — though not a wholly uncritical admirer. Shortly after my sixteenth birthday, I bought in a Yorkshire second-hand book shop a copy of the standard three-volume biography of the statesman published soon after his death by John Morley, and it turned out, as indicated by a signed inscription, to be the first set of the volumes issued to the public on the day of publication. The teenager found the detail of Gladstone's life enthralling, but the relationship between faith and politics in his career remained strangely obscure. Later I learned that Morley, though a colleague in the Liberal Party, was an agnostic, and so had been asked by the family not to analyze Gladstone's religious life. Since then, several scholars have made valuable contributions to understanding the statesman's religion, and much of what is novel in these pages falls in that category too. In the main, the book is derivative, owing an enormous debt to previous students of Gladstone, and particularly to Colin Matthew, the editor of the statesman's diaries and one of his latest biographers. Because of its short compass, the book is cursory in its treatment of several aspects of the man. It is a preliminary study for a work in preparation on the mind of Gladstone. In accordance with the conventions of the series, this book cites no sources for its quotations but includes a full annotated bibliography at the end. It is hoped that some readers may find the list useful as they read further round the subject.

Many debts have been incurred during the preparation of the book. Iain Hutchison, Mark Noll, and John Wolffe generously read a draft of the text, making wise suggestions for its revision, and Clyde Binfield and Ian Machin had kindly commented on a preliminary outline. None of them, however, is responsible for what has emerged. I am grateful to Sir William Gladstone, Bart, for permission to quote from unpublished manuscripts, and to Peter Gladstone (another direct descendant) for access to papers in the family home at Fasque, Kincardineshire. The British Academy, the Carnegie Trust for the Universities of Scotland, and the School of Arts of the University of Stirling gave much-appreciated financial support to the project, and Margaret Hendry word-processed the text with her customary professional expertise. Students from my special subject on Gladstone Studies at the University of Stirling contributed more than they knew; my mother-in-law, Margaret Lacey, prepared the index; and my wife, Eileen, provided encouragement, support, and a critical eye. My seven-year-old daughter Anne has already come to appreciate Mr. Gladstone, and so to her, with love, the book is dedicated.

D. W. Bebbington
Stirling, January 1992

A Gladstone Chronology

1809   29 December. Born in Liverpool.
1821   Attends Eton College (to 1827).
1828   Attends Christ Church, Oxford (to 1831).
1832   Great Reform Act.
       Elected M.P. for Newark.
1834   Junior Lord of the Treasury in Sir Robert Peel's first
       Conservative administration.
1835   Under-Secretary for War and the Colonies.
1837   Accession of Queen Victoria.
1838   *The State in Its Relations with the Church.*
1839   25 July. Marries Catherine Glynne.
1840   *Church Principles considered in Their Results.*
1841   Vice-President of the Board of Trade in Sir Robert
       Peel's second Conservative administration.
1843   President of the Board of Trade.
1845   May. Resigns from office over Maynooth grant.
       December. Secretary of State for the Colonies.
1846   Repeal of the Corn Laws.

1847 Elected M.P. for Oxford University.

1848 Year of Revolutions on the Continent.

1850 Gorham Judgment.

1851 Secession of James Hope and Henry Manning from Church of England.
Letters to Lord Aberdeen on misgovernment in Naples.
Death of Sir John Gladstone.

1852 Speaks against Disraeli's budget.
Chancellor of the Exchequer in Lord Aberdeen's Whig-Peelite administration (to 1855).

1854 Outbreak of Crimean War.

1857 Opposes Divorce Bill.

1858 *Studies in Homer and the Homeric Age.*
Lord High Commissioner to the Ionian Islands (to 1859).

1859 Chancellor of the Exchequer in Lord Palmerston's Whig administration (to 1865).

1860 Cobden-Chevalier Treaty with France.

1864 Speaks on Baines's motion in favor of parliamentary reform.

1865 Defeated at Oxford University but elected M.P. for South Lancashire.
Chancellor of the Exchequer in Lord Russell's Whig administration (to 1866).

1866 Introduces Reform Bill unsuccessfully.

1867 Second Reform Act carried by Disraeli.

1868 Prime Minister in his first administration (to 1874).

1869 Irish Disestablishment Act.
Juventus Mundi.

1870 First Vatican Council declares papal infallibility.
Franco-Prussian War.
Irish Land Act.

1874 Disraeli's second administration (to 1880).
The Vatican Decrees in Their Bearing on Civil Allegiance.

1875 Retires as Liberal leader.

1876   *The Bulgarian Horrors and the Question of the East.*
       Homeric Synchronism.

1878   Congress of Berlin.
       Homer.

1879   Midlothian campaign.

1880   Prime Minister in his second administration (to 1885).

1881   Irish Land Act.

1882   Occupation of Egypt.

1884   Third Reform Act.

1885   Death of General Gordon in Sudan.
       Lord Salisbury's first administration (to 1886).

1886   Prime Minister in his third administration.
       Introduces first Home Rule Bill.
       Lord Salisbury's second administration (to 1892).

1890   Fall of Parnell.
       The Impregnable Rock of Holy Scripture.
       Landmarks of Homeric Study.

1892   Prime Minister in his fourth administration (to 1894).

1893   Introduces second Home Rule Bill.

1896   *Studies Subsidiary to the Works of Bishop Butler.*

1897   *The Works of Joseph Butler, D.C.L.* (edited).

1898   19 May. Dies at Hawarden, Flintshire.

1 Gladstone and Victorian Britain

The career of William Ewart Gladstone spanned nearly the whole reign of Queen Victoria. The queen held the throne from 1837 to 1901, longer than any other British monarch; Gladstone entered parliament in 1832 and remained a member almost continuously until 1895. Although he retired about five years before the death of the queen, he had sat in the House of Commons for some five years before her accession. He was a commanding figure in Victorian politics, pursuing what by any standards was a remarkable career. No other person in British history has assumed the highest office in his eighties. He served four terms each as Prime Minister and as Chancellor of the Exchequer in charge of the country's finances. His cabinet colleagues included the Duke of Wellington and H. H. Asquith: Wellington had defeated Napoleon at the battle of Waterloo in 1815; Asquith was to be Prime Minister during the First World War a century later. In the 1830s, Gladstone was a junior minister in a Tory administration dedicated to preserving the existing constitution. By the 1890s, he was the leader of a Liberal administration and preparing a constitutional revolution, the limitation of the powers of the House of Lords. Many people become more conservative with age, but Gladstone, on the contrary, moved from convinced Conservatism to campaigning Radicalism. He was unusual in the evolution of his statesmanship and almost unparalleled in the length of his service in high political circles.

THE MAN AND HIS FAITH

Gladstone was a highly gifted man with a striking appearance. In his earlier years he was slim, erect, and had tousled black hair. In his old age, observers were most impressed by the majestic forehead and the piercing eye that made opponents quail. His mind was sharp, his memory excellent, and from an early age he was trained in precise reasoning. He worked formidably hard, applying himself to paperwork for long hours at a time. As Prime Minister in the 1880s, when he had the help of only four secretaries, he composed some twenty thousand letters a year. He was also an effective speaker. At private dinner parties, he was able to persuade eminent men to change sides on central political issues. Very often in the House of Commons he won over waverers with his skillful presentation and mastery of the facts. His public speeches up and down the country were perhaps his greatest triumphs, firing great audiences with zeal for a cause. Yet Gladstone did not restrict his interests to politics. He was also a scholar, a prolific writer, and a patron of the arts. The second volume of *The English Historical Review,* published in 1887, contains an article from his pen. He was an extremely versatile man.

The subject next after politics that most concerned Gladstone was theology. Even while Prime Minister, he composed articles defending the Christian faith. Religion was transparently the mainspring of his life; his evangelical home gave him a sense of mission that he never lost. During the 1830s, as his theological position developed, he decided that human beings could not be certain of their salvation. Consequently he felt all the more responsibility to be up and doing. Unremitting effort, together with constant vigilance, was essential to ensure the soul's welfare. Gladstone's diary, kept daily from 1825 to 1896, records some of his struggles with temptation. Self-discipline, he realized, was the antidote for his weaknesses, but one deficiency — a lack of personal sensitivity — he never remedied. To have no idea of what was going on in the minds of other people was frequently a serious handicap, not least in political life. Gladstone had another failing, but this one he did normally master: a hastiness inherited from his father. There were, according to Gladstone's wife, two sides to his personality, "one impetuous, impatient, irrestrainable, the other all self-control, able to dismiss all but the great central aim." Gladstone was only too aware of his defects, but by dint of prayer and self-examination he was usually able to keep himself in check. A severe spiritual discipline underlay the great political achievement.

The career of Gladstone therefore illustrates the interplay of Christianity with many aspects of nineteenth-century life. He wanted to enter the Christian ministry and would have done so had his father permitted it. He could well have become Archbishop of Canterbury, but he was destined for parliament instead. And he may well have served the Christian faith better as a statesman than he could have done as an archbishop. A religious professional is often suspected of being self-serving: religion earns him his bread and butter. But few suppose that a politician is devout for the sake of advancement. A person who succeeds in politics provides a more effective advertisement for Christianity. Again, a clergyman has to concentrate on church affairs. Even an archbishop, though to some extent involved in public issues, has to pay most attention to ecclesiastical questions. If Gladstone had pursued a clerical career, even as far as Canterbury, he would not have brought his faith to bear on a wide range of secular matters. By carrying the responsibilities of office, Gladstone was forced to deal with public order and administrative reform, economic growth and international affairs. In each sphere there were links — sometimes strong, sometimes more tenuous — between his Christian convictions and his political practice. As a lay statesman, Gladstone was able to show some of the ways in which Christianity can relate to power.

CONSTITUTIONAL DEVELOPMENT

Gladstone entered parliament at a crucial stage in the evolution of the British state. In the absence of a written constitution, there had been a gradual development of political conventions. Since the Glorious Revolution of 1688, there had been an uncertain balance between crown and aristocracy. Eighteenth-century Britain was undoubtedly more liberal than the major states on the Continent. Other European rulers governed according to their will, but in Britain the monarch had to rule through parliament. No monarch had rejected legislation passed by the House of Commons and the House of Lords since the days of Queen Anne (1702-1714). George I (1714-1727) and George II (1727-1760), both born in Germany, generally left the conduct of state affairs to their leading statesmen. The great aristocrats held authority. But George III (1760-1820) determined to claim power for himself and appointed chief ministers who would pursue policies of the king's choosing. One consequence was the independence of the American colonies, which had reacted strongly against royal despotism. In America the revolutionary solution was democracy, but in Britain there was no question of giving power to the mass of the people. In the late eighteenth century, the main constitutional issue was still between crown and parliament. Should the monarch be able to exercise personal rule, or should parliament determine policy?

A more radical question began to be raised in the 1780s.

Parliament had been unable to check the ambitions of George III in the earlier part of his reign. The government bureaucracy, "Old Corruption," had grown, and with it the burden of taxation. People wanted less government and lower taxes. At the time, a bloc of Members of Parliament, many of them in receipt of crown grants, regularly supported whatever Prime Minister the king selected. The existence of such "placemen" enabled the monarch to pursue his own policies. If more M.P.s were independent of royal favors, some began to think, the House of Commons could resist the king's demands more successfully. Why not alter the membership of the Commons? A section of the political nation began to call for parliamentary reform that would introduce a higher proportion of independent M.P.s. But then, in 1789, the French Revolution broke out in 1789, changing the whole political environment. The uprising against royal government in France created fears of a similar upheaval in Britain. The revolution soon turned against property, against aristocracy, and against the king himself, and in 1793 Britain entered a war against France that amounted to a counterrevolutionary crusade. In such an atmosphere, there could be no tampering with constitutional arrangements. Until some years after the final victory over Napoleon in 1815, parliamentary reform was put in abeyance. The issue did not emerge again until the 1820s. In that decade, when Gladstone as a schoolboy was scanning parliamentary reports in the newspapers, the question of reform returned to the forefront of political debate. After so long a period of delay, many thought it long overdue.

The Whig Party believed in reform. Out of office during nearly the whole period of the French wars and their aftermath, the Whigs were critical of royal power. They had no wild dreams of setting up a republic, but they did want to prevent the crown from abusing its authority. Their supporters, especially merchants and manufacturers in the growing cities, were often the keenest to bring in changes through a reformed parliament. The party in government during the 1820s, increasingly called "Tories," was divided. A few shared Whig hopes for reform, but more thought it was still unwise. A substantial number, the "ultra-Tories," feared that any change would unleash the forces of disorder. The aristocracy might be swept aside, the rabble would seize power, and, as in France, civilization would crumble. It was this apocalyptic vision that alarmed the young Gladstone, then still very much a Tory. As an undergraduate, he was the fiercest foe of parliamentary reform in his generation at Oxford. He argued that reform threatened "to break up the whole frame of society." He passionately believed in monarchy as the God-given mode of government, and he sought to defend the crown against its detractors. He held that aristocrats, men of inherited wisdom who were best fitted to serve the monarch, should continue to exert influence over the House of Commons. There was no need to alter the way in which parliament was elected, since the system had served the nation well for centuries. Why lay violent hands on it now? But all opposition was fruitless: after a protracted struggle, parliamentary reform was carried in 1832. The franchise was more widely distributed, and the placemen dwindled to a tiny band. Gladstone feared for the future. Yet, when offered a chance to enter the newly reformed House of Commons, he was glad to accept. He might be able to resist the most revolutionary schemes of the triumphant Whigs, standing in the breach as a champion of the crown and the established order. Gladstone opened his political career in stalwart resistance to the tide of constitutional change.

LIBERALISM AND NATIONALISM

During his lifetime, Gladstone gradually came to terms with the great political forces sweeping through the nineteenth century. One was liberalism. Stemming in part from the American and French Revolutions, liberalism was a questioning of traditional authority. Freedom of conscience, freedom of assembly, freedom of speech — these and other freedoms were increasingly claimed. The use of force, liberals argued, should be kept to a minimum. Rulers should be called to account, and governments should be subject to law. Gladstone was slowly drawn to the principle of freedom. His university education, he declared in 1878, had failed to teach him what he had since learned: "to set a due value on the imperishable and inestimable principle of British liberty." As his career progressed, Gladstone discovered that his early defense of the inherited constitution was one-sided. Change, he realized, need not be for the worse, and he began to urge broader liberties at home. Whereas he had opposed the Reform Act that extended the franchise in 1832, he proposed a more drastic Reform Bill in 1866 and carried another in 1884. He rejoiced when oppressive regimes abroad became more liberal. British influence in the world, he came to believe, should be exerted on the side of freedom. Although Gladstone never developed a systematic defense of liberalism in the manner of John Stuart Mill's *On Liberty*, his practical achievement was immense. As leader of the Liberal Party in Britain from 1868, he became an embodiment of the cause. Progressives throughout the world regarded him with reverence. President Woodrow Wilson of the United States hailed him as a model. He was more admired by Labour Party politicians in early twentieth-century Britain than any socialist theorist. Gladstone bequeathed a legacy of liberalism to the twentieth century.

Nationalism was another nineteenth-century trend championed by Gladstone. The popular patriotism of revolutionary and Napoleonic France added a new intensity to love of country. People speaking the same language began to look on each other as brothers. They aspired to rule themselves in accordance with their own traditions, throwing off the yoke of foreign oppressors. The various nationalities demanded their own freedom. Consequently, nationalism and liberalism often went together. In 1848 most of the revolutions that flared across Europe were as nationalist as they were liberal. The revolutionaries sought to carve out new nation-states in Germany, Italy, and elsewhere. The rights of peoples became the watchword. As a young man, Gladstone was touched by an intellectual variety of patriotism, and from the beginning to the end of his career he was deeply attached to the institutions of his country. But Gladstone also gradually developed a sympathy for nationalism outside Britain. By the 1860s, he was an ardent supporter of Italian unification. In the following decade, he became the leading defender of the Balkan peoples suffering under Turkish misgovernment. During the American Civil War, he publicly endorsed the Confederacy because, for a while, he saw it as an emerging nation. Gladstone was a champion of small peoples struggling to be free.

LANDED AND INDUSTRIAL SOCIETY

Gladstone's political career unfolded against the background of a country in transition. In his earlier years, Britain was still very rural. As late as 1851, half the people still lived in the countryside. Agriculture prospered during much of this period because a rapidly growing population increased the demand for food, especially cereals. Nevertheless, farmers feared that grain might be brought in from abroad to compete with their own crops. Up to 1846, so long as prices remained reasonable, imports were prohibited. Even after legislative protection was removed, in the 1850s and 1860s, farmers still managed to obtain good prices for their wheat. The buoyancy of agriculture meant in turn that landlords received a healthy income from their rents. The landlords of Britain — essentially the aristocracy and gentry — were secure in their social dominance. The aristocracy, consisting of about five hundred families with hereditary titles and seats in the House of Lords, continued to lead county society. In 1873 the peers of the realm owned 24 percent of the land in England and, in many cases, held great wealth. Aristocrats also dominated politics: they outnumbered commoners in every cabinet until 1886. The gentry, some twenty thousand families without seats in the House of Lords, formed the lower tier of the landed elite. In 1873 they owned 55 percent of English land. A majority of M.P.s in the House of Commons was drawn from the landed classes until as late as 1885. These families expected — and received — deference from lower social groups; it seemed natural that they should be at the head of affairs. And that was exactly how Gladstone saw things. He believed that the nation should be led by those with inherited wealth. He reasoned that they had the leisure to spend time in government and that they possessed sufficient wealth to lift them above the need for self-seeking. In Gladstone's early conservative social theory, the traditional elite had a central place. Although he later modified his views, he never lost his respect for rank.

The rural character of Britain, however, was being altered by the rise of industry. Increasingly it is being recognized that the process of industrialization was a long one. By the start of the eighteenth century, small craftsmen already constituted a large proportion of the population. But industry steadily gathered momentum, surpassing agriculture as a source of wealth early in the nineteenth century. The change was most evident in the northwestern county of Lancashire, where large cotton mills using steam power to manufacture textile goods sprang up on every side. The hinterland of Liverpool, where Gladstone spent his early years, was then the greatest industrial area in the world. Already Britain possessed substantial middle classes, some of them rich through commerce and finance. There were also the professionals — the lawyers, the physicians, the clergy, and the officers of the armed services. To their ranks were now added the industrial entrepreneurs, usually provincial and often unpolished. It was the manufacturers who in the mid-nineteenth century were least content with aristocratic government. They viewed the traditional order as corrupt and inefficient. In his earlier years, Gladstone shared little of their perspective except a desire to see aristocrats do their

9

duty, but his increasing attention to saving money in government closed the gap between them. As Chancellor of the Exchequer, Gladstone pursued policies that, by and large, earned the approval of industry. He was convinced that government should reduce its interference in economic affairs to a minimum. In the circumstances of the day, he rightly judged, that would provide the best environment for industrial progress. Gladstone served a nation growing rich through the triumphs of industry.

The wealth, however, was by no means evenly distributed. Working people received only a small proportion of the new prosperity in their wages. Those who had learned trades, by and large, did not fare too badly, although even they could be thrown out of work when demand for their products fell. Far less secure were the semi-skilled, such as the traditional handloom weavers whose craft was being superseded by the machines of the mills. In hard times, these men could become desperate. The unskilled — casual laborers, messengers, road sweepers, and the like — lived close to poverty at all times. Spouses and children commonly suffered more than the breadwinners, who by custom ate the lion's share of the household's meals. Women, increasingly squeezed out of the labor market, often had inadequate diets. Disease took the lives of many of the children; infant mortality rates were particularly high. In the inner cities that housed so many of the workers in the new industries, there was no pure water and virtually no sewerage. The average life expectancy for a baby in the Liverpool slums born in the same year as Gladstone was twenty-six. Such conditions virtually invited disorder. Almost no working men had the vote, and so agitation was the only way for them to make their demands heard. In the 1840s, when tensions had become acute, Gladstone was involved in efforts to ease the lot of working people. Subsequently he took the lead in proposing to give the vote to sections of the working classes. Their circumstances were inevitably a concern of Victorian politicians.

UNITED KINGDOM AND EMPIRE

Britain had enormous social variations; it also had significant geographical divisions. It is true that from the 1830s railways hugely reduced the time it took to travel from place to place. Nevertheless localities, even within England, held onto their distinctive customs, accents, and loyalties. Wales was generally treated during Gladstone's lifetime as a region, or set of regions, of England. The Welsh language was still spoken by most of the population even at the end of the nineteenth century, but it did not weld Wales into a single unit. South Wales became steadily more industrialized while nearly all of north and central Wales remained rural. Yet Gladstone delighted in Wales, where he lived from 1851 onward. It was one of his administrations that, in 1881, passed the first legislation that applied only to Wales, thus demonstrating that it could be treated as a political entity. There was no doubt, by contrast, that Scotland was a distinct nation. It had been united to England by a common monarch since 1603 and a common parliament since 1707, but many of its institutions remained separate. The legal system and various branches of administration, together with the established church and the education system, were different from those south of the border. Gladstone's ancestry was Scottish, and he lived in Scotland during the 1830s and 1840s. His greatest popular triumph came in 1879, when he delivered a series of political speeches in Scotland that won his party the subsequent general election. With a keen awareness of the preferences of the Welsh and the Scots, he was sensitive to the diversity of the United Kingdom.

That is just as well, for some of Gladstone's most demanding political problems arose in the other part of the United Kingdom, Ireland. Until 1800 the Irish possessed their own parliament in Dublin, subordinate to the British parliament at Westminster but enjoying a wide competence of its own. In that year the Act of Union abolished the Irish parliament and created a United Kingdom of Great Britain and Ireland. The

11

Dublin parliament had been controlled by the Protestant ascendancy, the pro-British elite of the Irish population, and so had not been popular with the Roman Catholics who constituted the larger share of the people. Yet in 1829 an agitation was launched for the restoration of a separate parliament. Repeal of the Union became a persistent Irish demand. For the rest of the century, public order in Ireland was a pressing concern of successive British governments. Some hoped to placate the Irish; others tried to suppress them; still others made an effort to combine conciliation and coercion. Nothing succeeded. It was partly because, in an overwhelmingly rural island, there was often too little work, food, or shelter. It was partly because of resentments against English conquest and dispossession long centuries before. It was partly because of religious discrimination. A few Irishmen turned to revolutionary methods, but more pinned their hopes on pressure through M.P.s at Westminster or the Catholic hierarchy. It was Gladstone who made the most constructive efforts to solve the Irish question. He carried reforms to deal with religious and agrarian grievances, and, when they proved insufficient, he proposed in 1886 to give the Irish a separate parliament once more. His final years in politics were spent advocating this "Home Rule." "My mission," he had once remarked, "is to pacify Ireland." It was an objective that only just eluded him.

At several earlier stages in his career, Gladstone was particularly concerned with the vast British Empire. Trading interests in many parts of the globe had led to the acquisition of territory. India, still technically administered by a commercial company until 1858, was economically important, buying nearly one-fifth of British cotton exports in 1850. Gladstone, however, was much more interested in other British territories overseas. The West Indian colonies, where small numbers of plantation owners presided over slave populations until their emancipation in 1833, were especially important to Gladstone, since his father owned properties there. He paid even greater attention to the other settler colonies. Canada, the Cape in southern Africa, New Zealand, and the Australian colonies were all lands where emigrants from Britain administered microcosms of the mother country. Gladstone applauded their efforts, viewing them as replacements for the lost American possessions. As Colonial Secretary in the 1840s, Gladstone did much to further their interests. Later in the century, he was far less satisfied with the course of colonial development. From the late 1860s, with empire being promoted as a means of bolstering national prestige, Britain and other European states became rivals in the quest for expansion. As Prime Minister, Gladstone presided over several stages in the process, but he disliked the expense, the risk of war, and the sheer bombast involved. In many ways Gladstone was a reluctant imperialist.

CULTURAL INTERESTS

Gladstone's idea of empire, like most of his other views, was shaped by his reading of ancient authors. He was given a thorough education in the classics of Greece and Rome, and it was natural for him to while away spare moments by translating an ancient poet. He published several books on Homer, the earliest poet of them all. Gladstone was well read in most aspects of Western civilization. He was a profoundly bookish statesman, and allusions to a variety of authors studded his speeches. His greatest delight, after the classics, was in writers of his own century. Gladstone was born in a generation deeply swayed by the Romantic movement. He valued the ability of the Romantics to go beyond the cold reason of the eighteenth century to explore the warmth of human experience, appreciating their delight in the dramatic and the supernatural. There was a close link, in fact, between Gladstone's taste and his religion. He always valued most highly the authors who showed a Christian awareness. He also appreciated an ability to evoke the past. Gladstone, like many others affected by Romanticism, had a love of history. But his interests ranged beyond literature to embrace many other arts. He enjoyed choral music and joined his wife in duets; he was a collector of paintings and a patron of artists; and, especially in later life, he frequently attended the theater. Gladstone had the cultural interests of an English gentleman, but he pursued them with greater zest than most of his contemporaries. He brought learning and refinement to the tasks of state.

A CHURCH IN NEED OF REFORM

Even more obviously Gladstone brought his religion into public life. He grew up in the Church of England at a time when many thought it was far more in need of reform than the state. There were conscientious clergymen and regular services in many Anglican congregations during the eighteenth century, but the extent of neglect was alarming. At the beginning of the nineteenth century, about six in ten parsons were permanently absent from the parishes they were supposed to serve. If they bothered to appoint deputies, these curates would receive a pittance while the absentee clergymen would pocket the parish income. A large number of clergy held more than one appointment simultaneously and so were not even theoretically capable of giving adequate pastoral care. The underlying problem was that the ministry provided a cozy career for younger sons of the gentry. Many "went into the church" without any sense of vocation. Their grand aim was to amass a substantial income from ecclesiastical sources. Because the right to appoint to clerical posts was commonly held by aristocrats or gentlemen, young clergy could secure lucrative preferment from family or connections. In 1830, private individuals selected the ministers of about half the parishes of England and Wales. Senior personnel in the church — archbishops, bishops, the deans and canons of cathedrals — were usually appointed by members of the government as advisers to the crown. These offices naturally tended to be rewards for political services, especially in the case of bishops, who automatically had the right to vote in the House of Lords. All stemmed from the position of the Church of England as an established church. It was not just that the monarch was automatically its head. The church was intertwined with the state and so operated according to secular standards. Promoting relations and supporters came naturally. By the early nineteenth century, critics were denouncing the Church of England as corrupt.

Further problems arose from socioeconomic change. Population growth meant that, especially in the large towns, there were too few places in church for the people. There were more church buildings in the south and east of England, regions that had always been richer and more densely populated. In the north, however, industrial expansion swelled the populations of parishes covering huge areas in which places of worship were sometimes located far from the main settlements. It was difficult and expensive to build new parish churches. The Church of England desperately needed to reconstruct itself, but the task was daunting. There were too many vested interests. A clergyman serving a parish church in a growing northern town, for example, might well be reluctant to give up part of his income to endow a chapel near a new factory. He might argue that the property was his in trust for his successors in office. There was no way of enforcing reform, because clergymen had absolute ownership of their parish rights. "Parson's freehold" was immovable. Ultimately the Church of England was unable to set its house in order because it did not govern itself. The bishops did not act together. Convocation, the collective voice of the church, had not transacted business since 1717, and so the church was controlled by parliament. It was only through statesmen concerned for the Church's welfare that there were serious hopes of improvement. In 1835, Sir Robert Peel, the Conservative Prime Minister, made the momentous decision to create an Ecclesiastical Commission to assess the finances of the Church and channel money to where it was needed. Gladstone, a junior minister in Peel's government, applauded the move toward reform. It was one of the reasons why he chose to model himself on Peel as a Christian statesman.

SECTIONS OF THE CHURCH OF ENGLAND

Change in the Church of England, however, came more from below than from above. Peel's initiative could affect only the institutions of the church; it would take a new spiritual movement to bring fresh inner life. Such a movement had in fact begun in the 1730s. For almost a century, the Evangelical Revival had brought individual clergymen to personal faith in Jesus Christ and reintroduced congregations to the old Reformation doctrine of justification by faith. At the same time and in parallel, John Wesley's preaching had created societies of men and women in earnest about salvation. Although most of Wesley's Methodists effectively left the Church of England in the 1790s, the zeal for conversions that they represented continued to fire a growing number of clergymen in the Church. They occupied more and more pulpits during the early nineteenth century, and sometimes patrons erected new church buildings for their ministries. Among the patrons was John Gladstone, William's father. It was therefore an evangelical clergyman that Gladstone regularly heard at home when he was a teenager. The growing boy had already shown signs, according to his mother, of the seriousness expected of those who had been converted. He was marked by the movement's spirituality, which sprang from an awareness of a personal relationship with Christ. He had a profound sense of gratitude for Christ's sacrifice on the cross which had won salvation for mankind, and he had an acute sense of responsibility to his Savior, especially in connection with the use of time. In his younger years, Gladstone was part of the rising tide of evangelicalism, a movement that brought renewed vigor to the Church of England.

Alongside the evangelicals in the Victorian Church of

England there were High Churchmen. Some were of a stiff and traditional variety. This body had been prepared to operate within the unreformed structures of the Church, constantly trying to resist the secular spirit. They had contended that the Church was a divine society that should not be the plaything of politicians but should encourage a strong devotional life through its appointed services. From the 1830s, furthermore, there was a fresh current of High Churchmanship. At Oxford a group of clergymen centered on John Henry Newman urged that the Church of England must rediscover its Catholic heritage. Initially this "Oxford Movement" had no particular sympathy for the Roman Catholic Church. Rather, its adherents believed that the Church should show how different it was from the state by demonstrating its continuity with the early church. Like the Christians of the first few centuries, Anglicans had a commission from Christ. Their teaching was valid because Anglican bishops were in a direct line of succession from the apostles. With this doctrine of apostolic succession, Newman and his circle laid stress on the crucial role of the clergy, the value of the sacraments as channels of grace, and the need for holy discipline in life. The *Tracts for the Times* containing the doctrines of the Oxford Movement gained a wide audience, especially among the younger clergy. "Tractarian" convictions steadily spread. Although he was never a disciple of Newman, Gladstone's mind moved in a similar direction. By the 1840s he believed passionately in the Catholicity of the Church of England. His purpose in life, he believed, was support for "Church principles."

The third section of Victorian Anglicanism was the Broad Church. Those under its umbrella deplored the incessant doctrinal wrangling between evangelicals and High Churchmen. Their own aim was not to render precise statements of dogma but rather to bring Christian teaching up to date. Religion must be shown to have relevance to everyday life. There must be an open door to new knowledge — to philosophy and to science. New trends of thought should not be treated with

17

suspicion but warmly welcomed, and it was hoped that biblical criticism in particular would unlock fresh truth. There were many shades of opinion among Broad Churchmen, ranging from a position approaching the orthodoxy of the other two parties to virtual agnosticism. A large number, like many High Churchmen, were strongly marked by evangelical piety. No two Broad Churchmen thought alike; they were individualists and rarely operated as a party. It was characteristic of their stance, in fact, to deplore parties in the Church. That conviction was shared by Gladstone, who never gave his entire allegiance to one school of thought. In his later years, while retaining his evangelical dynamism and his High Church Catholicity, he adopted more of the open-mindedness of the Broad Church. The great task at hand, he held toward the end of his life, was the defense of basic belief in God. He was unwilling to condemn fresh Christian ideas because of the Broad Church tinge to his thinking.

Gladstone was more aware than most Anglicans of other Christian traditions. His Scottish background gave him personal acquaintance with Presbyterian worship. In Scotland the Established Church had repudiated bishops in the seventeenth century and preferred more austere orders of service. But when in Scotland, Gladstone was a devoted son of the Episcopal Church. Although it was proud of its distinct High Church traditions, the Scottish Episcopal Church was the counterpart of the Church of England and so seemed to Gladstone his natural spiritual home north of the border. Despite his High Churchmanship, from the 1860s onward, Gladstone took pains to appreciate the Nonconformists of England and Wales. The Methodists, the Congregationalists, and the Baptists, together with a number of smaller denominations, constituted almost half the English churchgoers at mid-century, and in Wales they were dominant. The Methodists sprang from the Evangelical Revival; the Congregationalists and Baptists, though originating around the start of the seventeenth century, had also grown because they adopted evangelical beliefs in the eighteenth.

These Dissenters from the Church of England eventually came to be Gladstone's most dependable political allies. Britain also contained a significant number of Roman Catholics. During the nineteenth century, the tight-knit Catholic groups who inherited their faith from pre-Reformation times were overwhelmed by an influx of poor immigrants from Ireland. Gladstone had dealings with their leaders and also with Roman Catholics abroad, particularly scholars whom he sought out on his travels. His time on the Continent even brought him into personal contact with the Greek Orthodox. Gladstone was a man with wide knowledge of the Christian world and wider sympathies.

GLADSTONE THE STATESMAN

The rich tapestry of Victorian Britain provides a backdrop for the career of a fascinating statesman. Gladstone stands out as a central figure in a variety of fields. He is a good example of the qualities that a liberal education could produce in the early nineteenth century. He carefully worked out his views on political and ecclesiastical questions during his first decade in parliament. He survived, though with great personal pain, the collapse of his early ideals, and then, in mid-career, he took up the reform of government policies and institutions with typical vigor. He was responsible for the colonies and, with his cabinet colleagues, for overseas relations in general. At the same time, Gladstone was pursuing scholarship and leading a contented family life. From 1868 he was the Prime Minister of an energetic government, and over many years he campaigned for the welfare of small nations. He became the revered leader of the Liberal Party, and at the end of his active career he threw his energy into seeking justice for Ireland. He also spent much of his time in old age defending the faith. Gladstone brought his Christianity into every sphere. His mind was shaped by a Christian worldview, and his actions by a Christian conscience.

His spirituality disciplined the awkward aspects of his personality and channeled his restless dynamism into productive channels. Gladstone's religion enabled him to wield power not with total success but with a remarkable degree of integrity. A close friend in his later years, Lord Acton, is well known for the comment that power tends to corrupt and absolute power corrupts absolutely. Gladstone did not possess absolute power, but the great power he did exercise never corrupted him. His faith was a strong preservative.

2 Gladstone's Formation, 1809-1832

The Gladstone family came from Scotland. William's father was a Lowlander, his mother a Highlander. There was no drop of his blood, he used to remark in later life, that was not Scottish. In the century before he was born, the spirit of enterprise was rising in Scotland. In the Lowland belt between Glasgow and Edinburgh, new industrial ventures were springing up, and agricultural improvement was penetrating even the fringes of the Highlands. Adam Smith was composing his classic text on economic growth, *The Wealth of Nations* (1776). Possibilities of prosperity were in the air, especially in the growing centers of population. So, in about 1746, it was natural for Gladstone's future grandfather Thomas, then a teenager, to move from the family home in the small town of Biggar, Lanarkshire, to the bustling port of Leith, Edinburgh's outlet to the sea. There he became a modestly successful corn merchant. Devout and thrifty, he was an elder in the Church of Scotland who never felt he could afford to employ a clerk in his firm. He passed on his business acumen to his oldest son, John.

WILLIAM EWART GLADSTONE

GLADSTONE'S FAMILY

It was John, William's father, who dropped the final *s* from the family name "Gladstones" to make it "Gladstone." He was a man of vigor, decision, and resolution. He possessed, according to William, "a large and strong nature, simple though hasty, profoundly affectionate and capable of the highest devotion in the line of duty and of love." John put most of his enormous energy into expanding his father's corn business into a substantial mercantile empire. Born in 1764, John moved seventeen years later to Liverpool, the rapidly growing seaport of Lancashire. In the era when Lancashire cotton goods were increasingly being exported to the whole world and the burgeoning population of the county called for a variety of imports, there was no better place for making a fortune. John built up interests in shipping and eventually bought West Indian sugar estates worked by slaves — whose condition of life William was to defend in parliament on behalf of his father during the 1830s. In 1795, John Gladstone was worth about £16,000; by 1828, the figure was over £500,000; and it was to rise higher still. Many a contemporary peer of the realm owned property worth no more than £200,000. Even if, in William's view, his father's talents deserved much greater rewards, John ranked as one of the most successful of Liverpool businessmen.

John Gladstone set about establishing a social and political position worthy of his economic achievements. By 1811, he was building a large home, Seaforth House, in the countryside outside Liverpool. There he could imitate the life-style of the landed gentry even if he was too tainted with commerce to be accepted among them. He became the leading local supporter of George Canning, M.P. for Liverpool from 1812 to 1822, who had already held office as Foreign Secretary. Canning's beliefs in efficient administration and the relaxation of restrictions on trade recommended him to John Gladstone. He, in turn, gained standing in the vicinity from being Canning's lieutenant, and was disappointed not to secure the nomination to parliament as Canning's successor. Nevertheless, John did become an M.P., sitting for Lancaster from 1818 to 1820, for Woodstock in Oxfordshire from 1820 to 1826, and for Berwick-upon-Tweed from 1826 to 1827, when he was unseated for election offenses committed by his supporters. He made little mark in the House of Commons except, predictably, as a contributor to committees on commercial affairs. Business loomed too large in his mind for him to find much fulfillment in politics, but he was determined that one of his sons should play the part in public affairs that he had been unable to assume. His political mantle was to fall on William.

The future Prime Minister's mother, born Anne Mackenzie Robertson, was John Gladstone's second wife. His first wife, who had suffered from infertility and rarely enjoyed good health, had died in 1798 after only six years of married life. The wedding of John and Anne took place in 1800. She came from Dingwall, a small town on the east coast of Ross-shire in the north of Scotland, and was descended from Highland gentry on both sides of the family. For John to secure her hand was itself a sign that he was moving upward in the world. Anne was mild, beautiful, and, like John's first wife, frequently an invalid. She attempted to keep detailed household accounts, but she had to give up the effort in the later 1820s because of insufficient strength. She eventually died in 1835 at the age of sixty-three. Between 1802 and 1814 she bore six children. William was the fifth, arriving on 29 December 1809. Despite being distanced from his mother by nurses and servants — or perhaps because of it — William developed a warm devotion toward her tinged by a tender regard for her weakness and a deep respect for her spirituality. It was Anne Gladstone who shaped the Christian upbringing of her son.

The oldest child of the marriage, another Anne, was like her mother in character as well as name, both sensitive and sensible. She enjoyed play-acting and novels such as Sir Walter Scott's *Ivanhoe*, and she maintained a cheerful spirit despite perennial ill health that led to death when she was only twenty-six. Anne was William's godmother, and, as we shall see, she took seriously the resulting responsibility for his spiritual welfare. William's three brothers had very different personalities. Thomas, born in 1804, found the burden of his father's expectations hard to bear and proved a disappointment both at school and in parliament. Robertson, born in 1805, inherited his father's aptitude for business, identified with the public concerns of Liverpool, and rose to become its mayor. John Neilson, born in 1807, entered the Royal Navy at thirteen, retired before he was thirty, and lived as a country gentleman in the southern county of Wiltshire. In part because the three older brothers were born within three years of one another and William was born three years later, none of them was especially close to him during childhood or, for that matter, in later life. William had more to do with his younger sister Helen, born in 1814. She shared the tendency to poor health of the female members of the family but possessed something of William's combative intelligence. William was to be hard on Helen when he believed that she failed to show either his mother's patience in suffering or his own dedication to duty.

FAMILY RELIGION

The religion of the home was a paramount influence on the young William. At the end of his life, Gladstone recalled his early environment as strictly evangelical. The Gladstone household received *The Christian Observer*, the monthly periodical of the evangelicals in the Church of England. William's father erected new churches in Liverpool and selected evangelical clergymen to serve in them. William could remember being taken to seek advice on clerical appointments from Charles Simeon, the doyen of the evangelical party in the established Church. Nevertheless John Gladstone was no straightforward evangelical Anglican. As a Scot newly arrived in Liverpool, he had naturally attended the Presbyterian chapel, which by this date was well advanced on the path toward Unitarianism. He subsequently helped to found a separate Scottish Presbyterian cause in the town, and in Scotland during the 1830s he contentedly worshiped in the local congregation of the Church of Scotland. It is clear that John Gladstone was not a dedicated Anglican; nor was he exclusively attached to evangelical belief. "In religion," he wrote in his later years, "but not in politics, I am no party man." His doctrinal views were less precisely formulated than his son might have wished. William noted anxiously in his diary that in 1848 his elderly father stated that "he had endeavoured to live in the performance of his duty and he placed his trust in the 'compensation' which had been made for our sins." The son was distressed when in his last hours the doughty Scotsman declined to receive holy communion but called for a plate of porridge. Christian convictions were hardly the mainspring of his life. Though commanding unreserved respect, John Gladstone did not influence his son's religious views in any significant measure.

The evangelical tone of the home was set by William's mother. It was Anne, for instance, who prevailed on her husband to establish churches with evangelical clergymen. "My dear and noble mother," wrote William in old age, "was a woman of warm piety." Her home town of Dingwall had been noted for its zeal for vital religion since at least the beginning of the eighteenth century. Anne's mother came from Episcopalian stock, but her immediate family was molded by the traditions of Highland Presbyterian faith. Puritan spirituality was still flourishing in and around Ross-shire when Anne was growing up. A saving knowledge of Christ was held to be so important that individuals were called to direct their chief efforts to determining whether or not they possessed it. Salvation must not be assumed, for that might imperil the soul. There must be scrupulous and sustained introspection to determine whether or not a person was enjoying a state of grace. Anne Gladstone undoubtedly modified this inheritance when she came south. She sat under ministers, Congregational as well as

Anglican, who taught that faith brought assurance of salvation more readily in its train. Yet she maintained links with the piety of the north. It is not surprising that she was delighted to learn that William, when a young man at university, had formed a compact with his younger sister Helen to point out defects of Christian character in one another. Careful self-examination of this kind was to be a prominent feature of Gladstone's life.

An older William was able to recall only a few religious incidents from his childhood, such as praying to be spared the loss of a tooth when he was about six and asking his mother in church when a sermon would be over. He was much struck by *Pilgrim's Progress* when about ten. At about the same time, in 1818 or 1819, Anne Gladstone wrote to a friend that she believed her son William to have been "truly converted to God." In the evangelical Anglican circles that Anne had entered, conversion was normally conceived to be a gradual process, and so William's experience is unlikely to have been a sharp crisis. Although there is no other direct evidence, it seems likely that he was committed to Christian discipleship from boyhood. By the age of twelve or so, he was teaching local children in a Sunday school erected by his father. His own early education was conducted by William Rawson, the Seaforth clergyman, who preached what he called "the pure Gospel of Jesus." Rawson was an uninspiring teacher and a sober personality who always read his sermons from a written text. William's chief memory of the man was his anti-Catholicism. At sixteen, William noted in his diary, in the combination of French language and Greek script he reserved for entries that might prove embarrassing if discovered, that, according to Rawson, Roman Catholics ask pardon of saints and angels — "a piece of bigotry & I grieve to say untruth." In old age, when his judgment was colored by political antagonism, Rawson used to claim that Gladstone as a pupil had been unoriginal and verging on the insane. It is clear that the two developed no rapport and that Rawson did not exercise a significant influence over the boy's religious development.

ETON COLLEGE

In 1821, at the age of eleven, William was sent to Eton College. Standing in a village on the bank of the Thames opposite Windsor Castle, Eton could claim to be the premier school of England. Founded in the fifteenth century by King Henry VI, the school had trained the sons of the aristocracy and gentry ever since. By sending his sons to Eton, John Gladstone was taking the best possible step toward ensuring that they might enter the nation's elite. Like other great schools of the time, Eton operated on the principle of anarchy tempered by terror. The boys were allowed their "liberties" — that is, almost unrestricted freedom to organize their own affairs. The hope was that the pupils would learn responsibility, self-reliance, and an ability to govern a small commonwealth that would give them experience for public affairs in later life. The reality was that many were victims of the cruel whims of their seniors. Occasionally there were deaths and even full-scale rebellions against the teaching staff. In order to contain the potential chaos, the headmaster would indulge in frequent floggings that marked him as the seat of ultimate authority. Punishment was usually excessive and commonly arbitrary. The school was a terrifying place for a young child.

Thomas, William's oldest brother, had found Eton bewildering and distasteful. In 1818 he had been swept into a rebellion against a case of victimization by Dr. Keate, the headmaster, and was close to expulsion. Robertson stayed for only two years before moving on to Glasgow for a commercial education. John Neilson avoided Eton by entering the navy. Consequently, when William arrived, only Thomas, five years his senior, was still at the school. Every young entrant was assigned to an older boy as a fag, a personal servant who could be given menial tasks. William was cushioned during his first year against the harsher side of Eton life by being fag to his brother. By the time Thomas left, in the summer of 1822, William was better able to cope with the brutalities of the place.

27

He was flogged only once in his school career, for the offense (perhaps characteristic) of refusing to report on the misdeeds of others. Nevertheless he shared Thomas's dislike of Keate. On one occasion, when taken by his father to the London church of the immensely popular preacher Edward Irving, he had the satisfaction of observing from a spacious gallery pew the undignified efforts of his headmaster to stand upright in the crowded aisle below. Unlike his oldest brother — and in large part thanks to him — William gradually emerged as one of the pupils for whom the license of Eton provided the first of life's opportunities for self-fulfillment.

The curriculum, which consisted overwhelmingly of the Greek and Latin classics, had its effects on the young Gladstone. Translation work cultivated an eye for detail, an awareness of the nuances of language, and a capacity for recall that were to stand him in good stead for life. He developed a liking for a number of classical authors and laid the foundations for a critical appreciation of their work. At school he also learned French; mathematics was relegated to the home. Crucially, in 1825, he was elected to the Literati Society, the school debating society organized by a handful of the abler senior boys. Contemporary political topics were prohibited, but with some adroitness the members contrived to express their partisan views through discussion of past issues, especially the constitutional struggles of the seventeenth century. Gladstone's views were formed largely by the liberal Tory principles of George Canning, his father's political hero. Camaraderie developed with other members, such as James Milnes Gaskell and Francis Doyle. Gladstone admired Gaskell, "a sort of walking Hansard," for his political enthusiasm. Doyle, who later became Professor of Poetry at Oxford, also shared literary interests with Gladstone, helping him edit *The Eton Miscellany,* a collection of schoolboy pieces. Literature more than politics formed the chief bond with Gladstone's closest school friend, Arthur Hallam. The son of the greatest Whig historian of his generation, Hallam was two years junior to Gladstone but already showed precocious signs of the genius that Tennyson was to celebrate in the poem *In Memoriam*. In this circle, Gladstone's natural eloquence blossomed into a formidable power of debate. Sharp intelligences sharpened each other.

School religion was a formality. Chapel was admittedly frequent — twice on Sunday, twice on every holiday, once on every half holiday. But the building was drafty, the prayers mechanical, and the sermons (according to one contemporary) "mumbled and jumbled by aged men with weak, smothered voices." Gladstone's diary, begun when he was fifteen, confirms that the preachers were often almost or entirely inaudible. Religion in the curriculum was treated as an extra chance for translation practice. Keate read five minutes weekly from one of the sermons of Hugh Blair, the preacher of the late eighteenth century most celebrated for his style. Blair was one of the Moderates in the Church of Scotland whose elegant teaching concentrated on classical themes of human duty rather than on the biblical drama of salvation. Gladstone began to examine Blair for himself and gradually realized the discrepancy between what he was reading and what he believed. In an entry in his diary for May 1826, he wrote that Blair "seems to have formed too high an estimate of our character as 'men'." Gladstone, now aged sixteen, was engaging in discussion of religious themes with his friends. "Long talk with Hallam," he had noted in the previous month, "on subjects of Trinity, Predestination, &c." Despite the unpropitious circumstances at Eton, Gladstone was beginning a lifetime's reflection on the great doctrines of the faith.

There were two school religious events that impinged significantly on William. The first was the service of confirmation conducted by the Bishop of Lincoln in 1827. Virtually the whole school was confirmed, since in a vast diocese, episcopal visits were infrequent. Despite perfunctory official preparation, William took the occasion seriously, praying that he might be helped to keep the baptismal vows he was assuming. The second event was William's first communion. The school custom was that members of the sixth form, and only the sixth form, received communion, whether or not they had been confirmed. It so happened, however, that Gladstone was sent up into the sixth form shortly after the confirmation, and consequently his first communion took place only a month later. Circumstances therefore encouraged him to value the sacrament. He recorded taking part thankfully in this "work worthy of Divine Grace." The religion of Eton just managed to avoid being a nullity for him.

THEOLOGICAL EXPLORATION

One result of William's confirmation was a deepening of his relationship with his sister Anne, his senior by seven years. Anne clung for support in physical weakness to her devotional life, nurtured by the standard evangelical authors of the time such as Hannah More and Thomas Chalmers. As William's godmother, she took a special interest in his confirmation, the occasion when he accepted personally the promises she had made on his behalf at his baptism. She sent him a letter following his confirmation that he described in reply as "instructive." Although he was sincere in appreciating her guidance, Anne felt a little uncomfortable at his use of this term. "I was far from meaning to teach you," she wrote back, "who could well teach me in most things." Thereafter she tried to treat William as an equal while having at the same time a sense of living vicariously through her clever brother. They became closer. During the following summer, William regularly drew Anne about in an invalid chair, and by the end of the vacation she would not allow Thomas, Robertson, or Helen to take his place. When William left Eton in December 1827, it was Anne who made most of the arrangements for him to go to a private tutor for several months in preparation for university. William, for his part, canonized Anne as a model of Christian patience in affliction.

The private tutor was an evangelical clergyman, J. M. Turner, Rector of Wilmslow in Cheshire and soon to be Bishop of Calcutta. His chief service to Gladstone was probably to improve his mathematical skills. From Wilmslow, Gladstone moved in the spring of 1828 to join his family at the townhouse his father had bought in Edinburgh. Turner had urged Gladstone to get in touch with his Edinburgh friend and fellow evangelical Edward Craig. It was Craig who introduced Gladstone to a controversy that was to perplex him for more than a year. The theological issue that divided evangelicals most sharply from other Anglicans was the question of baptismal regeneration. *The Book of Common Prayer* of the Church of England includes a prayer that pronounces a newly baptized infant to be regenerated. Upholders of High Church teaching therefore insisted that all who receive infant baptism are born again and hence that they need no subsequent rebirth to begin the Christian life. Evangelicals were equally convinced that people did not become Christians until they experienced self-conscious conversion. Embarrassed by the phraseology of the Prayer Book, evangelicals sometimes contended that the prayer for the newly baptized should be understood merely as expressing confidence that regeneration would take place in the future. It was an issue of vital importance to evangelicals, since it called into question their right to preach for conversion within either the Church of England or the Episcopal Church in Scotland. The controversy stirred England from time to time between 1812 and 1851. It flared up in Scotland in 1825 when James Walker, who was soon to become Bishop of Edinburgh, published a sermon against evangelicals who were rejecting baptismal regeneration. Edward Craig, the clergyman whom Gladstone visited frequently during his stay in Edinburgh, wrote a response on behalf of the evangelicals. Within a week of first meeting Craig, Gladstone was delving into the debate.

He found the issue compelling. On the one hand, he was predisposed to side with Craig in rejecting the concept of baptismal regeneration, but on the other hand, his respect for authority, ingrained alike by home and faith, inclined him to give weight to the text of the Prayer Book. At home in Liverpool after his stay in Edinburgh, Gladstone studied an article on an earlier stage of the English controversy in the Tory periodical *The Quarterly Review*, taking careful note of the opinions of the fathers of the Church of England cited there in favor of baptismal regeneration. The question was by no means settled in his mind when he left Liverpool in August to take up residence at Cuddesdon, just outside Oxford, for further mathematical coaching. The whole matter, he believed, called for further exploration.

Why did the subject loom so large? The explanation is that William was considering becoming a clergyman and so pondering whether he, like Craig, should summon the baptized to conversion. There can be little doubt that the seed of Gladstone's aspiration to enter the ministry was sown by Craig. A year later, in response to a request for guidance from William, Craig replied that it was proper for college students to hold prayer meetings, since it was the practice of pious natives in Tahiti and Sierra Leone. "Prayer in college chambers," he went on, "is a good preparation for serious & efficient ministration in the church of God." Clearly he assumed that Gladstone was intending to become a clergyman. On the last night before he left home for Cuddesdon, William mentioned his hopes for the future to his sisters. Two months later, the fourteen-year-old Helen blurted out to Thomas, the oldest brother, that she knew William wanted to enter the ministry. Thomas was hurt that William had not told him, and it must have been Thomas who passed on the information to their father. John Gladstone, already nursing political ambitions for William, warned him not to choose a profession too early. Although William obediently refrained from mentioning the subject again for eighteen months, the responsibility of serving God in his church was to remain his ideal for life.

CHRIST CHURCH, OXFORD

Gladstone entered Christ Church, Oxford, in October 1828 and was to remain for just over three years. Christ Church was the largest and richest of the Oxford colleges. Founded by King Henry VIII in the sixteenth century as a training school for the royal service, over the centuries it had produced more eminent statesmen than any other college. About half the graduates of the whole university, however, went on to be ordained as clergymen, and Christ Church was a particularly clerical institution. Its college chapel doubled as the cathedral church of the diocese of Oxford, and the clergy who served the cathedral as canons were automatically senior members of the college. Nevertheless, as William reported to his father, the chapel service was "more shamefully profaned here than at Eton." In any event, William was to be more influenced by his contemporaries than by any religious teaching given in the college. Arthur Hallam had gone to Cambridge, and so Gladstone's relations with him necessarily became more distant. All the same, a number of other close Eton friends, including Francis Doyle and (from Gladstone's third term) Milnes Gaskell, joined him at Christ Church. They formed one of the circles in which Gladstone regularly spent his leisure time, often attending wine parties or going for long walks. Beginning in October 1829, this group formed the nucleus of an essay club called, after Gladstone, the "WEG." Its members met regularly for discussion of broad cultural topics. In February 1830, Gladstone proposed proposed at the club — unsuccessfully — that philosophy is superior to poetry. By the strange magic of universities, Gladstone and his friends provided an education for each other.

The formal curriculum was almost as classical as that at Eton, but the emphasis shifted from literature to philosophy. Gladstone was fortunate in his tutor, Robert Biscoe, who instilled in him an esteem for Aristotle that never faded. Nevertheless, there was no automatic deference to the opinions of the Greek philosopher whose dominance in Oxford studies had recently been reinstated. Aristotle's views were compared not only with those of other ancient writers but also with those of such modern authorities as John Locke and William Paley. Gladstone gained a capacity for precise reasoning, abstract but analytical, that was to mark his contributions to Commons debates. He worked hard, often spending up to twelve hours a day at his desk. Efforts to win prizes for classical scholarship during his career at Christ Church were frustrated, but an academic triumph came at the close of his university studies. In the autumn of 1831 he won a double first, a much-coveted but rarely achieved distinction. One of his first-class honors was in classics; the other, for which he engaged in intense study at the very end of his course, was in mathematics. The answer to one of his philosophy questions survives, for, with typical Gladstonian thoroughness, he wrote it out in summary on the evening of the examination. A long and elaborate essay on Aristotle's teaching, it is carefully organized and highly persuasive. Gladstone fully deserved his success.

A preoccupation with theological questions was particularly strong during William's first year at Oxford. He was drawn into a different circle, the hearers of Henry Bulteel, the Curate-in-Charge of St. Ebbe's Church in the city. Bulteel was on the extreme wing of the evangelical movement, a high Calvinist who in 1831 was to denounce the Church of England as apostate and eventually settle down to preach on Strict Baptist lines. On the Sunday of the first of his visits to hear Bulteel, conversation with the undergraduates of his congregation led Gladstone to jot down some good resolutions: "Not to eat more than one fish at any dessert. . . . Exclude from conversation devil, defile, 'whoring rant', 'infernal'." Friendships in this group made him long for a nobler life. He was also influenced by the theology he heard from the pulpit of St. Ebbe's. Bulteel's teaching had no place for baptismal regeneration, which to the Calvinist preacher seemed a soul-destroying heresy. Gladstone realized that he could no longer remain undecided about the doctrine. He determined to pursue the subject to a conclusion.

He had hardly begun the task, however, when he was summoned home, in February 1829, by the shattering news of Anne's death. Over the Christmas vacation, William had read John's Gospel daily with both his sisters. Now the older one was dead, and William thought of her as a "departed saint." On the day of her funeral, William took up J. B. Sumner's *Apostolical Preaching* to examine the question of baptismal regeneration. Sumner was a respected leader of the evangelicals who had accepted the dedication of Edward Craig's chief collection of sermons. Anne had shared delight with William when, in the summer of 1828, this evangelical champion was made Bishop of Chester, their own diocese. Unusually for an evangelical, Sumner asserted that baptism could regenerate, though he added some cryptic reservations. Gladstone copied out the passage, which went far toward neutralizing the growing sway of Bulteel's teaching over his thought. With memories of Anne's esteem for the bishop hovering around him, Gladstone was persuaded by Sumner's views on baptismal regeneration. Ironically, it was an evangelical author that had nudged his mind out of its evangelical groove. A close reading of the sixteenth-century Anglican divine Richard Hooker during the following summer served to confirm his opinion. It was the beginning of William's divergence from the religious views of his boyhood.

For the remainder of his time at Oxford, however, Gladstone remained an adherent of the evangelical school. Like Sumner, he was eager to accommodate his views as closely as possible to those of other sections in the Church of England, but he continued with typical evangelical activities, attending prayer meetings, reading religious newspapers, and attempting personal evangelism among his friends. He harried Doyle and Gaskell with spiritual talks till midnight. He took Doyle to hear Rowland Hill, an undenominational evangelist, at New Road Baptist Chapel, after which, he recorded, the conversation was "not very direct." He persuaded them both to visit the village of Toot Baldon, about seven miles outside Oxford, to hear a Mr. Porter, whom, as Gaskell told his mother, Gladstone declared to be the finest preacher he had heard. "This Mr Porter," Gaskell went on, "preaches for an hour and a half, so Doyle and I think that if we arrive in time for the sermon, it will be as much as the bargain." Gladstone also took Doyle regularly to the university sermon on Sunday afternoons — until the day when Gladstone fell asleep. The next week Doyle assured Gladstone he could sleep as well in an armchair as at the university church, and Gladstone (he recalled) troubled him no more. Still entertaining the hope of becoming a clergyman, Gladstone remained earnest in matters of faith.

It turned out to be Gaskell the political enthusiast who exerted a decisive influence over Gladstone the intending minister of religion rather than the other way around. Gaskell characterized Bulteel's followers as "only fit to live with maiden aunts and keep tame rabbits." He redirected Gladstone's energies into the university Debating Society, later called the Oxford Union. Unlike its Eton equivalent, this society made contemporary politics the staple of its debates. Gradually public affairs became William's primary fascination outside his work. It was through the Debating Society that he gained sufficient confidence to differ from his father. John Gladstone supported the Duke of Wellington as Prime Minister from 1828 to 1830, but William questioned Wellington's ability to govern the country. In November 1830, at an excited meeting of the Debating Society, William carried a motion of no confidence in Wellington by one vote. William also disagreed with his father about reform. John Gladstone was prepared to see modifications in the machinery of parliamentary representation, but William, with the passionate intransigence of youth, was utterly opposed to any such change. He feared that reform of the state would be followed by reform of the Church, and who could tell what would then ensue? In the spring of 1831, the predominantly Whig government of Earl Grey that had succeeded Wellington's administration introduced a Reform Bill into parliament. Gladstone was determined to do all in his power to resist the alteration of a system of representation that went back to the fifteenth century. He prepared posters for public display, organized an anti-reform petition from members of the university, and spent day after day in drumming up support. In May, as president of the Debating Society, he delivered a powerful speech denouncing reform as likely to undermine the social order. He emerged from university a much higher Tory than his father.

A POLITICAL CAREER

It was the speech against reform that sealed William's future. In the summer of 1830 he had once more raised with his father the possibility of becoming a clergyman, but John Gladstone had asked that the matter should be left in abeyance until William's graduation. It was a shrewd move. William's inclination toward politics steadily grew, fostered by his debating experience and his passionate aversion to parliamentary reform. In January 1832, the month after his second examination triumph, he determined to follow his father's wishes by undertaking a political career. In a sense he was not abandoning his earlier intentions, for it remained his purpose to advance the interests of the Christian faith. He was now convinced, however, that the defense of the Church in the public arena was the pressing need of the hour. As the reform crisis came to its climax in the spring of 1832, Gladstone was completing his education by traveling the Continent with his brother John Neilson. At Milan, on 6 July, he received a letter from a Christ Church friend, Lord Lincoln, conveying an astonishing offer. The Reform Act had passed; a new parliament was to be elected; would Gladstone accept nomination for the constituency of Newark from Lord Lincoln's father, the Duke of Newcastle? Lincoln had conveyed his admiration for Gladstone's anti-reform speech to his father, an arch-opponent of tampering with parliament, who had decided that Gladstone would make a fine defender of his point of view in the House of Commons. There was no need for an M.P. to live in a constituency or to have had any previous connection with it. Whoever received the Duke of Newcastle's nomination — despite reform — was almost certain to be elected. So it happened. On 13 December

1832, Gladstone was declared M.P. for the Nottinghamshire market town of Newark. It was the start of the most distinguished parliamentary career in British history.

The young politician possessed enormous advantages deriving from his early years. Eton and Christ Church gave him intellectual interests and analytical skills. They also provided a circle of contacts in the governing classes and, perhaps equally important, the social confidence necessary to move among them. Yet, as contemporaries were to remark, if he was Oxford on the surface, he was Liverpool underneath. Gladstone was molded primarily by his home. His energy, ambition, and sheer capacity for hard work came from his father. John Gladstone was forty-five when William was born and an immensely busy man, so there was little intimacy between father and son, but the gap between them generated in William a desire to emulate and to please. John also pointed his son toward politics. William could not avoid attaching weight to contemporary issues when family meals often resembled public debates. Although there were sisters in the home, education in all-male institutions helped ensure that the opposite sex was long a mystery to William. His ideal of womanhood was created by his mother and his older sister Anne, both of them remarkable for gentleness and patience in suffering. He was closer to them than to his father, especially on matters of faith. It was through his mother's influence that he early became a committed Christian. His personal religion deepened with the years, flowing in evangelical channels. Self-scrutiny, which was part of its mainstream, is evident in many of the daily entries in his diary. While still an undergraduate, however, William made a declaration of intellectual independence in religion by accepting the doctrine of baptismal regeneration. In a similar fashion, he moved away from his father's flexible Toryism toward a much more rigid variety. He saw public life as a sphere in which the established order in church and state had to be defended. Gladstone turned to mastering the theory needed for his chosen role.

3 Gladstone's Thought, 1832-1841

Gladstone spent much of his first parliamentary decade erecting an intellectual framework for his approach to life. His appetite for work found an outlet in mental activity as well as in the debates of the House of Commons. The habit of using spare moments to read or jot down ideas was deeply ingrained. He used the technique he had learned at Eton and practiced at Oxford — of taking extensive abstracts from more demanding books — with as much zeal as if he had still been in full-time education. Gladstone believed the political battles being fought around him were fundamentally ideological. The tendencies of the age that he abhorred were the result of principles that had to be combated. A revitalized Tory Party would have to stand for a set of convictions or else be swept away by the tide of history. Crucially, the Church of England had to be defended against threats to despoil it or to sever its connection with the state. A theoretical justification was essential for its effective protection. Meanwhile William was wrestling with his own understanding of the Christian faith and, in particular, a fuller

grasp of the doctrine of the church. Serious and sustained reflection was the priority of the decade.

THE WHIG PARTY

Throughout the 1830s, the Whigs, the victors in the parliamentary reform struggle of 1831-1832, remained in power. With
varying degrees of conviction, they believed in continuing a
program of reform. Some, even of those in the administration,
had been Tories in the 1820s, and their commitment to reform
was tempered by caution. On the opposite wing of the party
were others who had been kept out of government, avowed
Radicals who wished to press on with dismantling the antiquated state apparatus. The core of the administration and its
supporters inherited the purest tradition of eighteenth-century
Whiggery with "civil and religious liberty" as their watchword.
There had to be constant vigilance, they believed, lest the crown
and its officials restrict freedom by exceeding their powers. The
constitution had to be upheld, but it was their duty as
enlightened men to keep a check on royal authority. In the 1820s,
King George IV had so distrusted them that there was no question of their taking office; only under the more liberal William IV,
who became king in 1830, had they been able to come into their
own. Yet the Whig leaders were far from inclining to democracy.
Many of the greatest aristocrats, men of vast acres, were Whigs,
and family connections counted for a great deal in the higher
echelons of the party. A large proportion of its support came
from electors who, as the tenants of Whig landowners, voted in
accordance with the wishes of their social superiors. Only in the
growing towns and cities, overwhelmingly supportive of reform
in the early 1830s, were the party's adherents outspoken in their
demands for change. Much backing for the Whig administrations came from Scotland and Ireland, where Daniel O'Connell
combined patriotic claims with advanced Radicalism. Equally
loud calls for change came from the Dissenters of England and

Wales, Whigs or Radicals almost wherever they possessed a vote. Their pressure ensured that the question of continuing reform was inextricably bound up with religion.

Many of the more traditional Whig leaders tended to secular views. Lord Melbourne, Prime Minister briefly in 1834 and again from 1835 to 1841, maintained a disarmingly skeptical stance that was part of a broader relaxed attitude toward men and affairs. But a younger generation, touched by the rising religious temperature of the era, contained many sincere Anglicans who believed the state and its agencies existed to promote the moral welfare of the people. Typical was Lord John Russell, Home Secretary in the later 1830s and a man with whom Gladstone was to have many dealings. Russell and his contemporaries saw toleration as a key Christian value and education as a powerful agency of change. They were eager to modify the state Church in a manner that would avoid antagonizing Dissenters and, ultimately, bring them back into its fold. A few Dissenters, almost entirely urbane Unitarians, shared similar ideals. The great body of Dissenters, however, had different objectives. The Test and Corporation Acts that had theoretically excluded Dissenters from town councils were repealed in 1828. In the wake of the Reform Act, they saw no reason why remaining restrictions should not be thrown off, and beginning in 1834 many of their leaders called for the separation of church and state. The Whig administration was entirely averse to so drastic a constitutional change, but it did propose remedies for a few of the most urgent Dissenting grievances. The relationship of the Church of England to Dissent was near the center of political debate in the 1830s.

The sharpest controversies of all surrounded the Church of Ireland. About 80 percent of the Irish population belonged at least nominally to the Roman Catholic Church. About 9 percent were Protestant Dissenters, chiefly concentrated in Ulster. Only about 11 percent adhered to the Church of Ireland, which, since the Act of Union passed in 1800, had been constitutionally part of the Church of England. The anomaly of a state church cater-

41

ing to only a small minority of the population was one of the grievances dwelt on by Daniel O'Connell and his followers, who wished to repeal the Union. In order to placate the repealers, the Whigs greatly desired to reduce the causes of ecclesiastical friction in Ireland. Accordingly, in 1833, Gladstone's first parliamentary session, the government introduced a bill to reduce the costs of the Church of Ireland by merging several of its dioceses. It was this measure that provoked a sermon of denunciation from John Keble and kindled the flame of the Oxford Movement. To Keble and his friends it seemed that the state was committing sacrilege by laying hands on the Church. Gladstone agreed, and although there was no hope of defeating the overwhelming Whig majority, he spoke sharply against the bill in the Commons. Once the act was put into operation, there was a prospect of surplus revenues for the Church of Ireland. When the Whigs proposed to use the money for Irish schools that taught nonsectarian Christianity rather than the distinctive doctrines of the established Church, the cry of sacrilege went up again. In fact, the changes never actually produced a surplus, but the debate over what should have been done with it had it arisen sufficiently agitated parliament in 1834 and 1835 to cause a secession from the government benches to the Tory opposition. Gladstone warned the Commons in 1835 that the use of the Irish Church surplus for secular purposes was a precedent that would ultimately lead to "the recognition of the Roman Catholic religion as the national one." The generous instincts of the Whigs on religious questions were anathema to him.

THE CONSERVATIVE PARTY

Gladstone's Tory Party had been reduced to a small remnant by the wave of reforming enthusiasm at the 1832 general election. The pressing task for the party was to undertake the sort of reconstruction that would enable it to hold power again. The Carlton Club, founded in 1832 as a social center for Tory partisans in London, rapidly evolved into the organizational fulcrum of the new party. William joined as soon as he entered the House of Commons. From 1834, the leader of the party was Sir Robert Peel, an able statesman and a dynamic administrator. His address to his constituents in 1834, the Tamworth Manifesto, was an attempt to shake off the party's image as a set of disgruntled opponents of reform. Peel aimed to win over moderate opinion, even to the extent of conciliating Dissent. The preferred title for the party was henceforward to be "Conservative," not "Tory." Peel wanted the party to conserve existing institutions, in part by judicious concessions. Despite the leader's efforts to refurbish the party's image, its appeal remained substantially what it had been ever since the French Revolution. It naturally drew support from the landed interest and the Church of England, the twin pillars of the existing social order. It was also backed by most of the financial and professional middle classes together with the dependents of all the other groups. Conservatism stood for property rights, the due authority of the crown and House of Lords, and the maintenance of the established Church. If its program was essentially defensive and many of its supporters looked back wistfully to more stable times, it nevertheless managed to regain confidence steadily during the 1830s. The party's leadership was eager to make up lost ground.

Gladstone was marked out by Peel as one of the talented young men who would make the revival possible. In 1834, William IV dismissed his Whig ministers, the last occasion on which a monarch rather than the electorate determined the fate of an administration. Peel was summoned to form a government. Gladstone, though only twenty-five at the time, was appointed a Junior Lord of the Treasury, an office in which he was directly responsible to Peel. He remained there barely a month before being made an Under-Secretary of State to the Colonial Secretary, Lord Aberdeen. It was hoped that the family's experience of trade with the colonies would stand Gladstone in good stead. There was too little time, however, for him to make an impact as a member of the government. The Conservatives had no majority in the Commons, and, lacking the ability to carry legislation, Peel recognized after less than four months that there was no point in persevering in office. For the next six years the party was in opposition. During this period, Peel chose to sustain the Whigs in government, if necessary by voting for them against their own Radical supporters, until his party had mustered sufficient strength in the country to bring it victory at the polls. He was a politician who always appreciated the need for flexible tactics. But that was not Gladstone's way in these years. Although for purposes of debate he was able to put across a case temperately, at heart he was intransigent. Gladstone saw the reinvigorated Conservative Party primarily as a means of shoring up the Church of England. "Reflection shows me," he wrote in his diary during 1840, "that a political position is mainly valuable as instrumental for the good of the Church; and under this rule every question becomes one of detail only." An unflinching partisan, William was in hearty sympathy with his party's objective of conservation all round, but he defined his purpose more precisely than most of his colleagues. With defense of the Church his overriding aim, Gladstone was ideologically committed.

WIFE AND HOME

As he participated in the annual parliamentary sessions that stretched from February to the summer, Gladstone lived in central London in a bachelor flat. Increasingly he felt a loneliness that could be remedied only by finding a wife. The task proved more difficult than entering a political career. The problem was not that William remained aloof from entertainments and social gatherings, even if he did wonder whether dancing was at all proper for a Christian. It was rather that he was unable to form relaxed friendships with women; his earnestness frightened them away. Between 1835 and the beginning

44

of 1838, he seriously courted two well-born Scottish ladies, Caroline Farquhar and Lady Frances Douglas, but achieved nothing except his own frustration. In 1836 he also met Catherine, the sister of an Eton and Christ Church friend, Sir Stephen Glynne. Two years later William fell in with her party on a tour of Italy and, in less formal holiday circumstances, a friendship blossomed. It took Catherine five months to accept his proposal of marriage. The wedding took place on 25 July 1839, the bride being twenty-seven and the groom twenty-nine. There can be no doubt that Catherine was good for William. Her natural vivacity brightened his home life, which now included rather more of the music she enjoyed. They were bound together by their common faith and, beginning with the birth of their first son on 3 June 1840, by a growing family. William had found the person with whom he wanted to share his life.

Home for Gladstone during the 1830s and 1840s meant Fasque, the country estate that his father had bought in Kincardineshire, south of Aberdeen in Scotland. Regularly in summer he escaped from London to spend the months until Christmas at Fasque. It seemed an idyllic haven where, in August 1836, he "found all well — haymaking, cherries & gooseberries ripening." It was a place for recuperation, not least after his first two failures in love before he had found Catherine. He frequently sang after dinner; he enjoyed conversation with the family and visitors; and he played billiards, backgammon, and whist with his father and chess with his wife. He undertook long walks and drives through the surrounding countryside. He had a liking for outings on the lake with the ladies, and he went shooting with the men, though he enjoyed that less (in 1842 he was to lose his left forefinger in a shooting accident). Although he took an interest in horses, he never attained much skill as a horseman, despite his perseverance. When Francis Doyle, later William's best man, came on a visit to Fasque in 1834, the two went riding for a day. William's lively chestnut mare frustrated his attempts to open a gate and, even though Doyle could easily have unlatched it for him, William insisted on spending forty minutes until he had mastered the mare and opened it himself. At Fasque, Gladstone also fulfilled paternalist responsibilities toward his father's tenants. He surveyed their needs for the estate manager, examined the ground for almshouses, and visited cottagers who were ill, elderly, or dying. Often he prayed with them. On one occasion he took his first baby to see a woman in her nineties, noting that she was nearly two hundred times the infant's age. Gladstone put down deep roots in the Scottish countryside.

William had more leisure for study when he was at Fasque. In the throng of business in London, he would rarely pass a day without a bloc of serious reading, but at Fasque he aimed for a total of nine hours' reading and writing each day. On occasion he could manage eleven hours or even more. Sometimes he was forced to call a halt because his eyesight was too weak, and then he would warn himself against the self-indulgence of reading. Yet he rarely took up a book without a specific end in view. The coverage of his reading was wide. Contemporary affairs at home and abroad necessarily occupied a good deal of time. He enjoyed history and biography. He read and reread Boswell's *Life of Johnson*. After completing a life of George Washington, he pronounced him "a Roman in wonderful degree." Ancient literature was another favorite field. He noted, for example, having borrowed a volume of Plato from a neighbor. Modern philosophy was represented by, among others, Francis Bacon. And there was more modern literature in his reading than might be expected. He gave Sir Walter Scott's novel *Waverley* "a fresh perusal by way of a treat." Henry Wadsworth Longfellow's poems, he concluded, "show decided genius." William Makepeace Thackeray's novel *Vanity Fair* received a more qualified verdict: "a work of genius, and to be admired in some other respects." Theology, in works great and small, was constantly being devoured. In the late 1830s, he particularly applied himself to the systematic study of Augustine, the greatest of the fathers of the Western church. Gladstone was perpetually stocking his mind with fresh reading.

UTILITARIANISM

Gladstone's program of study was designed to extend the inquiries he had begun at Oxford. As an undergraduate, he had come to see in utilitarianism a dangerous foe to be resisted. Best known today as the core of the moral theory taught by the philosophers Jeremy Bentham and John Stuart Mill, utilitarianism had become widespread in Gladstone's day, not least because a variety of it was officially taught in the University of Cambridge. Utilitarianism often also appeared in the pages of *The Edinburgh Review*, the journal of the more advanced and more intellectual Whigs. This school of thought, as Gladstone perceived matters, provided the rationale for the political practice of his parliamentary opponents. It held that the rightness of an action can be rationally assessed only by an analysis of its effects. All the consequences for each of those affected by the action must be taken into account. The undesirable consequences could be quantified in terms of the amount of pain produced for anybody involved; the desirable consequences, on the other hand, could be weighed in terms of the amount of pleasure that was generated. The sum totals of pain and pleasure could then be compared. If there was more pain than pleasure, the action should be avoided: it was wrong because it would detract from the overall happiness of the human race. If it would produce more pleasure than pain, however, the action was to be commended: it was right because it would add to human happiness. The greatest happiness of the greatest number was the goal of this system of ethics. It was a briskly straightforward approach to moral issues designed for the age of reason. The implication was that institutions should be reformed so as to maximize their efficiency as agencies of happiness. Political structures and established churches needed to be remodeled along rational lines — a conclusion that was anathema to Gladstone. Institutions hallowed by tradition, he believed, should not be dismantled by the pride of one generation. Accordingly, Gladstone set out to scrutinize the premises of the system. He elaborated in his private papers a critique of the whole intellectual approach.

His first objection was that the utilitarian scheme left the will of God out of consideration. In the Bible, human beings are summoned first of all to turn from their wicked ways. Since holiness, not happiness, is the supreme value in life, repentance from sin must take precedence over maximizing pleasure and minimizing pain. Hence there was a flaw, Gladstone insisted, at the heart of the utilitarians' case. The principle of utility could not be valid, for the proper goal of any action should be to promote not the greatest happiness for the greatest number but, as he put it, "the greatest holiness of the greatest number." Furthermore, he argued that, contrary to the utilitarian view, the morality of an action is determined by its motive, not by its effects. According to most ancient schools of ethics as well as Christianity, the intention of the agent determines the rightness of the deed. Even though there might be calamitous consequences, the agent possessing a sound motive should enjoy a clear conscience. And he argued that the utilitarian criterion for evaluation was also mistaken. Pain is not in itself an evil, and pleasure is not intrinsically a good; rather, both pain and pleasure are morally neutral. They may enhance the strength of an experience, but they do not determine its moral value. No doubt with his mother and sister in mind, William asserted that the pain of suffering can exalt the moral quality of endurance. He condemned utilitarianism for being at odds with Scripture and the ablest writers on ethics.

SOCIAL AND POLITICAL THOUGHT

The philosopher from whose armory Gladstone drew his chief weapons for the campaign against the utilitarians was Aristotle, whose works he had studied most closely at Oxford. He took the assertion that pain and pleasure are morally neutral, for instance, directly from this authority. Aristotle molded Gladstone's mind just as he had shaped the thinking of Thomas Aquinas in the thirteenth century. Consequently, Gladstone's social and political theory belongs to the same natural-law tradition as the thought of Aquinas. According to Aristotle, society and government are natural institutions. They exist not because of arbitrary human whims but because of the needs of human nature for company and authority. What is natural, Gladstone and other Christian disciples of Aristotle down the centuries have agreed, is divine. The Creator fashioned human beings to live in communities. Hence there is a strong corporatist emphasis in Gladstone's thinking. The individual is virtually inconceivable as a unit in the abstract, since each one is part of a family and of a nation. It could not be objected, according to Gladstone, that conditions in the modern world prevented the application of ancient thought to the present. He held that the recently developed rapid communications rendered the modern state scarcely less tightly knit than the small city-state of Aristotle's day. One ought to begin political theorizing not with the individual but with the community.

Another influence pointed Gladstone in the same direction. His mind was deeply swayed by the currents of Romantic opinion flowing in his day. During the first thirty years of the nineteenth century, received taste had been challenged and then superseded by the Romantic poets. William Wordsworth, Samuel Taylor Coleridge, and their contemporaries had broken with the literary forms of the past in order to give vivid expression to their personal experience. In 1833, Wordsworth visited Gladstone, who especially admired his poem "The Old Cumberland Beggar." Coleridge was particularly influential in transmitting the social theories of the Romantics to subsequent generations. They influenced educated opinion later in the nineteenth century in a number of directions. The Romantics characteristically discerned the divine in the world of nature, emphasized the corporate dimension of human life, and nurtured a nostalgia for the glories of the past. Gladstone was swept along by this wave of new attitudes. He showed from time to time a sense of God's presence in the natural world, although this faculty was less developed in him than in many of his contemporaries. More important for the substance of his thought were the corporatism and the nostalgia he drew from such writers as Coleridge. He began to think of the state not as a mechanism, as the eighteenth century had normally conceived it, but as an organic body, a natural entity rooted in the past and growing over time. Coleridge reinforced Aristotle in persuading Gladstone that a nation is not an aggregation of individuals but a community with a character of its own. Furthermore, Gladstone displayed a strong historic sense, an awareness of the distinctiveness of particular eras. Like many in his generation, he looked back to the Middle Ages — a period brought to life by Sir Walter Scott — as a time not of deplorable Gothic gloom but of laudable solidarity in the Christian faith. Traditions going back to the medieval period, as Thomas Carlyle was soon to teach, were likely to have value for the nineteenth century. A respect for tradition in national life gave backbone to his Toryism.

In private memoranda of the 1830s, Gladstone described the resulting political thought as a "moderate monarchism." Like Tories in previous ages, he believed in supporting the existing constitution with the crown at its apex. He held that the inherited pattern of government possessed the sanction of nature and, ultimately, of God. The monarch had to be restrained from tyranny, however, because government is meant to exercise paternal responsibilities for the welfare of its subjects. While the popular will was not (as the Whigs maintained) the creator of government, it did serve to provide a check on the potential for abuse of power. There was no question of a contract between governors and the governed, according to Gladstone, since an individual does not share in deciding his relations with society. He can no more choose the form of government than select a family in which to be born. Gladstone dismissed the American practice of popular sovereignty as a fiction. He argued that because the Senate and House of Representatives are elected at substantial intervals, democracy functions for only a brief while around the elections. Most of the time these representatives ignore the wishes of the people who choose them. Where a mixed constitution embraces a monarchy and a popular assembly, a third element is called for to hold the balance between the other contending powers: the aristocracy. For a state to be healthy, the aristocracy must play a prominent part in public affairs. Wealth, leisure, and education accorded peers particular responsibilities which they were bound to discharge at a national level as well as on their own estates. In Gladstone's view, rank was another of the natural features of society, and that made egalitarianism a foolish and unattainable nostrum. Gladstone's overall theory was traditional but not too doctrinaire. It was sufficiently flexible, for example, to allow for future expansion of the role of the popular will. During the 1830s, however, Gladstone's political thought, a Romantic flowering deeply rooted in natural law, was highly conservative.

THEOLOGICAL DEVELOPMENT

Gladstone's churchmanship was affected by similar influences — the Romantic spirit of the age and the communitarian ideal of the ancient world. "Community," he wrote, "is the very essence of the Church of Christ." As the 1830s advanced, he laid increasing emphasis on the corporate expression of the Christian faith, on "Church principles." Romantic sensibility also created the atmosphere in which the Oxford Movement began to propagate a revitalized High Churchmanship in those years. The same Whig threats to the Church of England that Gladstone resisted in the Commons provoked a group based in the University of Oxford and headed by John Henry Newman to issue a series of tracts urging the clergy to assert the sacred dignity of their office. The church was a divine creation, argued these Tractarians, not a plaything of politicians. The

apostolic succession of the bishops from the very days of Christ
ensured that his teaching was still authoritatively transmitted
to the faithful. The sacraments of the Church were to be revered
as God's means of conveying grace. And his servants were to
show great holiness of life. It was a compelling ideal that animated, for instance, Henry Manning, an Anglican clergyman
who was later to become a Roman Catholic cardinal, and James
Hope, an ecclesiastical lawyer. Because of their devotion to
Church principles, Manning and Hope became Gladstone's
two closest friends in the late 1830s and 1840s. Yet Gladstone
was never wholly at one with the Oxford Movement. Although
he learned from Newman's writings, Gladstone was troubled
that the leaders of the movement undervalued the state connection of the Church of England. He disliked even more the
Oxford tendency to form a party in the Church. Gladstone
could not wholly favor a group of men who fostered a divisive
spirit within the Christian community. He sympathized with
the Oxford Movement from a distance rather than joining its
ranks.

During the 1830s, Gladstone's personal understanding of
the Christian faith developed slowly from its earlier evangelical
form toward a pattern more consonant with a higher churchmanship. His acceptance of baptismal regeneration had led
him to reconsider his attitude to conversion while he was still
at Oxford. Conversion, he decided, is not the beginning of real
faith but rather the gradual transformation of the behavior of
a believer. Next he reflected on the evangelical practice of
openly discussing religious experience. Questions addressed to
others about their spiritual state, he realized, can sometimes
violate sensitive feelings. Yet inward experience is an authentic
dimension of the Christian faith. What is not essential, he concluded in 1834, is the necessity of assurance. It is unusual for
Christians to be given supernatural confidence of their being
among those who will be saved. In fact, he believed that salvation might be truly possessed but then subsequently lost.
Gladstone rejected the Calvinist view that God's power is a

guarantee of heaven to true believers when he decided that free will is a divine gift. Even a careful reading of Jonathan Edwards, the great American Calvinist theologian of the previous century, failed to convince him otherwise. Gladstone grew to believe that only the ordinances of the church anchored the soul in a state of grace. Holy communion increasingly became the heart of Gladstone's spiritual life. By 1837 he was asserting the real presence of Christ in the elements of bread and wine when they are received by the communicant — though he did not yet go so far as to maintain that Christ is truly present in the elements before they are received. In his pilgrimage of faith, Augustine was his chief guide. It was through this father of the church that he retained a firm grasp on the doctrine of grace. Human merit, he was always to assert, has no part in making sinners acceptable to God. Notwithstanding the evolution of his theology, the kernel of his early piety, a sense of unworthiness in the divine presence, was to remain with him for life.

FIRST TWO BOOKS

Gladstone summed up his new religious position in a book published in 1840 entitled *Church Principles Considered in Their Results*. It is a massive tome of 528 pages, together with three appendices. In the book he contrasts four ecclesiastical positions. First there is the "cold theology of the last century," the counterpart of the utilitarianism in ethics that he rejected so firmly. The dominant theological stance in the eighteenth century had been tainted with rationalism, a downgrading of the supernatural. This view he dismissed as superficial. To the second position, that of the evangelicals, he gave his qualified endorsement. The evangelicals had recovered half the divine truths — those relating to the individual — that had been neglected by most others in the eighteenth century. But the evangelicals had themselves been infected by rationalism in denying the corporate dignity of the church and in failing to attach importance to the sacraments. To the third position, that occupied by the Tractarians, Gladstone granted almost entire approval, although he was careful to distinguish it from his own, the fourth position. He upheld the ancient Catholic teachings about the visible church, the sacraments, and the apostolic succession, but he remained eager to conciliate Dissenters who did not. Furthermore, he recommended the Church of England as a potential center of reunion for the whole church. He cherished the hope that national branches of the Roman Catholic Church would throw off their allegiance to the pope and so become virtual equivalents of the Church of England. Although Gladstone was careful to insist that, as a layman rather than a clergyman, he held no authority to teach the Christian faith, *Church Principles* is the book of an enthusiast for new views. It outlines the Anglican convictions that Gladstone was to uphold for half a century and more.

Two years previously, Gladstone had published a book that gained far more attention than *Church Principles*. The earlier work, *The State in Its Relations with the Church*, was a treatise on a leading topic of the hour. It reflected Gladstone's practical experience in parliament of rebutting Dissenting claims and Whig assaults on the Church of Ireland. It may also be seen as the culmination of his reflection on moral and political theory during the 1830s. The book is a defense of the principle of church establishment on Gladstone's corporatist premises. The nation, he argued, is "not an aggregation of individuals; it is a collective body." It is therefore capable of moral action, possessing a conscience that enables it to profess truth in religion. The state as much as the individual is bound to accept God's revelation embodied in the church. The state must therefore choose to support the church professing the truth. It follows that it is wrong for a government to give money to religious bodies outside the state church. This policy, often called "concurrent endowment," was already being practiced by the Whigs. Schools in England as well as Ireland were receiving state grants even though they did not teach Anglican doctrine. Gladstone was utterly opposed to such laxity. Yet, as the Whig writer Thomas Babington Macaulay pointed out in a trenchant review, Gladstone did not follow his principles to their logical conclusion. He ought, according to his critic, to have advocated persecution. "Why not roast dissenters at slow fires?" asked Macaulay. The state should have enforced religious conformity as it had tried to do under the Stuart kings. Gladstone argued in favor of toleration on the grounds that coercion is ineffectual and that there is no divine warrant for the use of force in religion. It is a concession that reveals the practical politician. In his book, as in his political activity in the 1830s, Gladstone was no fanatic. *The State in Its Relations with the Church* was nevertheless a dashing assertion of the principles that fired the young politician, still only twenty-eight when it appeared.

Principles were important for Gladstone. The politician, he realized, was habitually so immersed in detail that he was in danger of forgetting his fundamental convictions. The essential remedy was the systematic examination of underlying premises in which Gladstone spent a large portion of his first decade in politics. He took up with zest the hard thinking for which Oxford had trained him and his personality fitted him. He carefully dissected the utilitarian basis of Whig policy with the aid of Aristotle and Coleridge. Augustine seconded by Newman gave him a living theology that seemed to make sense of his Christian experience. He took pains to integrate his social theory and his theological convictions, and the result was a distinctly Christian perspective on public affairs. His view was conditioned by time and circumstances, but that is an unavoidable limitation on thought. Gladstone's Christian understanding had the great merit of engaging fully with the secular developments of his day. Although Peel feared that Gladstone's first book might ruin his career by chaining him to an untenable position, Gladstone's views about monarchy, aristocracy, and the wisdom of inherited institutions set him firmly within the ranks of Peel's revitalized Conservative Party. Nor was it foolish of Gladstone to see the Conservatives as the defenders of the Church. Peel himself, when in office in 1835, had set up the Ecclesiastical Commission to review the anomalous allocation of revenues within the Church and so to draw the sting of the most popular argument for disestablishment. The party was preparing itself to gain a majority in the House of Commons and then wield power. A new Conservative government might be expected to make ample provision for the future safety of the Church of England. That was Gladstone's hope when a general election was called in 1841. His powerful sense of mission, now encouraged by his wife, made him look to the Conservative Party as the future savior of church and state.

4   Gladstone and Crisis, 1841-1851

The Conservatives under Sir Robert Peel were returned to office by the electors in 1841. The government faced critical times. Industrialization had brought prosperity to Britain, but the poor, huddled together in the insanitary dwellings of the new urban areas, commonly suffered from inadequate food and rampant disease. Overwork alternated with periods when no work was to be found. Many people resented the Poor Law of 1834, which had been designed to reduce public spending on the needy. In some parts of the country the anti-Poor Law movement had developed into Chartism, the first mass working-class political organization in British history. It aimed, among other things, to win the vote for every man in the land and so make parliament more responsive to the demands of working people. Some Chartists were prepared to take violent measures to achieve their ends. In the twelve months after the Conservative election victory, many were thrown out of work by one of the periodic slumps of the economy. In Manchester, the heart of the Lancashire cotton industry, mobs of unemployed rioters roamed the streets damaging factories, and the authorities lost their grip on public order. Revolution seemed at hand.

Dissatisfaction was not confined to the working people. Many middle-class manufacturers disliked the way in which parliament, dominated by the aristocracy and gentry, pursued policies favoring agriculture rather than industry. In particular, they objected to the Corn Laws, which prohibited the import into Britain of foreign wheat until the price of its home-grown equivalent reached a high level. The effect was to protect domestic agriculture against overseas competition in order to guarantee farmers and their landlords a good income. The benefits for landed society, however, were bought at the expense of driving up the price of bread for the bulk of the population. Industrial wages had to be higher, and this expencse in turn raised manufacturers' costs. Agriculture was in effect handicapping industry. An Anti-Corn Law League had been created to agitate for the repeal of the offensive legislation and call for free trade. Its spokesmen, led by Richard Cobden and John Bright, contrasted the idle aristocracy with the "industrious classes," the capitalists and workers together. The League was not simply opposed to a policy but was voicing criticism of the whole social order that rested on the privilege of the landed classes. The Conservatives, however, stood for the traditional structure of society and staunchly resisted the arguments of the League. The small towns and the counties that benefited from agricultural protection formed the basis of their support in the 1841 parliament. But the new government was left with a problem. How was it going to reduce social tensions? The nation wanted to see how Peel the physician would try to heal its ills.

PEEL AND GLADSTONE

Peel's strategy was to move, gradually but firmly, in the direction of free trade. He had probably been convinced for some years that the Corn Laws could not be retained indefinitely, but he wanted to proceed cautiously and so allowed them to remain on the statute book for the time being. The first step was to reduce the other customs and excise duties that inflated the price of goods for the consumer. Lower prices would make people more content with their lot. The government department most concerned with financial policy, after the Treasury, was the Board of Trade. Gladstone was Peel's choice as Vice-President of the Board, responsible to Lord Ripon in the cabinet as its President. "I really am not fit for it," Gladstone told Peel; "I have no knowledge of trade whatever." Peel waved aside his qualms. He knew that the appointment of the son of a Liverpool merchant would reassure the country's commercial interests about the good intentions of his government. He also placed great confidence in Gladstone's ability to master a new field, and his trust was not misplaced. Gladstone set to work, in his own words, "as a reluctant schoolboy meaning well." He labored under Peel's direction to formulate new financial policies that were introduced in 1842. Duty was reduced on some 750 of the 1,200 articles then liable. Gladstone rapidly showed himself to be a skillful departmental administrator. So successful was his tenure of the post that in 1843 he was promoted to the presidency of the Board of Trade with a seat in cabinet. Gladstone was playing a major part in one of the most significant projects of reform undertaken in the first half of the century.

Peel's example left a lasting mark on Gladstone. The younger man admired the Prime Minister for his tactical skills. In parliament, for example, Peel was normally careful to agree as far as possible with opposition arguments in order to reduce the number of his critics. Gladstone made note of "the extraordinary sagacity of his political instinct." Likewise, Gladstone responded to Peel's advice about the method of parliamentary speeches. Peel urged him not to be short and concise but rather to be long and diffuse so as to convince men holding a variety of views. Gladstone was ever afterward to be noted for his ability to expound issues at length — at excessive length, according to opponents. His respect for Peel went beyond matters of technique: the Prime Minister seemed to him a model of Christian responsibility in public life. Peel shared none of Gladstone's evangelical past or High Church present, and yet his more sober Anglican piety was genuine. He kept a written prayer among the personal belongings in his dressing room, and his policies were grounded in a Christian vision of the world. Peel was not, as he has sometimes been depicted, simply a brilliant pragmatist; he was a man of conviction. His political credo, the inspiration for the new Conservatism of the 1830s and 1840s, rested on a belief in providence that we shall consider more fully in Chapter 5. And he imposed on himself a punishing regimen of conscientious hard work. Although Gladstone was to differ from Peel on particular points, his admiration for the man never dimmed. Peel showed his disciple, probably unconsciously, how the Christian faith could be applied to the tasks of government.

CHURCH AND STATE

While he was gaining experience of the practice of politics, Gladstone was beginning to realize that his theory of the proper relations between religion and politics could no longer be upheld. He had asserted in his book of 1838 that the state must give exclusive support to the Church of England and consequently that no other religious body should receive public financial assistance. Yet in 1840, even before the Conservatives entered office, he conceded that this principle had to be breached. In Canada it was determined that the proceeds from sales of land that had been reserved for the support of the Anglican clergy should be shared with other denominations, and Gladstone agreed that the wish of the colonial government should be respected. By Easter 1842, he was admitting to himself that in England itself church and state could not cooperate in the way that he had envisaged in 1838. Governments had to take account of too many contrary pressures. In 1843, Peel's administration attempted to introduce a national education system in which the schools were entrusted exclusively to the care of the Church of England as the established church, but vehement protests from Dissenters led to the withdrawal of the proposal. Gladstone voted nn cabinet to drop the measure. In doing so, he was accepting that even a Conservative government could not impose Anglicanism on an unwilling nation. In the following year the administration passed the Dissenters' Chapels Act, giving Unitarians secure possession of buildings erected by their orthodox Presbyterian predecessors. "The measure," Gladstone later recalled, "in some way heightened my churchmanship but depressed my church-and-statesmanship." His churchmanship was enhanced because the incident reinforced his belief that the Church of England alone could preserve orthodoxy, but his church-and-statesmanship diminished in that he acquiesced in state help to a religious community outside the state Church. His theoretical position was being compromised by government policies for which he was responsible.

The tension snapped over the Maynooth issue in the same year. It was proposed in cabinet that the grant made annually to the Roman Catholic seminary at Maynooth in Ireland should be made larger and permanent. The object was to attach the Catholic priests trained there more firmly to the government. Agitation led by Daniel O'Connell for the ending of the Union with Britain was posing a serious threat to the public order in Ireland. Peel believed that the goodwill of the priesthood would be a powerful weapon in the hands of the authorities. But the proposal provoked an outburst of passionate opposition. The Protestant sentiment of the nation would not tolerate the permanent endowment of popery. Gladstone spoke against the measure in cabinet, explaining that it conflicted with his principle that the state should give money to no ecclesiastical body but the Church of England. In February 1845 he resigned from the presidency of the Board of Trade. It was supposed by some that he might lead the public opposition to the grant, but that was far from Gladstone's mind. He recognized that the Irish Catholics had to be placated, and he agreed that Peel's policy was the wisest course; in fact, he actually voted for it in parliament. In the aftermath of the affair, he asked himself whether the state could still lay claim to a distinctive religious profession. No, he answered reluctantly, the state was no longer a Christian institution.

The Maynooth question marked an epoch in Gladstone's thought. Although he still clung to the pattern outlined in *The State in Its Relations with the Church* as the ideal arrangement, he recognized that in the conditions of the mid-nineteenth century it was impracticable. Irish Catholics and English Dissenters were both too powerful for the government to ignore in framing policy. Gladstone's theory foundered on the hard rock of religious pluralism. He was thrown into a protracted crisis about his role in politics. If the ideal sketched in his book was unattainable, what was his purpose in life? No clear answer was to emerge until the following decade.

CONSERVATIVE DISINTEGRATION

Maynooth opened a rift between Peel and many of his supporters. Many held that his willingness to finance Catholics made him a traitor to the Church of England that he had been elected to defend. Soon the rift widened. The other main reason for the Conservative success in 1841 was the party's championing of agriculture against the Anti-Corn Law League, but in the same year as the Maynooth question, Peel determined that it was time to repeal the Corn Laws. The background was provided by famine in Ireland. With the failure of the potato crop, continued restrictions on the import of grain could hardly be justified. The decisive factor, however, was Peel's desire to make the change at a time of the government's choosing rather than when the League's case became irresistible. Wary lest the authority of the executive should be undermined, the Prime Minister insisted that there must be no truckling to extraparliamentary pressure. But he could not carry all his cabinet with him on the point, let alone his party. Many of the most solid Conservatives were too attached to the interests of agriculture to consider abandoning protection. Yet Gladstone was convinced. His collaboration with Peel in reducing the tariff made the further step of repealing the Corn Laws seem natural. Accordingly, when the Protectionist Lord Stanley left the cabinet in December 1845, Gladstone was appointed to his place as Colonial Secretary. At the same time, however, he lost his seat in parliament. New cabinet members had to seek re-election by their constituents, but Gladstone's patron at Newark, the Duke of Newcastle, was a fierce opponent of the Maynooth grant and a stalwart defender of agricultural protection. Knowing that in supporting Peel he had forfeited the duke's favor, Gladstone declined to stand again. So he was left to administer the colonial affairs of the country (a topic that will be discussed further in Chapter 6) without being able to defend his policies in the House of Commons. Loyalty to Peel was threatening his political future.

In any event, Peel did manage to carry the repeal of the Corn Laws in 1846, and so opened a period of nearly a century during which free trade was the settled policy of British governments. Cheap bread did raise the workers' standard of living and so reduce unrest, but the achievement destroyed Peel's party. In June, when a combination of Whigs and Protectionist Conservatives defeated him in the Commons, Peel and his ministry resigned. The split in the party's ranks became permanent, with the Protectionists under Lord Stanley securing the allegiance of most Conservative voters. The more liberal followers of Peel gained fewer than half as many parliamentary seats as their rivals at the 1847 general election. Both groups continued to call themselves Conservatives, but their division allowed the Whigs to dominate parliament for the next twenty years. Peel, in fact, was happy to give advice on financial policy to the Whig Chancellor of the Exchequer during the late 1840s. A polarized system of politics in which government and opposition fought for power no longer existed. Gladstone, still a decided Conservative, deplored the change and held Peel responsible. The former Prime Minister, in Gladstone's view, failed to exert himself to reunite the scattered elements of his former party. Nevertheless, Gladstone remained devoted to Peel and, after his chief's death in 1850, to his memory.

Being faithful both to the broader Conservatism and to the narrower Peelite position created its own tensions. For more than a decade Gladstone was to be troubled by the contrary pulls on his allegiance, but political life retained all its fascination for him. In 1847, he returned to the House of Commons as M.P. for the University of Oxford, in effect a representative of the clergy who formed a majority of its graduates. He still hoped, though with much less clarity of vision than in the past, to serve the Church of England in public life. But there was now no single Conservative Party to act as the natural vehicle for his views.

CATHOLICISM, ENGLISH AND ROMAN

Between 1841 and 1851, the Church of England was being convulsed by several crises of its own. Most stemmed from the revival of Church principles at Oxford during the previous decade. Through his friendships with Henry Manning and James Hope, Gladstone was drawn during the 1840s into the slipstream of the Oxford Movement. Gladstone developed an intimate rapport with Manning, the godfather of his oldest child. Manning dedicated his book *The Unity of the Church* (1842) "affectionately" to Gladstone, and from 1836 to 1851 nearly four hundred letters passed between them. James Hope was even closer to Gladstone, taking the place once occupied by Arthur Hallam. William later recalled that Hope was "at the head of all his contemporaries in the brightness and the beauty of his gifts." Gladstone deeply respected Hope for his mental powers as well as for his moral qualities.

Both Manning and Hope fully identified, as Gladstone did not, with the Tractarian position of John Henry Newman. The difference emerged in the affair of the Jerusalem bishopric in 1841. The Church of England and the united Protestant Church of Prussia were to set up a joint bishopric in Jerusalem, its occupant being drawn alternately from the two Churches. The proposal entailed the cooperation of the Church of England with a body making no profession of Catholicity. Newman denounced the scheme, and Hope agreed with him, but Gladstone was more cautious in his response. He was prepared to attend the consecration of the first English bishop and agonized for a month about whether he could in conscience become a trustee of the project. Eventually he decided that he could not. Like Newman and his circle, Gladstone believed that the Church of England was part of the Catholic Church. Unlike them, however, he was reluctant to draw extreme inferences from the belief. He was a High Churchman, but a moderate one.

Gladstone's moderation was apparent in his entire lack of sympathy for the leanings toward the Roman Catholic Church that gradually appeared in the Oxford Movement. By 1841, Newman was showing clear signs of being drawn toward Rome. Gladstone, by contrast, wished "to catholicise the members of the Church of England, but without 'unprotestantising' them." Newman had turned against the sixteenth-century Reformers of the Church of England on the grounds that they had destroyed the medieval Catholic heritage. Gladstone, on the other hand, applauded their achievement of maintaining essential Catholic teaching while identifying the Church with the English nation. According to what has been called his theory of religious nationality, Gladstone believed that particular peoples express their religious genius in different forms and hence that there should be no imposition of international organization on national churches. He maintained that it was a major error of the papacy to dragoon different peoples into an artificial uniformity. The autocracy of the pope was hateful to Gladstone's patriotism. He also disliked the Roman Catholic doctrine of purgatory, the veneration of Mary, and the encouragement of sacramental confession, but papal claims always aroused his strongest objections. "I see in the Church of Rome," Gladstone wrote to Hope in 1845, "the very best and the very worst of all the Churches of Christ." When, in 1845, Newman was eventually received into the Roman Church, Gladstone was dismayed but not surprised. His own allegiance to the Church of England was certainly not called into question.

APPLIED CHRISTIANITY

With James Hope, Gladstone conceived a remarkable project for "extending Church principles in Scotland." The aim was ambitious: they wanted nothing less than to turn the country back from Presbyterianism to the Episcopalianism it had intermittently professed in the seventeenth century. The agency was to be a college that would simultaneously train clergy for the Scottish Episcopal Church and educate the sons of the well-to-do. Hope, who took the medieval statutes of his own Merton College, Oxford, as the model for the new institution, was far more interested in the clerical training side. He insisted that the college must be remote from any town in order to allow a semimonastic atmosphere of retirement from the world. Gladstone, on the other hand, paid more attention to the training of the laity. He wished to imitate Eton and so to generate an Episcopalian ruling class whose influence would permeate the whole of society. Hope had secured the sanction of the Scottish episcopate in 1840. Soon the promoters gained the financial backing of John Gladstone, William's father, who laid the foundation stone of the chapel in 1846 at Glenalmond, west of Perth in central Scotland. Trinity College opened in 1847 and developed into an independent school that still flourishes. Its training for the ministry, never very extensive, was merged with an Edinburgh college in the 1870s. Although the college did not succeed in re-Episcopalianizing Scotland, it was a major venture that consumed much of Gladstone's energies during the 1840s.

Another religious project of the period was what Gladstone called "the Engagement." Together with about a dozen other lay High Churchmen, he undertook to attend daily service, to observe the fasts of the Church, and to spend time regularly in prayer. Members also selected some charitable work, Gladstone's choice being the relief of the destitute of Soho in central London. Partly because the members of the Engagement assembled together only once a year, it faded away in the early 1850s, but in Gladstone's case it left a legacy: care for the destitute, and especially the rehabilitation of prostitutes, became a permanent feature of his life. Already by 1842, when he recorded in his diary seeing "the girl Rebecca," he was occasionally trying to befriend prostitutes, and in 1849 he undertook systematic rescue work. The girls were given financial help to start a job or else sent off to a home near Windsor for training. Gladstone's wife, Catherine, knew about the enterprise, and even invited some of the girls to the family home, but it was nevertheless a dangerous activity for a rising politician. On one occasion a blackmailer threatened to expose him to the press, but Gladstone immediately turned the correspondence over to the police. An even more acute risk was that Gladstone would lapse from his own high moral standards. He found the girls attractive and on one occasion recorded enigmatically "a strange & humbling scene" with one of them. He was to declare shortly before his death that he had never been unfaithful to his wife, but at the time he knew he was courting danger. So seriously did he treat the temptation that from time to time he would privately scourge his own back. Several High Churchmen of the period believed that such flagellation was the best remedy for the sins of the flesh. Gladstone also used the scourge after venturing into pornography not for information (as he had initially persuaded himself) but for titillation. He felt the need for ascetic discipline in order to restrain his sexual appetite. Gladstone was intensely aware of the power of temptation.

GLADSTONE'S SPIRITUALITY

The chief support of the Christian, Gladstone believed, came from the communion service. By the 1840s, in accordance with growing High Church practice, he tried to receive the bread and wine each Sunday. He noted in 1842 that Christians are commanded in Scripture to receive communion, and yet those who would never disobey other commands ignore this one. Here was a criticism of other schools of opinion in the Church, especially among evangelicals, that made communion less central to the spiritual life. Nevertheless, there was continuity with Gladstone's earlier religious phase in his understanding of the sacrament. The first sermon that he preached to his household, in 1834, was on the Lord's Supper. Fourteen years later, when the transition from evangelicalism to High Churchmanship was complete, he was content to preach the same sermon unaltered. Even so, by 1843 he was attributing more to the service than he had in the past. The climax of a sermon entitled "The Vision of God" dwelt on how the believer sees God at communion. "He that neglects the Eucharist neglects the Saviour," he wrote two years later; "he that rejects the Eucharist rejects the Saviour." The service had become by far the most important channel of grace. Gladstone composed a set of devotions to occupy the mind during communion. Their acute sense of sin and total dependence on Jesus Christ for salvation are well illustrated by the stanza of Augustus Toplady's hymn he chose to include:

> Nothing in my hand I bring,
> Simply to Thy Cross I cling:

Naked, come to Thee for dress;
Helpless, look to Thee for grace;
Foul, I to the Fountain fly;
Wash me, Saviour, or I die.

The words of a Calvinist continued to nourish Gladstone's soul.

He attempted to pass on spiritual food to his family and servants through the sermons he composed for household prayers on Sunday evenings. Most of them were written in the 1840s and reused up to the 1860s. Household worship, he admitted, was a poor substitute for a church service, and yet Gladstone, the former intending clergyman, put considerable effort into his sermons. "It is the duty of those who are placed at the head of a house," he explained in one entitled "Duties of Masters and Servants," "to see that God is reverently worshipped therein by all its inmates: to collect them for prayer: to lead them in an acquaintance with God's Holy Word." Repeatedly he warned his household against the unthinking assumption that because they had been baptized or lived in a Christian land their eternal future was secure. He preached for conversions, but not in the evangelical sense. Christians were not to look for unclouded assurance of salvation but for a growth in actual holiness. That alone, he urged, would make them fit for heaven. He also gave evidence of a significant shift away from evangelical doctrinal preferences. Instead of concentrating on the cross of Christ, he taught the importance of the resurrection that generates new life in the believer and supremely of the incarnation, "an idea or doctrine which has a title to rank before all others in the Gospel system." The incarnation, in which God became man, was "the medium of our living union with God." At the eucharist the believer is joined more closely to Christ and consequently to the Almighty. The twin emphases on incarnation and eucharist were to become the hallmark of Anglican theology from the 1880s long into the twentieth century. Gladstone was anticipating the pattern of the future when his own style of churchmanship was to become ascendant in the Church of England.

WILLIAM EWART GLADSTONE

THE GORHAM JUDGMENT

In the middle years of the nineteenth century, however, Gladstone was apprehensive about the future of an energetic High
Churchmanship. He feared that, far from promoting the interests of the Church of England in accordance with his earlier
vision, the state might meddle damagingly in its life. The
Roman Catholic Church, rather than reforming itself along the
lines of the Church of England, might draw away fresh Anglican converts in the wake of Newman. Both fears were realized
in the crisis provoked by the Gorham Judgment of 1850. George
Gorham, an evangelical clergyman, was in effect refused permission to assume the duties of a new parish by his bishop,
Henry Phillpotts, a doughty representative of the old pre-
Tractarian school of High Churchmen. Phillpotts's objection
was that Gorham did not believe in baptismal regeneration.
The case was taken through the ecclesiastical courts and then,
on appeal, to the Judicial Committee of the Privy Council, a
court of the state, not the Church. It determined that Gorham
need not accept baptismal regeneration in order to officiate in
the Church of England. Evangelicals were relieved; High
Churchmen were appalled. As they saw it, a secular court had
declared what they counted heresy to be authentic Anglicanism. The only refuge for those who upheld baptismal regeneration as essential Christian teaching seemed to be Rome. Accordingly, there began a trickle of converts to the Roman Catholic
Church. Gladstone's loyalty to the English Church was not in
doubt, but he was faced with a dilemma. He was outraged by
the legal judgment and wished to do something about it, yet
the obvious course of action, the suggestion that the Church
should be freed from interference by the state, pointed toward
disestablishment. Any politician adopting that remedy would
have no further credit with the Conservative Party. Gladstone's
conscience was at war with his career.

He unburdened himself in June 1850 by publishing *Re-
marks on the Royal Supremacy*. He argued that in the future

70

doctrine should be settled by a predominantly ecclesiastical body, although the Church of England should not abandon her established status "until she actually sees that the hour appointed for her to make that choice, is at hand." He was occupying ambiguous ground, dissatisfied with present arrangements and yet not wishing to propose drastic change. It was a measure of tension with which he learned to live. The greatest pain, however, was still to come. Henry Manning and James Hope, his closest friends, both saw no prospect of the Church of England regaining its spiritual freedom. They were drawn inexorably toward Roman Catholicism. Gladstone spent long evenings trying to dissuade the two men, but on 6 April 1851 they were received together into the Roman Catholic Church. "They were my two props," Gladstone lamented in his diary. "Their going may be a sign that my work is gone with them. God give us daily light with daily bread." Two days after their secession, he struck out Hope as executor of his will, and soon he returned the letters had had received from Manning. Ending these friendships was a desolating experience. Again Gladstone had recourse to publication. In a letter to the presiding bishop of the Scottish Episcopal Church, *On the Functions of Laymen in the Church,* written at the end of 1851, he recognized the threat from the state to the doctrine and discipline of ecclesiastical bodies. Hope for the future, he argued, lay in giving churches their own constitutional organizations for expressing their convictions independently of the state. He proposed a synod for the Scottish Episcopal Church in which laymen would have a share. Soon, in 1855, Gladstone was to welcome the restoration of Convocation, a similar body for the Church of England, though lacking a lay element. The Gorham crisis had compelled him to move further away from the view expressed in *The State in Its Relations with the Church.* There he had recommended close identification between the two bodies corporate in the title, but now he was urging a separate voice for the Church. The relationship between politics and religion was becoming more distant, more complex. For one whose vocation in politics was

71

essentially religious, the developments of these years caused immense strain.

FAMILY RELATIONS

Gladstone discovered some relief in his family life. In Catherine, as long-suffering as she was charming, William had found an ideal partner. From the start of their marriage, he shared with her his political secrets, although he kept the sharpest temptations of his personal life from her. When they were apart in 1851, Catherine wrote to her husband saying that he did not know half the evil in her life; he replied that "it sets me thinking how little you know the evil of mine of which at the last day I shall have a strange tale to tell." Disagreements between them were rare. On one occasion, William noted in his diary, they differed about when they should travel to a marriage in her family. William prevailed, but he was flurried by the incident. His diary reveals that he shared his wife's concern for the health and welfare of the expanding family. Eight children were born to them in regular succession: after William (1840) came Agnes (1842), Stephen (1844), Jessy (1845), Mary (1847), Helen (1849), Harry (1852), and Herbert (1854). The father sometimes played cricket with the children in summer and put up snow buildings with them in winter. Gladstone paid particular attention to the training of the oldest son, Willy, often giving him daily lessons and reading Scripture with him. Once, when the boy was seven, Gladstone whipped him for persistent inattention to his tutor. There were other troubles in running a household. In 1846, for instance, a nurserymaid had to be dismissed for theft. The greatest trauma, however, was caused by the slow death of four-year-old Jessy from meningitis in 1850, an experience that racked Gladstone in the weeks immediately following the Gorham Judgment. The child had been particularly promising and affectionate. Catherine was "cut up and tried" during the ordeal; flickers of hope for Jessy's survival, if anything, made the matter worse. The life of Agnes had been threatened by erysipelas two years before; and in 1851, the year of the secession of Manning and Hope, Mary's eyesight was so despaired of that the household traveled to Naples for her relief. If family often provided a channel of recuperation, its responsibilities also added to Gladstone's anxieties.

The greatest permanent worry in the family was Gladstone's younger sister, Helen. Since 1839 there had been complaints of erratic behavior on her part from the servants in the Scottish family home at Fasque, where she was expected to look after her father. It emerged that she was taking opium and other drugs. In May 1842 the problem of how to treat Helen was aggravated when she entered the Roman Catholic Church. The act was interpreted by others, especially William, as an attempt to spite the family. She also proved capable of causing further divisions in the household, twice turning William's aunt against his father. The truth seems to be that she was an extremely able person, sharing much of her brother's energy, who was doomed by bouts of ill health and her status as a woman to perpetual frustration. In 1839 it appeared likely that she would marry a Polish nobleman, but his parents forbade the match, and she remained a spinster. In 1845, she escaped the constraints of home by going to the German spa town of Baden Baden and, once there, ceasing to correspond with the family. William traveled to fetch her home. When he arrived, he found that she had just taken an overdose of laudanum, and for twelve days she refused to see him. In the end, he managed to arrange for her return to Britain. She was put under virtual house arrest at Fasque. Two years later she suffered a serious fit, her life was despaired of, and her mind became deranged. "She sent for me," Gladstone recorded in his diary, "to tell me of a plot formed to carry her off this night. She sees people coming in through the walls, 'little people' covering the drawers." By 1855 she had recovered sufficiently to take the vows of a nun, though remaining outside any nunnery, but

Helen was still liable to behave oddly. Often during the 1840s she taxed Gladstone's patience up to and beyond its limits.

Relations with his father were also problematic. The retired merchant was still a domineering personality in old age. The locals round Fasque referred to him as the prophet Elijah. In 1844 he celebrated his eightieth birthday. Two years later, on the advice of Sir Robert Peel, Queen Victoria made John Gladstone a baronet, allowing him to transmit the title "Sir" to his heir. William never permitted himself to criticize his father, even in the pages of his diary, but by the later 1840s he was evidently finding his demands irksome. Sir John expected his son to play whist with him almost every night they were together at Fasque. The father was less able to perform his business duties, and William was called in to assist. Most painful were disputes over free trade, for Sir John was incredulous when Peel repealed the Corn Laws. As grain prices in his area plummeted, he repeatedly launched intellectual assaults on his son for the part he had played in the decision. "Stood two batteries on free trade," noted William in his diary on one occasion. How was he to respond? Counterarguments caused overexcitement; silence encouraged his father to believe that he was winning the battle; pleas to escape provoked annoyance. William was relieved of the embarrassment only by the advance of senility in the final two years of his father's life. Sir John eventually died in 1851, adding to the trauma of a demanding year. William suffered from many of the difficulties encountered by those with aging parents.

GLADSTONE'S HOME

Gladstone was putting down roots at Fasque in these years. He entered into the activities of the area, attending a plowing match and speaking at a society aiming for agricultural improvement. He was powerfully attracted to country life, but Fasque lacked one thing needful: an Episcopal Church. On his early visits, Gladstone had been content to attend the village's Presbyterian Church, but the promoter of Trinity College, Glenalmond, could not rest content without Episcopal worship on the estate. The first task was to persuade his father, who was Church of Scotland by origin and the donor of a new spire to the local Presbyterians in 1838. William persevered, encouraging his father to take an interest in the design of the new building. St. Andrew's Episcopal Church was opened for worship in 1846, and the formal consecration took place in the following year. There was, however, an embarrassment. One of the three sermons was delivered by the Bishop of Aberdeen at short notice, and it turned out that the harried prelate had plagiarized from an American bishop. The sermon could not be published with the other two. Nevertheless, William greatly enjoyed planning the arrangements of the new building. Despite his father's disapproval, he attended on saint's days and twice in the week. Before the arrival of an organ, he acted as precentor, leading the congregation in the singing of the Psalms. In 1845 there were only thirteen Episcopalians in the parish apart from the landed proprietors, and so the building up of a congregation was a demanding task, but Gladstone was not daunted. St. Andrew's held a special place in his affections. The remains of his mother and older sister Anne were transferred there, and the body of his daughter Jessy was laid to rest there. Fasque became a sacred spot.

The estate turned into a bone of contention between William and his oldest brother Thomas. William stayed on more friendly terms with the two other brothers, Robertson and John Neilson, perhaps because they rarely met, but Thomas (Tom to the family) was different. William went shooting with him, but recorded no warm feelings for him in his diary, and he described Tom's wife, Louisa, as a "grand barbarian." The relationship was also strained politically. Tom had entered parliament at the same time as William but had achieved virtually nothing. In 1847, differing over free trade, he threatened not to support William in the election for the University of Oxford.

But the chief division between them was over Fasque. As the eldest son, Tom was due to inherit his father's estate, but William hoped that it might fall to him instead. In 1844, when Tom was living in Cheltenham and showing little interest in Fasque, William proposed to his brother that he might like to let him take over the Scottish estate on their father's death. He received a firm rebuff. In 1846, William urged his father not to make the title of the baronetcy include Fasque. Tom would automatically succeed as baronet, but William was clearly still hoping he would not take Fasque as well. Again William's suggestion was rejected. Tom noticed with dismay that, as business adviser to his father, William had access to his will, and the older brother was suspicious. Immediately after Sir John's death in 1851, Tom asserted himself. He assumed charge of the funeral arrangements, took over family prayers from William, and investigated complaints by the housekeeper against a nurse employed by William, sending for him in the process. The message was clear: William must regard his time at Fasque as a closed chapter in his life. Recognizing his position, William paid twenty-nine farewell visits and then left, not to return for seven years. Relations with Tom, later a Conservative parliamentary candidate when William had become a Liberal, were never entirely harmonious. The brothers went their different ways.

Gladstone was to make his permanent residence in Wales, not Scotland. His wife's home before their marriage was Hawarden Castle, a few miles west of Chester over the Welsh border in Flintshire. The castle — actually a large Georgian house to which castellations had been added at the turn of the century — stood in its own grounds on the edge of the village. It belonged to her brother Sir Stephen Glynne, who was unmarried, and his heir was his younger brother Henry, the clergyman at Hawarden. If neither Stephen nor Henry, who was a widower with only a single surviving daughter, had a son, the estate would pass through Catherine into William's family. At one stage Henry seemed likely to marry, and Gladstone, not without a touch of self-interest, expressed the view that the two possible prospects were unsuitable. No marriage took place. Consequently, on Stephen's death in 1874, Hawarden passed into the hands of the Gladstone family. Hawarden had been the main family base ever since the disappointment over Fasque, and in a sense the inheritance was earned. Gladstone spent many long hours wrestling with the intricacies of the business interests of the Glynne family, especially in the years 1847 to 1852. The Glynnes had invested heavily in the Oak Farm brick and iron works in Worcestershire, which had expanded too rapidly and gone bankrupt in 1847. Gladstone was examined before the Birmingham court of bankruptcy in the following year. By putting in hard labor and committing his own capital, he managed to secure the survival of the iron works and the retention of Hawarden by the Glynnes. Gladstone's inexpert support for the manager of the works had originally contributed to the over-expansion, but in turning round its fortunes he learned skills of financial management that were to stand him in good stead later when he ran the nation's finances. In the years round 1850, however, the affairs of Oak Farm formed another of the burdens he had to bear.

The whole period was for Gladstone a time of crisis. In every aspect of life there were serious problems. He shared in Peel's achievement of mollifying a discontented population by reducing the cost of consumer goods, but at the same time he gradually came to realize that his ideal of exclusive government support for the Church of England was untenable in the circumstances of the times. He believed with all his heart in Peelite Conservatism, but the party was shattered by the Corn Law issue. Even though the revival of Church principles gave him hope, the specter of Roman Catholicism haunted him with apprehensions. His voluntary work led to the creation of Trinity College, Glenalmond, yet his care for prostitutes exposed him to temptation that was difficult to resist. Although the sacrament of bread and wine and belief in the incarnation permanently upheld his spirits, the secession of his closest religious confidants dealt him a painful blow. Although his wife provided a haven in the storm, his family life was troubled by difficulties with Helen and Tom and the deaths of Jessy and Sir John. He lost Fasque, and he found his wife's home at Hawarden to be encumbered with debt. The various threads of anxiety, public and private, intertwined, leaving him few opportunities of escape. In his birthday reflections at the end of 1851, the culmination of the most testing period, he described it as a "sad year."

> If I have had in my soul any consolatory token it is this that the thought of God's presence & judgment is ever dear to me. But what things have I not done or trodden on the edge of while entertaining that thought. In truth the religious trials of the time have passed my capacity & grasp. I am bewildered, & reel under them. . . . But I am in thine hand: & Thou wilt show forth thy wisdom and justice, which is all one with thy long-suffering mercy, in me.

Gladstone had to endure a great deal of adversity, but his spiritual awareness was not eclipsed. His faith proved a sufficient support in years of stress.

5 Gladstone and Reform, 1852-1868

In 1852, Gladstone was still a Conservative, believing in the rights of the crown and the aristocracy and aiming to defend the existing institutions of the country. All his political affinities were with the Tory Party. By 1868, he had been transformed into the leader of the Liberal Party. His followers now included self-professed Radicals, Dissenters eager for disestablishment, and even men wanting to turn Britain into a republic. His administration of 1868 set about a program of systematic reform, for the Prime Minister was now committed to implementing change. Gladstone had moved from the right to the left of the political stage. The shift, however, was neither sharp nor sudden: it took time for him to alter his political associations so drastically. The initial stages of the evolution were already under way by 1852. He had taken his first steps along the road of reform under Peel's leadership in the 1840s. The reduction in protective duties and the repeal of the Corn Laws had set Gladstone on course to become a free trader, and he was now entirely opposed to the reinstatement of agricultural protection. Equally important was the fading of his vision of state support for the Church of England. Churches, he had come to believe, needed freedom from state interference more than they needed anything the state could give. By 1852 he wished to criticize the non-Peelite Conservative faction on two scores. "Protection and religious liberty," he wrote in that year, "are the subjects on which my main complaints would turn; shuffling as to the former, trading in bigotry as to the latter." Gladstone had already set out on his political pilgrimage from one allegiance to another.

THE ROLE OF THE PEELITES

At the beginning of the period, he was at the heart of the group of Peelite Conservatives, whose common bond was loyalty to the memory of Sir Robert Peel. At the 1852 general election, the "Liberal Conservatives," as the Peelites were sometimes labeled, were reduced to fifty-eight M.P.s. The core of those who regularly consulted about policies was much smaller, the dozen or so who had held office under Peel. In the early 1850s, the Peelites had the freedom to move in either direction. Some favored attempts to reunite the Conservative Party, arguing that the main Conservative grouping under Lord Derby (the former Lord Stanley) was committed only in theory to restoring protection: its members would never actually try to enact new Corn Laws, since they knew they would face too loud an outcry from the growing urban areas of the country. So the natural outcome, according to the advocates of Conservative unity, was a fusion of the two wings of the party. But other Peelites wanted to move toward the Whigs. The more traditionalist Whigs, they rightly argued, were as conservative in their views as the Conservatives themselves. Several Whig aristocrats were the greatest landowners of the country. The Whigs could be trusted to avoid rash innovations so long as the sober men in their ranks were able to restrain the hot-headed Radicals on their left wing. The merger of the Peelites with the Whigs would strengthen the prudent section against the wilder men. With two directions to choose from, individual Peelites were steadily slipping away to the left or to the right. Gladstone, however, held firm. His opinions, he later recalled, inclined him toward the Whigs, but his lingering sympathies drew him back toward the solid Conservatives. He recommended that his grouping should aim to be "liberal in the sense of Peel, working out a liberal policy through the medium of the conservative party." For the time being, Gladstone argued, the Peelites must remain together to see which way the wind would blow.

The Whig government under Lord John Russell that had held office since the collapse of Peel's ministry resigned in turn in February 1852. The Protectionist Conservatives formed a minority administration under Lord Derby. Hoping to increase their numbers, Derby called a general election in July, but the result was inconclusive. The new House of Commons contained some 284 government supporters and some 309 Whigs of various shades, and so the balance of power lay in the hands of the 58 Peelites. Which way would they cast their votes? It largely depended on the government's financial policy. Responsibility for drawing up the budget rested on the shoulders of Benjamin Disraeli, the Chancellor of the Exchequer. Disraeli, five years older than Gladstone, was a witty novelist, a *bon viveur*, and a brilliant political tactician. Born a Jew, though baptized a Christian at the age of twelve, he was an outsider who climbed by his own talents to the summit of parliamentary life. Disraeli stood for the traditional Toryism of rank and privilege that Gladstone was gradually abandoning. His novels, particularly *Coningsby* and *Sybil*, portrayed an idealized affinity between the lower orders and their social superiors that could be cemented by true Conservative values. It was common at the time to contrast Disraeli's flippancy with Gladstone's gravity. Disraeli had already earned Gladstone's dislike by mounting the rhetorical onslaught that brought down Peel's government following repeal of the Corn Laws. By 1849, Gladstone was describing

Disraeli privately as "a man whose objects appear to be those of personal ambition and who is not thought to have any strong conviction of any kind upon public matters." Their rivalry was to be a thread running through Victorian politics.

THE DISMISSAL OF THE CONSERVATIVES

When Disraeli introduced his budget on 3 December 1852, Gladstone set about preparing a counterblast. The scene was set for a duel. Disraeli ably defended his proposals on the evening of 16 December, producing what Gladstone admitted to be "superlative acting and brilliant oratory." When the Chancellor sat down, his rival rose to speak. With moral earnestness, Gladstone denounced the attacks that Disraeli had made on individuals in his speech and went on to dissect the provisions of the budget. A thunderstorm outside heightened the dramatic atmosphere. Disraeli's success, and with it the government's future, had seemed assured, but Gladstone destroyed both with his passionate speech. Directly after he sat down, a vote was taken on the budget, the government was defeated by 305 to 286, and Derby immediately resigned. Gladstone had rallied the Peelites to join the Whigs in dismissing the administration, a pivotal point in national politics. The Conservatives together, Derbyite and Peelite, had formed a natural majority in the 1840s, but with Gladstone's speech, most of the remaining Peelites turned decisively against their erstwhile colleagues. Over the next few years, the Whigs gradually absorbed the Peelite remnant, and they retained a parliamentary majority throughout the period up to the 1867 Reform Act. It is not too much to say that Gladstone helped to reshape the pattern of mid-century politics. The occasion was, as the press put it, "not merely the victory of a battle, but of a war." His parliamentary triumph brought Gladstone to the front rank of national life.

Directly after the resignation of Derby's administration, the Whigs and Peelites formed a coalition — what Gladstone called a "mixed government" — that allowed the Peelites to hold on to their identity. They provided the Prime Minister, Lord Aberdeen, and, despite their much smaller numbers in parliament, six out of thirteen cabinet ministers. At the express wish of Queen Victoria and her consort Prince Albert, whom Aberdeen consulted in creating the government, Gladstone was appointed Chancellor of the Exchequer. Prince Albert had formed a high estimate of Gladstone's abilities as a financier. There was a characteristic tussle with Disraeli over the official robes, which it was customary for one Chancellor to hand on to his successor. Gladstone repeatedly requested them, but Disraeli, smarting from his parliamentary defeat, sent a succession of evasive answers, and the robes never arrived. They are still displayed for visitors to see at Disraeli's former home, Hughenden Manor. There were also disagreements within the cabinet. Perhaps inevitably, Gladstone differed sharply with Lord John Russell, the Whig leader whom Gladstone had once considered the chief parliamentary opponent of his own views. The occasion of the dispute was a trivial one. Gladstone dismissed an official from the department of woods and forests. Russell demanded his reinstatement. Gladstone would not concede. It was clearly a symbolic issue in which the pent-up antagonism of representatives of differing political traditions found expression. In general, however, Gladstone was backed by the cabinet in the schemes that he undertook, with characteristic energy, as Chancellor. In the 1853 session of parliament, his speeches occupy 400 columns of the official record, far more than the next largest number, 286 columns by Lord John Russell as Leader of the House of Commons. His first task was to introduce a budget to replace Disraeli's.

THE BUDGET OF 1853

Gladstone's budget of 1853 was probably his greatest single achievement. In the short term it consolidated the standing of the coalition government, and in the long term it laid the foundations of the financial policy of subsequent administrations, what has been called "the social contract of the mid-Victorian state." Gladstone was aware that taxation directly affected the fortunes of different groups in society. He was dealing, he explained in his budget speech of 18 April, with "the relations of classes brought into the nicest competition one with another." Accordingly he sought to institute a careful balance between various interests. For the sake of the poor — and in order to ensure that they were content with their lot — Gladstone wished to continue Peel's policy of decreasing the customs and excise duties that drove up the price of basic consumer goods. That meant retaining the income tax, as Peel had done, which fell most heavily on the middle classes. In order to satisfy the Radical champions of the middle classes who wanted the complete abolition of the income tax, he sought compromise in a plan to phase out the tax by 1860. And, in order to ease the burden on existing income tax payers, he sought to extend the tax for the first time to the lower middle classes. The cost of contributing to annuities and life assurance, chiefly taken out by professional people, was to be exempt from income tax. Landlords were to be liable to a new legacy duty but were not to pay income tax at a higher rate than the middle classes. That was crucial. Gladstone had taken Disraeli severely to task for proposing that land should be taxed at a different rate from salaries. Such a measure was calculated, Gladstone believed, to stir up social resentments between the landed gentry and aristocracy on the one hand and the middle classes on the other. Gladstone suggested, with good reason, that all would benefit from his budget. It was a masterly scheme of fiscal reform.

Behind Gladstone's desire to avert interclass friction was his organic vision of society. The different social groups, he believed, needed each other and had to work together. The landlords had to be respected, for from their ranks the governing elite would continue to be drawn. Gladstone was attempting to entrench the position of the traditional ruling class, for he was still upholding a conservative social theory. Yet he was also trying to ensure rewards for "the classes of professional men and of persons who are dependent upon their own exertions." He knew that society benefited from the skill and enterprise of such middle-class individuals, and he honored their efforts at self-help. Most fundamentally, his reforms favored the working classes. He wished to improve their standard of living by decreasing their relative contribution to the exchequer and so insisted, as he put it, that income tax should not "trench on labour." The taxation paid by the working classes would be of the indirect variety, on their purchases, not direct, on their income. Gladstone's achievement was to create a balance between indirect taxation falling chiefly on the working classes and direct taxation on the better off. The government was following intelligible principles designed to be fair to all — a policy, Gladstone hoped, that would increase popular respect for the institutions through which the nation was ruled. Furthermore, once principles of taxation were settled, there would be no need for bargaining with extraparliamentary pressure groups such as the Anti-Corn Law League of the previous decade. Power would be firmly located in parliament. Gladstone's scheme was modeled on Peel's method, the maintenance of existing institutions through carefully executed reforms. The Chancellor was acting as a true liberal Conservative: conservative as to ends, liberal as to means.

ADMINISTRATIVE AND UNIVERSITY REFORM

During his tenure of office under Aberdeen, Gladstone had two other reforming preoccupations. One involved the civil service, the bureaucracy that administered the departments of state. It was tiny by twentieth-century standards, but Gladstone feared it was growing and so costing the taxpayer more. Many of its officials were noted for political bias that hampered the work of governments of a different allegiance from their own. Gladstone's central complaint about the civil service was its inefficiency. He found the chief official at the Treasury, the department over which he presided, incompetent to advise him in the preparation of the 1853 budget. The root of the problem was the system of patronage whereby politicians nominated recruits to the service without regard for their aptitude. The administrative machine was often staffed by the relatives and friends of great men in government. The "high aristocracy," it was commented at the time, "have been accustomed to employ the Civil Establishments as a means of providing for the waifs and strays of their Families." Gladstone declared war on this relic of "Old Corruption." The aim was to create a disinterested public service in which places were held on grounds of merit alone. He appointed Sir Stafford Northcote, his former private secretary, and Sir Charles Trevelyan, permanent head of the Treasury, to recommend ways of reforming the bureaucracy.

The Northcote-Trevelyan Report, submitted to Gladstone in 1854, urged the introduction of competitive examinations for entry to the civil service. Henceforward the well-connected should have no automatic advantage, and only the ablest would be allowed to serve the state. Gladstone gave the report his enthusiastic backing. He did not view its proposals as an assault on the privilege of the higher classes; to the contrary, as he explained in a remarkable twenty-two-page letter to Russell defending the scheme, he intended that reform would strengthen their hold on the nation's administration: "I have a strong impression that the aristocracy of this country are even superior in natural gifts, on the average, to the mass; but it is plain that with their acquired advantages, their *insensible education*, irrespective of book-learning, they have an immense superiority." Gladstone's conservative social theory was intact. He was hoping that the traditional elite would continue to exercise its sway, but that only those individuals in its ranks who were diligent enough to succeed in the examination would hold responsible office. Although his intended legislation to implement the Northcote-Trevelyan Report was abandoned by the government for lack of time, in 1855 there was created a Civil Service Commission empowered to test potential recruits according to standards set by the various departments. Further reform was deferred until 1870, in Gladstone's first term as Prime Minister, when the principles of the report were systematically enforced.

Gladstone's other reforming preoccupation involved the University of Oxford. It was the university Gladstone had attended; it was the constituency he represented in parliament. He was devoted to its interests, but he was forced to admit that there were many time-encrusted anomalies at Oxford. Positions were often restricted to people from particular places or even particular families; fellows of colleges frequently did not have to reside in order to qualify for their stipends; and, most seriously of all, the importance of the university as a distinct entity was vastly diminished as control had passed to its constituent colleges. Its professors' duties were minimal, and instruction was in the hands of college tutors. Change, however, was likely to threaten the Anglican monopoly of the university, since Dissenters, hitherto excluded from admission by religious tests, were demanding the right to be educated there. As the institution that trained a high proportion of the clergy, its welfare was essential to the Church of England. A Royal Commission, appointed by the Whigs in 1850, had reported in 1852 with proposals for reform. Two years later, Gladstone took charge of preparing a bill and steering it through long sittings in the Commons. His purpose, as he told a cabinet colleague, was to set up "competition as against restriction or private favour." That is to say, the measure was designed to sweep away the hoary abuses that prevented the ablest from coming to the fore. It was part of the same campaign as the reform of the civil service, with which it was closely connected in Gladstone's mind. Oxford should be reconstructed so as to inculcate the skills necessary for success in the civil service examination. On the other hand, there was far less strengthening of the role of university professors as against college tutors than Radicals desired and virtually no tampering with Anglican exclusiveness. Gladstone was by no means drastic, least of all at the expense of the Church he served. Yet a commission established by the act set about reforms that nurtured fresh vigor at Oxford. Once again Gladstone was pruning away the indefensible in order to make a traditional institution work efficiently.

FROM THE PEELITES TO THE WHIGS

The coming of the Crimean War in the spring of 1854 was the major event in the life of the Aberdeen coalition. We shall turn to Gladstone's views on the issues surrounding the conflict in Chapter 6, but some consideration of its impact on the government is relevant in this context. First, the war affected financial policy. As Chancellor, Gladstone had to determine how money was to be raised to support the war. He adopted the basic principle that those responsible for going to war must pay for it themselves. Future generations should not be burdened with the cost, and so the extra government expenditure should not be financed by loans. "The expenses of a war," he told the Commons, "are the moral check which it has pleased the Almighty to impose upon the ambition and the lust of conquest that are inherent in so many nations." Nor, he held, should the poor suffer unduly. He tried at first to avoid entirely increases in the tariff that would push up the cost of living, though he was forced, in a supplementary budget, to raise the duty on three articles. The main means of raising money for the war was therefore the income tax. Its rate was doubled, effectively undermining Gladstone's hope of eliminating it by 1860. Second, the war destroyed the government itself. The rickety bureaucratic machine over which it presided was altogether incapable of servicing the military campaign mounted in southern Russia. In January 1855, a motion condemning the administrative chaos was carried in the Commons, and Aberdeen's government gave up office. Gladstone was induced to continue as Chancellor under Lord Palmerston, the bellicose Prime Minister who succeeded Aberdeen, but he resigned after only a month. Palmerston was supporting the appointment of a committee to investigate the earlier conduct of the war, a decision that implied criticism of the previous administration. Gladstone could not countenance such a slur on the coalition and so entered the political wilderness.

Palmerston's first ministry, which lasted two years, avoided introducing contentious domestic measures by concentrating on an assertive foreign policy. Gladstone found the Prime Minister as personally distasteful as the policy was objectionable. Palmerston lacked seriousness, displayed an overbearing manner, and had led a profligate life. His Chancellor of the Exchequer, Cornewall Lewis, abandoned Gladstone's approach to finance by raising both loans and duties. It was all immensely frustrating. Gladstone knew precisely what he would do if he were Chancellor, spelling it out first in a private memorandum and then in a public, though anonymous, article. There can be no question about his ambition in these years; but equally there can be no doubt that his ambition was directed toward measures for the public good. "I greatly felt being turned out of office," he wrote to a friend in 1857. "I saw great things to do. I longed to do them. I am losing the best years of my life out of my natural service." His feelings were, if anything, accentuated when the Chancellor reversed his policies in 1857. Cornewall Lewis announced a sharp reduction in the rate of income tax with the aim of ending it in 1860. It was galling for Gladstone to see his own strategy adopted by another man. The 1857 general election, which strengthened Palmerston's parliamentary position, also reduced the Peelites to a tiny coterie. The future of Gladstone's immediate political circle was therefore uncertain. When in the following year Lord Derby's Conservatives returned to office, Gladstone was sounded about joining the cabinet but could not bring himself to accept. There was now the further mortification that his rival Disraeli was once more Chancellor. It was a doleful period.

The wilderness years came to an end in 1859, when Palmerston returned to office and offered Gladstone a cabinet place. Although it was a Whig government rather than a Whig/Peelite coalition, Gladstone overcame his dislike of the Prime Minister's personality and resumed the Chancellorship. Frustration had induced him to change sides in politics, and he never again spoke for the Conservative Party. Yet his conservative instincts remained, even while he was pursuing major financial reforms. "It is true," he wrote to his wife in 1861, "that I seem to be both at the Conservative and at the Radical ends of the Cabinet." There were repeated sharp clashes in cabinet with the Prime Minister during 1860 and 1861. Palmerston wished to increase military and naval spending in order to strengthen his hand in foreign affairs. Since defense already swallowed up well over a third of government expenditure, Gladstone strongly desired to resist. Nevertheless, Palmerston usually possessed the authority to circumvent his Chancellor. There was also tension between the two men over church patronage. The Prime Minister had the duty of advising the crown on whom to appoint to senior positions in the Church of England. Generally Gladstone avoided pressing his ecclesiastical views on Palmerston, just as he had when serving with Lord Aberdeen. His opinions as a High Churchman, he knew, would be unwelcome. But when there was a vacancy in the Archbishopric of York, the second most senior position in the Church, Gladstone did exert pressure on the Prime Minister. Gladstone's candidate was Samuel Wilberforce, a son of the champion of the slaves and a bishop who shared his own convictions about Church principles. In this, as in most other tussles with Palmerston, Gladstone was unsuccessful. Yet the two men learned to live with each other. Palmerston was adept at using the political platform as a way of appealing directly to the people and enhancing his own popularity. Gladstone had at first been skeptical of this technique as an undignified undervaluing of parliament, but he learned to recognize its value. As they commended the government's policies to the nation, Palmerston and Gladstone even began to echo one another.

A REFORMING CHANCELLOR

Once in office as Chancellor, Gladstone launched out on the program he had planned in advance. His basic strategy was to follow through the fundamental principle of the 1853 budget, the attempt to strike a fair balance between the various social groups. He argued that "the labouring classes should bear their share of the burden" but that "the bulk of the burden should fall on the shoulders of those having property." The 1860 budget reduced the number of substantial articles liable to duty to a mere fifteen, but retained the duties on tea and sugar so that the working people would still contribute significantly. He aimed to phase out income tax, but he always intended to replace it with some alternative tax that would fall on the propertied classes. Each budget was the result of his own meticulous preparation. In every year following 1860, Gladstone consolidated all his tax proposals in a single Finance Bill, resulting in a streamlining of the nation's fiscal affairs. The change in procedure also had the effect of giving greater prominence to the Chancellor of the Exchequer. Previously the post had been one cabinet responsibility among many; afterward it became the second or third most important office after the Prime Ministership itself, and so it remains today. Throughout Gladstone's administration of the Treasury, the grand object was the saving of public money. "Economy," he told his brother Robertson in 1859, "is the first and great article . . . in my financial creed." He hated all forms of extravagance, directing, for example, that particular attention should be paid to the preservation of paperclips for future use. A Chancellor, he later declared, is "not worth his salt if he is not ready to save what are meant by candle-ends and cheese-parings in the cause of the country." The principle of retrenchment, the cutting back of public expenditure, was to be one of the slogans of Gladstonian Liberalism.

Gladstone's underlying purpose was to minimize the taxation of the man in the street. Cheap government would leave more money in the pockets of the people. Their ability to spend would mean greater demand for goods and higher investment by producers. The result would be a thriving economy and, in turn, a contented population. The state, in fact, should interfere very little in a system of self-regulating capitalism. It was a formula that, at a time when Britain's industry was enjoying dominance of the world, was almost bound to foster even greater prosperity. Gladstone, however, was no laissez-faire ideologue who ruled out government initiatives in economic life. While Chancellor, for instance, he set up the Post Office Savings Bank under government auspices (1861) and passed the Industrial Classes Annuities Act (1864). Both were intended to foster savings, especially by skilled workers, that would tide them over in difficult years. Yet most of Gladstone's new undertakings were designed to ensure financial responsibility by the state. In 1861 he created a Public Accounts Committee of the House of Commons to investigate how government agencies were using their money. The committee had unlimited powers "to send for persons, papers and records" and so immediately became an effective check on departmental spending. In 1866 Gladstone carried the Exchequer and Audit Departments Act, creating the new post of Comptroller and Auditor-General. The Comptroller was to prepare detailed audits of government expenditures for the Public Accounts Committee. Henceforward all departments were restrained by the vigilance of the Treasury from unwarranted expenditure. The result was to entrench the principle of Treasury control, an axiom of British government that, like the structures designed to implement it, has stood the test of time down to the present day. Gladstone was the architect of the financial machinery of modern Britain.

A CHRISTIAN WORLDVIEW

Gladstone's policies were the result of careful study of the state apparatus and contemporary economic conditions, and so in one sense his reforms were dictated by the needs of the hour. In another sense, they were the fruit of his upbringing, for his father had impressed on young William the importance of careful accounting. In a further sense, however, the policies were the application of a Christian worldview. The liberal Conservatives of Gladstone's younger days, Peel and his circle, had been deeply impressed by the economic teachings of Thomas Chalmers (1780-1847), the leader of the Scottish evangelicals. Chalmers had blended political economy with theology. The relations of commerce and the state, he argued, must be seen in the light of the divine government of the world. Chalmers favored free trade and direct rather than indirect taxation, since they accorded, he believed, with the will of God. Providence watched over human affairs, bringing good out of evil, order out of chaos. The universe was designed by its Creator for the welfare of human beings so long as they did not abuse their trust. Government regulation of trade constituted interference with the ways of providence. It amounted to human laws infringing the sphere of divine laws. The right policy was for the state to abandon as far as possible such restrictions as Corn Laws and customs duties. Chalmers held that there should be no compulsory poor law either. Charitable relief should be a voluntary affair, binding together the rich and the poor in mutual affection. The pinch of poverty would be a spur to able-bodied men to work for a living. Self-help was not only a maxim of prudence: it was the wisdom of the Creator.

Such a Christian social theory, kindly in aim though hardheaded in method, provided the mental framework within which Peel moved toward free trade. Gladstone, who had met Chalmers and respected his writings, went through his apprenticeship in financial policy when such ideas were in the ascendant. He argued in an article in 1843 that "religion and Christian virtue" have the first place in political economy "as the means of creating and preserving wealth." They prompted the energy and self-reliance necessary in the entrepreneur. Free trade, low taxation, and minimum government interference in the economy were the conditions under which wealth could best grow. Thus Gladstone looked askance at the factory legislation of the period. By restricting for their health's sake the hours that employees could work, the government was reducing factory production. Gladstone accepted the need for some limits on working hours, but he was wary of pushing the principle further. He was convinced that working people would be helped most by the natural increase of prosperity. As time went by, his views on political economy were influenced more by the secular Radicals, with John Stuart Mill's *Principles of Political Economy* (1848) particularly drawing his admiration. Yet economic policy remained closely linked in Gladstone's mind with the operations of providence. It was his task as an executive politician to see that the state conflicted as little as possible with "the moral government of the world." Financial rectitude became an overriding ethical imperative. In earlier years he had been guided in politics by the ideal of the state upholding the Church. From the 1850s he turned instead to reorganizing the nation's finances, but in doing so he was no less guided by a Christian vision.

"THE PEOPLE'S WILLIAM"

Gladstone's achievement as Chancellor brought him popularity. At the start of his term of office, he had been under a cloud of suspicion. Conservatives thought him a renegade; Whigs resented him as an ambitious upstart; Radicals suspected his past. Concerning the new administration in 1859, J. J. Colman, a Baptist mustard manufacturer, wrote, "The appointment which perhaps Reformers would most object to is Mr. Gladstone's, but . . . I think we must . . . hope his position may induce in him a more liberal tone." His 1860 budget, though certainly welcome to Radicals, did not rouse enthusiasm outside the House of Commons. The turning point in his public reputation was his struggle with the House of Lords in 1860 and 1861 over paper duties. Gladstone proposed to abolish the excise duty on the manufacture of paper, but in 1860 the Lords, fearful of the widespread circulation of possibly subversive ideas that would follow, rejected his bill. The conflict turned into a constitutional issue: Could the House of Lords legitimately reject a financial measure passed by the Commons representing the mass of the people? By incorporating the proposal in a larger Finance Bill, Gladstone secured its passage in the following year. As the leader in a mighty struggle for progress, he earned a great deal of favor, and, crucially, he won the praise of the press. The paper duties, "taxes on knowledge," had made newspapers expensive; their abolition vastly increased newspaper circulation. The press, and especially *The Daily Telegraph*, showed its gratitude by giving Gladstone favorable coverage. Gladstone expanded his popularity by delivering speeches at meetings of bodies such as the Social Science Association and on civic occasions in major centers of population. As the country prospered — largely because of developments beyond his control — Gladstone won greater applause. By the conclusion of his period as Chancellor in 1866, he was well on the way to becoming a national hero, "the people's William."

Gladstone's newfound popularity was soon yoked to the central cause of reform a further increase in the size of the electorate. The Reform Act of 1832 had been intended as a permanent settlement of the franchise, but the act itself formed a precedent for more drastic change. The middle classes generally had the vote. Why should the responsible sections of the working classes not receive it? Already in 1851, a Radical motion calling for fresh parliamentary reform had been carried in the Commons, putting the issue firmly on the political agenda. On behalf of the Whigs, Lord John Russell tried to preempt the Radicals by proposing minor reforms in 1852, 1854, and 1860.

For the Conservatives, Disraeli introduced a bill in 1859 designed to extend the franchise but at the same time to increase the proportion of voters who would defer to the wishes of their landlords. No measure commanded the support of the House of Commons, and so there was stalemate. In 1859, Gladstone was still a supporter of Disraeli's bill to shore up the existing constitution, but in the following year, as a member of a Whig administration, he spoke in favor of Russell's bill and of giving the vote to some of the working classes. "The quality of that body of our working men," he told the Commons, "is good enough to entitle them to a share in the privileges of Parliamentary representation." The remark was not noticed by the public. Four years later, however, Gladstone spoke again on the subject. He declared that "every man who is not presumably incapacitated by some consideration of political danger is morally entitled to come within the pale of the Constitution." His language, deliberately opaque, was misunderstood. He was thought, even by Palmerston, to be saying that universal suffrage was morally right. In reality, however, he was merely remarking that *in principle* (which is what he meant by "morally") men should be regarded as potential voters until the reasons against that principle had been taken into account. He was saying little more than he had in 1860, but because he appeared to be enunciating a broad principle and because he was now in the public eye, his words created a stir. "I have unwarily," he wrote, ". . . set the Thames on fire." Gladstone was identified as the champion of reform.

THE PARLIAMENTARY REFORMER

Social circumstances made him welcome the new role. Whereas earlier in the century many in the working classes had shown disaffection, by the 1860s, as Gladstone put it, "the fixed traditional sentiment of the working man has begun to be confidence in the law, in Parliament, and even in executive Government." In particular the artisans of Lancashire were clearly fit to vote. The Civil War in America prevented the import of cotton during the early 1860s, and this left Britain's chief industry slack. Families were thrown out of work, yet there had been virtually no rioting. Gladstone admired the Lancashire operatives for displaying "self-command, self-control, respect for order, patience under suffering, confidence in the law, regard for superiors." Such qualities deserved the reward of the franchise. There was another consideration in Gladstone's mind. As Chancellor of the Exchequer, he had deliberately tried to link liability to tax with the right to vote. Those who paid for the government, he held, should be able to choose it. The working classes contributed a significant part of government revenue through taxes on consumer goods, and so there seemed a logical case for enfranchising some men from their ranks. Their desire to keep down taxes would increase the pressure for retrenchment of government expenditure. Consequently, parliamentary reform would strengthen any Chancellor's demands for economy. If reform was to come, as Gladstone had learned from Peel, it should be undertaken at a time and in a manner of the government's choosing. There must be executive action before any popular agitation arose so that the benefit would be appreciated. There would be, in Gladstone's phrase, a "knitting of hearts together." The result would be social harmony.

No proposal of reform was possible while the elderly Lord Palmerston remained Prime Minister, since he was implacably opposed to any significant extension of the franchise. While popular expectations of reform were gathering force, parliament could do nothing. At this stage there was a major change in Gladstone's position. At a general election in July 1865 he was defeated as M.P. for the University of Oxford. His increasing identification with reform was not appreciated by many of the electors. For the first time, furthermore, it was possible to vote by post rather than by appearing in Oxford, so that clergymen with traditional views participated in much larger numbers than before. The pain of parting from Oxford was mitigated by Gladstone's awareness that he was now able to speak his mind much more freely. No longer would he have to scruple over whether the graduates of Oxford would approve. He was, as he put it, "unmuzzled." Gladstone was returned instead for South Lancashire, the constituency surrounding his native city of Liverpool and the heart of industrial England. His views were now far closer to those of his new electors. He was acceptable, as the advocate of cheap government, to the most Radical in their ranks. Then, in October 1865, Palmerston died, and the political scene was transformed. With parliamentary reform seeming inevitable, voices called for Gladstone to succeed as Prime Minister, but it was too soon. He was only a recent recruit to the Whig cause, and some of his new colleagues doubted, with reason, whether his views sufficiently coincided with those general in the party. Although he had visited many Whig country houses during the early 1860s, he was not yet trusted by all the party's grandees. In any case, Russell, who had been created an earl in 1861 and so now sat in the House of Lords, had a prior claim. Russell, the champion of moderate reform for fifteen years, was appointed Prime Minister. Gladstone, while remaining Chancellor, also became Leader of the House of Commons. The stage was set for a dramatic struggle over reform.

THE REFORM CONTEST

The Reform Bill of 1866 was drawn up by Gladstone and Russell together. It embodied Gladstone's principle that a section of the working classes should be enfranchised. He drew the bottom line of the new urban electors firmly at those who paid £7 a year for their homes in rent, for he intended that only the elite of the working classes was to receive the vote. But this proposal went further than most of the cabinet wished. His colleagues were still influenced by Palmerston's fears that the

diluting of the electorate by the working classes was a dangerous concession. Outside the cabinet there was stern opposition
from the ranks of the more traditionalist Whigs. Robert Lowe,
a witty intellectual, poured scorn on the political capacity of
working people: "if you wanted venality, ignorance, drunken-
ness," he asked, "— if you wanted impulsive, unreflecting, violent people — where do you look for them?" Gladstone, by
contrast, spoke of "our fellow-subjects, our fellow-Christians,
our own flesh and blood." While the government party was
divided, the Conservatives were solidly opposed. It was an
uphill struggle for Gladstone, and his performances in the
Commons were sometimes lackluster, especially against Lowe.
He was working fourteen hours a day as well as speaking
regularly for the bill. It was predictably defeated in June. The
government resigned, and the Conservatives under Lord Derby
came into office once more. It was now their turn to propose a
Reform Bill that would satisfy parliament.

Disraeli, taking over as Chancellor, accepted the challenge. In working closely with Derby, he wanted to impress his
leadership qualities on the Conservative Party by a major triumph, and he also wished to outdo Gladstone. He was prepared to go to almost any lengths to achieve his goals. The
Conservatives had been reluctant to engage in any parliamentary reform, yet in 1867 Disraeli was willing to introduce a bill
enfranchising (though with certain limitations) all male urban
heads of households. That proposal went far further in enlarg-
ing the electorate than Gladstone's measure of the previous
year. Furthermore, in his eagerness to pass any bill, Disraeli
accepted a variety of amendments that gave the vote to even
more men. Virtually the only person from whom he refused
amendments was Gladstone. Outside parliament, mass rallies
began to call for the bill to be carried, and so, despite its drastic
provisions, the House of Commons did not dare reject it. Consequently, the 1867 Reform Act was a far more radical measure
than Gladstone would have wished. Since every male house-
holder in a town was given the vote, a new age of mass

democracy had opened. It was a remarkable achievement for Disraeli. He had trounced the Whig opposition, outmaneuvering Gladstone; he had secured his position among Conservatives, assuming the Prime Ministership in February 1868; and he now trusted that the new electorate would show its gratitude by returning him to power. Gladstone had other intentions. He prepared the ground during the 1868 session by carrying resolutions against the Conservative administration. Despite the events of recent months, Liberalism was generally recognized as the cause of further reform, and at the ensuing general election it was Gladstone, not Disraeli, who gained the support of most new voters. In December 1868, Gladstone took office for the first time as Prime Minister.

He was now unequivocally the Liberal leader, for in the contest surrounding parliamentary reform he had stamped his authority on the party. Its members were now generally known as Liberals rather than Whigs. During the 1850s and 1860s, the two terms had been used interchangeably in reference to the party as a whole, though "Whig" had overtones of the party's past as a stronghold of landowners, and "Liberal" was associated with its future as the party of progress. Although in 1868 a substantial section of the party remained Whig in character, its overall identity was Liberal. Gladstone was definitely Liberal rather than Whig: he stood above all for active reform and economy in government. Yet there was continuity with his own past. "I have never swerved," he told a Lancashire audience as late as 1865, "from those truly conservative objects and desires with which I entered life." His evolution had been gradual. The Peelite schism in the Conservative Party had allowed him to develop certain liberal views without incurring criticism from the backbench traditionalists of his own party. Following the financial policies of Sir Robert Peel had eventually enabled him to become a welcome recruit to the Whig administration of 1859. Those policies were designed for practical ends — less government spending, more economic growth, and greater social harmony — yet they reflected an understanding of where political economy fitted into God's world. Retrenchment, in Gladstone's eyes, was a profoundly Christian aim. In his emergence as a Liberal as much as in his earlier Conservatism, Gladstone was applying his faith to the conduct of public affairs.

6   Gladstone and Overseas Relations, 1835-1868

In the early nineteenth century, Europe was trying to recover from the twin shocks of the French Revolution and Napoleon. Both had undermined the traditional order, one by subversion, the other by expansion. The Treaty of Vienna (1815) following Napoleon's defeat at Waterloo was designed to put an end to such threats. The leading states of Europe agreed to send representatives to regular congresses where they would monitor the condition of France, lest it should turn again to the quest for military glory, and they would concert efforts to keep potential revolutionary forces in check. Austria, Prussia, Russia, Britain and, after a period of probation, France created a structure designed to maintain international stability. There were no permanent power blocs within this European order but rather shifting patterns of cooperation that sustained a rough balance of power. Yet there were settled differences of approach between the five great powers. Austria, Prussia, and Russia were autocracies fearful of change, whereas Britain was a constitutional monarchy proud of its liberty. France moved from the former to the latter camp with its revolution of 1830, which established a more liberal constitution. Because of its less apprehensive stance, Britain tended to adopt more pragmatic policies, moving earliest, for example, toward the recognition of the independence of the former Spanish colonies in Latin America. The liberal Tories of the 1820s believed in European cooperation, but they also welcomed the progress of constitutional government. John Gladstone's political hero George Canning, Foreign Secretary from 1822 to 1827, put national interests before the defense of the European order. Canning believed that domestic opinion should be a major concern of a Foreign Secretary, and he earned popularity by pursuing distinctive British goals. The young William Gladstone had been brought up to admire Canning's approach.

THE GLOBAL POSITION

Canning ceased attending the meetings of representatives of the great powers on the grounds that such congresses "necessarily involve us deeply in all the politics of the Continent." As an island, Britain could shun the entanglements that might lead the other European powers into conflict. The avoidance of Continental commitments remained a hallmark of policy throughout the century. Britain's major interests were commercial and, to a great extent, global rather than merely European. The nation's industry depended on non-European sources for many of its raw materials. It is "the business of the Government," wrote Palmerston in 1841, "to open and secure the roads for the merchant." Ensuring access to overseas markets and, as far as possible, maintaining peaceful conditions for the benefit of trade were among the priorities of successive administrations. The defense of the realm was also a primary preoccupation. It was axiomatic that no foreign power must be allowed to threaten national security. Sea power was considered essential for the protection of international trade and the British coastline. The Royal Navy remained an efficient fighting force throughout the century, never possessing fewer than two hundred vessels. Spending on the army, however, was far less generous, and land forces were proportionately smaller than those maintained by other great powers. The effect was to reinforce the instinct to escape from European involvement. "Ships sailing on the sea," Palmerston remarked in 1864, "cannot stop armies on land." Overseas policy was therefore directed toward minimizing the risk of military confrontation with other powers. It was in Britain's interest to maintain the peace of Europe.

In the rest of the world, Britain possessed an extensive empire in which India held pride of place. It was ruled until 1858 by a commercial organization, the East India Company, and so fell outside the responsibilities of the Colonial Secretary. Nevertheless, the welfare of India was necessarily a concern of government, since there was a succession of minor wars in the region, especially on the frontiers, and India was a major trading partner. More directly under government control were the settler colonies such as Canada and Australia, regulation of which was the chief duty of the Colonial Secretary. In addition, there were many smaller territories — coastal settlements such as Gibraltar and islands such as Mauritius in the Indian Ocean, which were essential to the maintenance of the nation's naval power, serving as bases for the fleet. As yet there were no large swaths of Africa under imperial control, but British possessions were expanding steadily. Between 1841 and 1851, for instance, Britain acquired New Zealand, the Gold Coast in western Africa, Natal in southern Africa, Punjab and Sind in India, Labuan off the coast of Borneo, and Hong Kong. There was little or no greed for empire during this period. On the contrary, whenever possible the government wished to avoid fresh annexations, since new colonies always entailed extra expense. Britain preferred to encourage trade without assuming the burdens of administration, but when commercial interests or existing frontiers could not be secured without adding to the empire, new colonies were tolerated. The growing empire added to Britain's interests overseas.

COLONIAL POLICY

The colonies were one of Gladstone's chief concerns during his earlier years in parliament. His father's estates in the West Indies inevitably engendered an interest on his part in colonial affairs. The family connections were also the reason why Sir Robert Peel chose Gladstone as Under-Secretary of State at the Colonial Office in 1835. Although, as we noted in Chapter 3, he held office only briefly — just over two months — and so was unable to initiate any significant policies, he did nevertheless develop respect for his senior, Lord Aberdeen, the Colonial Secretary. Aberdeen was to influence Gladstone's attitude toward overseas issues in subsequent years. As an opposition M.P. in the later 1830s, Gladstone spoke frequently on colonial affairs. He joined a succession of parliamentary committees — on the treatment of the native people of southern Africa, on colonial waste lands, on the apprenticeship system that had replaced slavery in Jamaica, on military spending in the colonies, on colonial accounts, and on the colonization of New Zealand. He built up expertise that was rewarded in 1845, when Peel appointed him Colonial Secretary, Lord Aberdeen's former post, with full cabinet responsibility. He later admitted that not all his decisions in this position were wise. Characteristically, he placed undue confidence in reports from an Australian bishop about the inefficiency of the local governor. Gladstone recalled the governor, remarking in a private letter that he had heard rumors against the man's character. When the letter came to light, Gladstone's opponents seized on the unjustified slur as a weapon against him. Nevertheless, much of his work was admirable. He planned to put pressure on Spain, and through Spain on Brazil, to end the continuing slave trade across the Atlantic. He devised an elective assembly for

New Zealand, and he organized a survey of Canada with a view to building railways there. During the 1850s, some still thought of Gladstone as primarily a colonial specialist.

He held a view of colonial affairs that differed from the prevailing policy of recent times. The colonies had been subject to close supervision — over their lands, their finances, their defense, their relations with native peoples. Gladstone advocated what he held to be the more generous policy of earlier years. It was the business of parliament to define the areas outside the purview of the colonial authorities and then "to leave them free in everything else." Colonies should govern themselves. Their relations with Britain should be based on voluntary attachment rather than formal bonds. "Experience has proved," he said in 1855, "that if you wish to strengthen the connection between the colonies and this country — if you want to see British law held in respect and British institutions adopted and beloved in the colonies, never associate them with the hated name of force and coercion exercised by us at a distance, over their rising fortunes." Gladstone, like his father, was content if colonies should choose to move toward independence, but he believed that allowing a large measure of self-government would be the best way to avoid rebellions such as those in Canada in 1837-1838. It would also save money: if colonies were responsible for their own defense, they would be motivated to keep costs down. There was a close link between Gladstone's attitude toward the colonies and his developing convictions about the need for economy in government. Both policies formed part of an evolving worldview.

COLONIAL THEORY

Gladstone shared the belief of progressive writers in his day that colonies should be planted throughout the world in order to advance civilization. Cornewall Lewis, later a rival Chancellor of the Exchequer, swayed Gladstone with his *Essays on the*

Government of Dependencies (1841). Each colony, according to Lewis, should reproduce in a distant land the culture of the mother country. It must therefore share the constitutional liberties of Britain. The model in the minds of Lewis and Gladstone alike was the Greek colony of ancient times, when citizens were sent out not to be subject to the sending city but to flourish in independence. The effect of such colonization had been to spread a superior civilization throughout much of the ancient world, and they hoped the same might happen in the modern world. Gladstone wished to encourage emigration to the settler colonies, which, by being thrown on their own resources, would form the character of their inhabitants. So it had been, Gladstone claimed, in the eighteenth century. The colonies on the eve of "the great American Revolution . . . bred and reared men of mental stature and power such as far surpassed anything that colonial life is now commonly considered to be capable of producing." Self-help, he believed, strengthened a community. There is a connection here with the liberal Tory economics that Gladstone had absorbed through Peel from writers such as Thomas Chalmers. The removal of state regulation was good for trade and industry; it was also good for colonies. If the rich were compelled to help the poor, according to Chalmers, then bad feeling would arise on both sides. Likewise, Gladstone argued that if the mother country were forced to support the colonies financially, there was certain to be mutual resentment. Give the colonies freedom, on the other hand, and there would be bonds of affection.

Gladstone stated the case in scriptural language. "For all true, genuine, wholesome and permanent resemblance," he wrote, "we must depend upon a law written not upon stone, but on the fleshy table of the heart." The biblical allusion is not accidental. Gladstone's colonial theory was grounded in the Christian social theory he had drawn from the school of Chalmers. Human regulation, in colonial as in other matters, risked interference with divine laws. Providence had ordained that good relations between a state and its dependencies should grow up naturally, while attempts to control a community at a distance were doomed to frustration. The union of hearts that Gladstone envisaged was a Christian goal. But it would be achieved only if Christian truth was propagated in the colonies. Accordingly, Gladstone was, as he put it, "anxious to see the Church of England take a strong and healthy root" in their soil. While in opposition between 1847 and 1852, he put forward several parliamentary bills to establish bishoprics in the colonies. None was carried as he wished, but the form of his proposals is significant. He planned that the colonial bishops should be independent of control from England so that there would be no reason for friction between the Church of England and its daughter churches abroad. The other major provision was that the colonial churches should not have the privilege of establishment. A state connection, he explained, would be "nothing but a source of weakness to the church herself and of discord and difficulty to the colonial communities." Gladstone's trust in freedom had supplanted his youthful belief in the establishment principle. He hoped that the colonies would be Christian societies; he believed they would be all the more Christian if they were freed from interference by external authority, whether ecclesiastical or political.

ABERDEEN, BRIGHT, AND PALMERSTON

In 1841, Gladstone became a junior minister in Peel's government. Gladstone originally had qualms about joining, since he feared that the government might recognize the legitimacy of the opium trade between British India and China. Palmerston as Foreign Secretary in the previous administration had just fought a war with China to defend the right of British merchants to sell opium there, but Gladstone, aware of the effect of opium in his own family, had protested against "our national iniquity against China." The Prime Minister settled his doubts, inducing him to join the administration with a good conscience.

Peel's Foreign Secretary was Lord Aberdeen, Gladstone's former chief at the Colonial Office. Aberdeen, like the Conservative Party in general, believed in maintaining the order created by the 1815 settlement. In particular, he favored a strong Austria as a bulwark against French or Prussian ambitions. He saw no essential difference between his own strategy and that of Palmerston, but there certainly was a difference of style. Whereas Palmerston was blustering and assertive, Aberdeen was cool and reserved. He was an intelligent, fair-minded man who felt a horror of war after having witnessed the battlefield at Leipzig in 1813. He counted his greatest achievement under Peel to be the avoidance of war with the United States over the Canadian boundary and with France over Greece and Spain. Aberdeen was a natural diplomat, making allowances for the point of view of the other side in negotiations. He had a strong sense of the unity of Europe through a common inherited civilization. His personality appealed to Gladstone, who thought he possessed a "dignity . . . tempered by a peculiar purity and gentleness." Although formally a member of the Church of Scotland, Aberdeen declared, to Gladstone's satisfaction, that he preferred the Church of England. Gladstone had visited his Scottish home, offering him a pair of swans for the lake, and the younger man developed a son's respect for the older. The Foreign Secretary's approach to international relations coincided with Gladstone's natural inclinations — toward conciliation, concession, and peace. Aberdeen was Gladstone's tutor in foreign affairs.

Gladstone felt a moral revulsion against the use of force to settle disputes between nations. By war, he declared in 1853, we mean "that the face of nature is stained with human gore; we mean that bread is taken out of the mouth of the people; . . . we know that it means that demoralisation is let loose, that families are broken up, that lusts become unbridled in every country to which that war is extended." An awareness of the human cost of war strengthened his Christian belief in the maintenance of peace. Interference in other nations, he believed, must be kept to a minimum lest conflict should break out. Establishing peace as a priority, however, did not make Gladstone a pacifist. His contemporary John Bright, a Lancashire mill owner and leader of the Anti-Corn Law League, was a Quaker for whom all war was abhorrent. Bright, together with his friend Richard Cobden and other members of the so-called Manchester School, argued that there should be no contact at all between governments. They held that formal diplomacy produced only friction and that relations between nations might better be established by merchants. Commercial interests, they contended, always dictated peace. Despite his growing sympathies for their principle of free trade, Gladstone was too much of a realist to accept the analysis of the adherents of the Manchester School. He continued to believe that sometimes force had to be deployed against wickedness. "One great advantage of a peaceful and temperate foreign policy," he wrote in 1860, "is that it reserves and husbands power to spend it upon great occasions." Restraint was nevertheless the rule, coercion the exception. After all, the deliberate avoidance of conflict yielded benefits. It kept down military spending, a principle in harmony with Gladstonian finance. If retrenchment was to be one slogan of the Liberal Party under Gladstone's leadership, peace was to be another.

His admiration for Aberdeen's diplomatic techniques and his desire for harmony between nations turned Gladstone into a stern critic of Lord Palmerston. The Whig peer succeeded Aberdeen as Foreign Secretary in 1846 and was therefore in office during 1848, "the year of revolutions." Europe exploded in a series of rebellions against existing rulers, most of them successful. Gladstone, still a Conservative, had no sympathy for insurgents, but Palmerston was more pragmatic, awarding British recognition, for instance, to the new republican regime that had overthrown the monarchy in France. What irritated Gladstone far more, however, was Palmerston's characteristic gunboat diplomacy. When an incident seemed likely to affect even the most trivial of British interests, a naval task force was sent to impress the local rulers. The classic case was the Don Pacifico affair of 1850. Don Pacifico, a Maltese Jew of doubtful character who was nominally a British subject, lost some property during a riot in Athens. Without waiting for redress through the Greek legal system, Palmerston dispatched the Royal Navy to the Piraeus, the port of Athens, to demand compensation from the Greek government. The action of the Foreign Secretary was popular at home, where it was viewed as an assertion of British resolve against a corrupt regime. To Gladstone it seemed a scandalous overreaction indicative of "a spirit of interference." In a magnificent parliamentary speech lasting two and a quarter hours, he denounced Palmerston for having "set the mischievous example of abandoning the methods of law and order, in order to repair to those of force." Although Palmerston's defense of his policy triumphed when it came to a vote, Gladstone had set out the principles of a morally founded foreign policy.

EXPERIENCES IN ITALY

In the following year, Gladstone's name was first brought to the attention of overseas statesmen. In the autumn of 1850, Gladstone was traveling with his family in Italy, a land he had come to love as one of the seats of European culture. It had produced Dante, his favorite poet, and the school of "Primitive" Christian painting he most admired. In the early nineteenth century, the peninsula was a checkerboard of minor states. In one of them based on Naples, King Frederick II, known as Bomba, ran a severely repressive regime. He had nearly been toppled from his throne by liberal forces in the turmoil of 1848-1849 and would tolerate no further opposition. Liberal leaders had been arbitrarily arrested, tried with little show of justice, and thrown into prison. Gladstone visited several of the prisons and was horrified to discover that respectable politicians of constitutional views were chained up with thieves in insanitary conditions. On his return to Britain early in 1851, Gladstone reported on the state of affairs in Naples to Aberdeen, asking the former Foreign Secretary to exert pressure on Bomba for reforms. Aberdeen opened contacts with the Austrians, whose conservative government was in a position to sway the Neapolitan king. While this private diplomacy was beginning, however, Gladstone's impatience led him to publish a *Letter to Lord Aberdeen* censuring the king. The Neapolitan regime, he announced, was "the negation of God erected into a system of government." A fortnight later he amplified his charges in a second public letter. The revelations created a sensation in many parts of Europe. Critics of autocracies, including Palmerston, were delighted; their defenders, at home and abroad, were appalled. Aberdeen, his private efforts hardly begun, was sorely embarrassed, and the Austrians refused to act further. The immediate effect of the published letters was probably to prolong the sufferings of the political prisoners in Naples, but in the longer term Gladstone gave fresh hope to the Italian liberals. His aim had been to urge reform by a conservative government in order to reinforce its legitimacy. Paradoxically he had earned the reputation of being a champion of European liberalism.

There was another result of Gladstone's Italian holiday in 1850-1851. He spent time, as always on Continental tours, observing local religious affairs, and on this occasion his attention was particularly drawn to the papacy. The secular authority of Pius IX over the Papal States in central Italy had been overthrown in another revolution of 1848, but it had been restored by French troops in the following year. Gladstone was convinced that only this outside force prevented the entire collapse of papal rule. "The temporal power of the pope," he wrote exuberantly in 1851, "that great, wonderful and ancient erection, is *gone.*" It was not that he was carried away by popular anti-Catholicism. In fact, Gladstone took a stand during 1851 against the greatest legislative expression of anti-Catholicism during the nineteenth century, the Ecclesiastical Titles Act.

When the Whig government, buoyed up by mass resentment in the country, carried the act prohibiting the newly appointed Roman Catholic bishops from taking territorial titles for their sees, Gladstone vigorously protested against this instance of Erastian interference by the state in a Church. Yet that did not make him a friend of the pope's claims to secular authority, which was as distasteful to him as Erastianism. The church and the state, he was persuaded, fulfilled distinct roles, and neither should trespass on the province of the other. Furthermore, he had seen that the Papal States were administered unjustly and chaotically. After his return from Italy, he set about translating into English the four volumes of a history of the Roman state from 1815 to 1850 by Luigi Carlo Farini. They were published between 1851 and 1854 and helped to confirm British educated opinion in the belief that Roman rule was hopelessly corrupt. They formed the first of several assaults by Gladstone on ultra-montanism, the exaltation of papal authority, religious and secular, that was gaining ground in the Roman Catholic Church. He became a determined foe of the temporal power of the pope.

THE CRIMEAN WAR

From the end of 1852, in office under Aberdeen as Prime Minister, Gladstone shared in the decisions that led to British involvement in the Crimean War. Russia had long entertained ambitions of expanding southward toward the Mediterranean, and the Turkish Empire, ill-administered and already breaking up into lesser political units, seemed fruit ripe for picking. Russia proclaimed itself the champion of the Eastern Orthodox Christians subject to an Islamic power. Conflict actually broke out in October 1853, when Russian troops marched into Romainian provinces of the Turkish Empire. The aggrandizement of Russia was unwelcome to the other great powers, who feared that this was the first step of many against Turkey. Britain and France, as signatories of the Treaty of London (1841) that regulated the waterways into the Black Sea, felt a particular responsibility to take action. Palmerston, predictably, favored the use of force against Russia, but Gladstone, as Aberdeen reported of a cabinet meeting, was "active and energetic for Peace." The destruction of the Turkish fleet by the Russians in December, however, turned the balance against him. Gladstone continued to have doubts about the legal justification for a British naval presence in the Black Sea, but he was persuaded that Russia must be prevented from swallowing up Turkey. By February 1854, he was stiffening the resolve of the Prime Minister to fight. It was, he had decided, a defensive and fully justified struggle. Britain declared war on Russia in March 1854.

The joint Anglo-French military expedition to the Crimean peninsula in southern Russia was not an abject failure. Victories were won; but progress was slow, disease ravaged the army, and there was administrative incompetence on a vast scale. In July, Aberdeen was sharply criticized in the House of Commons and, to his dismay, none of his cabinet colleagues rose to defend him. Gladstone excused himself on the ground that he was not "fully master" of the situation. Aberdeen began to feel that, although just, the war had not been necessary: the same objectives might have been achieved by diplomacy. Gladstone, however, continued to argue that the struggle had been right because it withstood Russia's aggression. Few wars, he told the Commons, had been "begun and continued with such perfect purity of motives." Although Palmerston brought the hostilities to a conclusion after the fall of the Aberdeen coalition in January 1855, the experience of managing the war left a permanent mark on Gladstone's thinking. He believed that Britain, as one of the belligerents, had a duty to maintain a continuing interest in the affairs of the region. There could be no shirking of what was called the Eastern Question because, in having helped to defend the Turkish dominions, Britain had accepted a responsibility to ensure that subsequent Turkish rule was just. The Christian peoples of southeastern Europe must be Britain's concern. In 1858, he defended the newly created Romanian state against efforts by Turkey and Austria to suppress it. Britain, in Gladstone's view, had incurred a moral responsibility for greater European involvement.

EUROPEAN CIVILIZATION

A European outlook transcending narrow British interests came naturally to Gladstone. He made his own a phrase first formally used in the Treaty of Paris (1856) concluding the Crimean War: "the concert of Europe." Cooperation on agreed terms between the largest possible number of great powers was most likely to achieve the just settlement of disputes. A concert of these powers could enforce what in 1850 he had called "that great code of principles which is termed the law of nations." Small countries such as Greece or Romania deserved special protection; there should be an "equality of the weak with the strong." Britain, he argued, should take the lead in promoting cooperation to uphold the brotherhood of nations. In keeping with this point of view, Gladstone was critical of Lord Malmesbury, the Conservative Foreign Secretary in 1858 and 1859, for trying to solve the Italian question alone rather than appealing to what Gladstone called "the general sentiment of the civilized world." After all, Europe enjoyed a common culture. As a classical scholar, as a fluent speaker of French and Italian, and as a rather less fluent speaker of German, Gladstone was particularly aware of the shared inheritance. The European nations, he held, instinctively acted on similar principles not least because they shared the same religion. Echoing Scripture, Gladstone had urged in 1850 that the British should "do as we would be done by." No state should take independent action against another that it would not wish to suffer itself. Common action in the name of justice, he often asserted, was the best restraint on national selfishness. Gladstone's vision of the concert of Europe was an expression of his ideal of a community of Christian nations.

In 1858, Gladstone was entrusted by the Conservative

government with the investigation of a colonial question that was also a European issue. At the end of the Napoleonic wars, Britain had accepted a protectorate over the Ionian Islands, an archipelago off the west coast of Greece that included a naval base on Corfu. There had been a rebellion in 1849, and subsequent reforms had failed to settle unrest. An elective assembly voiced the aspirations of the people, but the executive was not responsible to it. The aspirations, furthermore, were becoming definite: the ending of British rule and union with Greece. During the Crimean War, the Archbishop of Corfu had introduced prayer for the Tsar of Russia into the liturgy. Gladstone, with his experience of colonial constitution-making and his love of Greece, was sent out to recommend fresh arrangements. Frustrated at the time by exclusion from office, he was glad to accept a commission that entailed visiting Ithaca, the home of the hero of Homer's *Odyssey*. He also had the chance to observe a branch of the Eastern Orthodox Church. On Paxos, kissing the bishop's hand, he inclined his head forward for a blessing. The nonplused bishop hesitated. Gladstone decided no blessing would be forthcoming, raised his head sharply and collided with the bishop's chin! He took away from the islands an impression of the simplicity of popular devotion. But his mission proved a failure. Gladstone proposed an extension of the rights of the assembly over the executive, but the tide of Greek nationalism had swept opinion beyond a stage where constitutional tinkering was acceptable. In 1862, Palmerston's government, with Gladstone a member, resolved to allow the islands to merge with Greece. The union was consummated in 1864. At the time of his visit to the Ionian Islands, Gladstone was still underestimating the power of national feeling.

THE ITALIAN QUESTION

His understanding was soon to be deepened by events in Italy. Throughout the peninsula, as in Naples and Rome, the nationalist revolutions of 1848 had been repressed. Only in the north-western kingdom of Piedmont, which also embraced the island of Sardinia, had constitutional government been established. Gladstone met the Piedmontese Prime Minister, Cavour, in March 1859 on his return journey from the Ionian Islands. Gladstone sympathized with the Italian statesman's ambition of ending Austrian control of northeastern Italy and papal control of the central states, but he was wary of Cavour's further schemes for consolidating the whole of the peninsula under Piedmontese leadership. Gladstone favored a gradual evolution of liberties in the various parts of Italy, what he called "the slow growth of the oak." The pace of events, however, soon quickened. Piedmont, backed by Napoleon III, went to war against Austria in May 1859, only to be deserted in July by Napoleon, who made a separate peace with the Austrians. The minor Italian states now began to declare in favor of union with Piedmont. The "Risorgimento" of Italy was in full swing, and Gladstone recognized that deep-seated changes were inevitable. In cabinet during the years 1859 to 1861 he became, with Russell and often Palmerston, a leading champion of the pan-Italian cause. He found himself in opposition to the bulk of the cabinet members who took the traditional British line of backing Austria. Gladstone had been weaned away from defending the authoritarian powers, Austria, Prussia, and Russia, together with their satellites. The upsurge of Italian nationalism had forced him to shift his outlook on foreign affairs.

During 1860, the Italian situation was transformed when the quixotic liberal nationalist Garibaldi invaded Sicily and then Naples. The power of Frederick II of Naples, Gladstone's old antagonist, collapsed, and papal rule also disintegrated. Naples and the Papal States were both annexed to Piedmont, which emerged as the kingdom of Italy. Only the reduced northeastern territory of Austria near Venice and a small area round Rome under the pope remained outside the new kingdom. Palmerston toyed with supporting France against Garibaldi, but Gladstone, together with Russell, withstood him.

Gladstone was now convinced that Italian unity was the only practicable solution. "The miseries of Italy," he told the Commons in 1861, "have been the danger of Europe. The consolidation of Italy, her restoration to national life . . . will add to the general peace and welfare of the civilized world a new and solid guarantee." Italy was a welcome recruit to the concert of Europe. The unification of the peninsula had another great advantage in Gladstone's eyes, for it undermined the residual political authority of the papacy. Gladstone was to call on Pope Pius IX twice in 1866 on a further visit to Italy, but he remained a stern opponent of the pope's temporal power. The whole Italian episode was important for Gladstone. It turned him from a pragmatic defender of existing governments in the manner of Aberdeen into a willing apologist for freedom movements in the style of Russell. It was part of the process that pointed him toward Liberalism.

FRANCE AND AMERICA

During the early years of the Palmerston ministry, relations with France slipped perilously toward war. With the Emperor Napoleon III pursuing blatantly expansionist policies in order to win a tighter grip on domestic power, fear of a French invasion mounted in Britain during 1860. Gladstone, like Russell, was eager to avoid conflict, and at the same time, as Chancellor, he wished to move further toward free trade. The result was the Cobden-Chevalier Treaty of 1860. On the French side, Napoleon III wanted to secure British friendship, not least while he dabbled in Italian affairs. On the British side, Richard Cobden, the apostle of free trade, negotiated the reduction of customs duties on both sides to a bare minimum. Gladstone steered the treaty deftly through cabinet and the Commons by making it part of a package with his budget, which neither body was willing to reject. The treaty greatly reduced the risk of war between Britain and France. The more pacific atmosphere in turn strengthened Gladstone's ability in cabinet to resist Palmerston's demands for additional spending on the army and navy. Although Gladstone did not wholly trust the French emperor, his growing liberal convictions made him prefer France to the more authoritarian powers. He explained in a cabinet memorandum of January 1860 that "the alliance with France is the true basis of peace in Europe, for England and France never will unite in any European purpose which is radically unjust." Such moderately pro-French views were to remain with Gladstone in later years.

During the Civil War that tore America apart between 1861 and 1865, opinion in Britain and the cabinet was divided. There was widespread regret at the outbreak of hostilities. On the other hand, Palmerston, with typical *raison d'état*, hoped that the Southern Confederacy would become a separate state, supposing that the United States, a potentially dangerous rival, would consequently be weakened. Russell believed that the Confederacy carried the flag of liberty. When in the early months of the conflict the North seized two Southern envoys from a British vessel on the high seas, there was a definite risk that Britain would go to war against the Northern states. Russell wrote a demand for satisfaction that might well have precipitated hostilities. Prince Albert toned it down before it was dispatched, however, and the affair was patched up.

Gladstone was less pro-Southern than his two colleagues. Yet by the summer of 1862 he was hoping for concerted mediation in the Civil War by Britain, France, and Russia — mediation that implied the existence of a legitimate Confederate government. In a speech delivered in October, Gladstone went further. There was no doubt, he declared, that the leaders of the South "have made a nation." The statement created a great stir, since people imagined that the government was about to recognize the Confederacy. This was not the case: Gladstone was speaking for himself alone, and he later deeply regretted his words. He did not share Palmerston's wish for the permanent breakup of the United States; nor did he harbor any sympathy for slavery, which he said was founded on the "detestable" principle of white supremacy. His motive was humanitarian, a desire to move toward mediation "for the avoidance of further bloodshed." In retrospect, he felt the greater pain because he had subsequently "received from the government and people of America tokens of goodwill which could not fail to arouse my undying gratitude." In return, Gladstone developed a high regard for President Lincoln. He was to take a close interest in the progress of the United States.

Humanitarianism was one of the enduring components of Gladstone's attitude toward overseas affairs. If the horrors of war were to be avoided, peace must be pursued as a central objective and conciliation as the way of achieving it. Yet he realized that in the relations between states force cannot be ruled out. Originally, like other Conservatives, he saw the preservation of the existing regimes of Europe as another overriding aim. Gradually, however, Gladstone's conservatism was sapped. His views on colonial self-government allied him with progressive thinkers at an early stage in his career, and his experience of Italian affairs subsequently moved him to a more liberal overall stance. But his early respect for order was by no means extinguished. When the Italian hero Garibaldi visited Britain in 1864, Gladstone was alarmed at the mass ovations he received and helped arrange for him to be sent home early. His crime was to excite too much enthusiasm for a cause that had recently been revolutionary. Gladstone was still no friend to insurrection. Yet he did favor the emergence, by natural and peaceful processes as far as possible, of national states. His own sense of organic nationality made him appreciate similar patriotic feelings in others. Even small nations — perhaps especially small nations — deserved support for their spirit of independence. The concert of Europe, the voice of classical-Christian civilization, should be their protector. Already in the 1850s and 1860s, Gladstone's defense of the liberties of the oppressed had gained him international acclaim. He was subsequently to win far more fame worldwide in the same cause.

7 Gladstone's Private Life

Gladstone remained throughout life a classical scholar, never shaking off the influence of his undergraduate studies at Oxford. At dinner parties he would discourse on aspects of the ancient world, and in public speeches he would quote classical authors. In quieter moments on the front bench of the House of Commons, he would translate English hymns into Latin. Reading the classics was a natural relaxation for a gentleman. Both Lord John Russell, one of his Whig cabinet colleagues, and Lord Derby, the leader of his Conservative opponents, published translations of Homer. If many of Gladstone's contemporaries enjoyed similar pursuits, he took them further than almost any other amateur. Human beings, he argued, must be trained by the study of things human in "the most typical forms" — forms that are "principally found among the ancients." Because there is a close relationship between thought and its expression, the languages of the ancients must be studied alongside their ideas. Language, literature, and philosophy, he held, form a single cultural legacy. Gladstone continued to respect Aristotle, on whose principles he had based his social theories in the 1830s. He contended that Aristotle was a powerful agent of ethical and, indirectly, of Christian teaching. Even in his most private reflections, when wrestling with sexual temptations, Gladstone would employ Aristotelian terminology in his diary. Yet when Gladstone settled into a sustained scholarly enterprise in the 1840s and 1850s, it was not Aristotle that he studied but Homer. The transition paralleled the move from his early defense of the Church to his later advocacy of financial austerity. In both cases, the change was from theory to application, from abstract ideas to practical affairs. Homer depicted human beings in actual situations, just as policies of retrenchment affected real social groups. The classics, Gladstone passionately believed, could impinge on nineteenth-century life.

HOMERIC STUDIES

Homer was traditionally understood to be the author of the two earliest Greek epic poems, the *Iliad* recounting the story of the Greek siege of Troy and the *Odyssey* describing the subsequent wanderings of Odysseus. At the end of his life, Gladstone claimed to have read through Homer about thirty times. His feeling for the poet was part of a wider development of taste in his day. Whereas there had been only one verse translation of Homer into English in the generation prior to 1854, twelve were published in the period up to 1877, and the poet was to become even more popular with the Edwardians. Gladstone's partiality for Homer is nevertheless surprising in view of the remarkable absence of ethical considerations in the overt action of the epics. There is nothing, for instance, of the moral dilemmas to be found in the drama of Sophocles. The characters are actuated not by morality but by honor. Gladstone's fascination is to be explained by Homer's stark representation of the interplay of human motives. Homer's society is at once primitive and elaborately organized, and so it readily yielded instruction about human nature. The Homeric world, according to Gladstone, was "fresh and true to the standard of its nature, like the form of an infant from the hand of the Creator, yet mature, full, and finished . . . like some masterpiece of the sculptor's art." The values assumed by Homer are those of an aristocratic society. Heroes and their feats of valor are acclaimed; wealth is presumed, not sought after; allegiance to the community is sacred. The application of the *Iliad* to nineteenth-century society was, in Gladstone's eyes, quite direct. The poem provides case studies of an elite in critical times. The British landed classes could learn from it courtesy and decision, generosity and hard work — the qualities demanded by the hour. The honorable temper that Gladstone deemed to be so conspicuously absent in a Disraeli could be cultivated by the study of Homer. The poet provided a liberal education.

Gladstone designed the three volumes of his *Studies in Homer and the Homeric Age* (1858) with at least one eye to practical application. In the first volume, it is true, Gladstone launches into an elaborate discussion, lasting well over five hundred pages, of the racial composition of the Greeks. The inquiry is based on careful comparison of passages in the Homeric text and is of some enduring scholarly value. But this close textual work is preceded by a vindication of the importance of including Homer in a regular education. Fresh from reforming the University of Oxford, Gladstone wished to commend the expansion of Homeric studies in England. The second volume, on the religion of the Homeric world, takes up the issue of why a Christian society should trouble with pagan gods. Gladstone is forced to admit the immorality of the gods of Olympus, but he contends nevertheless that they exercise a watchful care over the world, upholding right and punishing wrong. There Gladstone discerns the essence of the Christian doctrine of providence. Contemporary preoccupations are most striking in the third volume. In ancient Greek customs Gladstone thought he could recognize "the germ of the law of nations." He also convinced himself that the assemblies, the equivalents of parliament, were superior to the kings as embodiments of the common life. "I know not where else in all antiquity," he remarked in a later article, "to find a living exhibition so much in harmony with the fundamental conceptions, and even institutions, of the English-speaking races of the world." A more popular summary of the three volumes appeared in *Juventus Mundi* ("The Youth of the World") in 1869. Gladstone was eager to transmit the lessons of his Homeric researches to a large audience.

THE SIGNIFICANCE OF HOMER

Behind Gladstone's enthusiasm for Homer lies a theological motive. After the painful crisis of 1850-1851, when the Church of England was rocked by the Gorham Judgment and his closest friends went over to Rome, Gladstone wrote much less than before on ecclesiastical issues. Yet, instead of abandoning the theological enterprise, he broadened it. Homer was charged with religious significance. Gladstone held that the divine revelation recorded in the Bible had also reached the Greeks. They received from neighboring lands the knowledge of God that had been given to the Jews. In Greece, however, the original creed had "fallen into dilapidation" as elements of the worship of nature and animals had corrupted right religion. Even so, traces of truth could still be discerned in the beliefs of the Homeric world. Thus the triad of Greek gods, Jupiter, Neptune, and Pluto, is a pale reflection of the Holy Trinity. Homer therefore accorded in large measure with biblical teaching. Gladstone admitted that the Old Testament was more accurate in its portrayal of the divine government of the world and that the Greeks lacked a sense of sin, but he maintained that Homer was clearer in his account of the operations of human society and that Greek religion "tended powerfully to produce a lofty self-respect, and a large, free, and varied conception of humanity." It also taught that the future life holds retribution in store for misdeeds committed on earth. The heroic age of Greece even pointed toward the incarnation. There is in Homer's depiction of Achilles as the ideal man exalted to semidivine status a foreshadowing of the ultimate revelation in Christ that would unite Godhead and manhood. Gladstone's sympathetic interpretation of the poet may sometimes have gone beyond reasonable conjecture, but he stood in a long tradition of Christian scholarship. The early Church Fathers contended that ancient literature contained anticipations of the coming of Christ. Like them, Gladstone was fitting classical works into an integrated Christian worldview.

It was important for Gladstone's purpose to argue that Homer was an accurate reporter. Only if the detail was trustworthy could guidance be gleaned for contemporary affairs. Consequently, sections of *Studies in Homer and the Homeric Age* contend that the poet was trying to describe faithfully a whole way of life. Gladstone had no doubt that the epics were composed by a single author, and he wished to make few concessions to the newer view that the poems had been remolded by a subsequent oral tradition. His *Homeric Synchronism* (1876) was an attempt to root the Trojan War in a particular period. In it he publicized the recent archaeological work of Heinrich Schliemann at Troy and Mycenae. Schliemann believed he had unearthed both the city the Greeks captured and the palace of their leader, Agamemnon. Gladstone hastily claimed that the excavations demonstrated the reality of Homer's world. Later discoveries, however, established that the city and the palace were of different dates. Homer's Troy was probably on the site examined by Schliemann, but at a different level. Yet Gladstone obstinately defended Schliemann in the face of mounting evidence that he was mistaken. It was an instance where the will to believe got the better of Gladstone's judgment.

Another work he published in 1876, called simply *Homer*, was a more valuable book. It was a straightforward primer, surveying the various aspects of the poet's achievement with a patent enthusiasm that soon infects the reader. Over a century later, the book is still a stimulating introduction to its subject. In 1890, Gladstone published a rather less successful volume entitled *Landmarks in Homeric Study*. Even the well-disposed Lord Acton found reading the work "a hard trial." Although it has to be admitted that Gladstone's opinions about Homer were sometimes farfetched or simply wrong, they were founded on an intelligent appreciation of the text as an avenue into archaic Greece. His efforts broke with the increasingly pedantic scholarship of the day that concentrated on points of grammar and syntax. Gladstone deserves to be seen as having anticipated the late twentieth-century approach of reconstituting Homer's whole social world.

BOOKS AND LIBRARIES

The range of Gladstone's reading was immense. Even when hard-pressed by cabinet business, he normally allocated a portion of the day to books unconnected with any current task. "Books," he once wrote, "are the voices of the dead." Through the written word he was heir to the wisdom of the ages. Theology, classics, history, and biography formed the core of his huge personal library, but it also embraced a large number of other subjects. Anthropology, for example, was well represented. Although the discipline was in its infancy, Gladstone took pains to absorb the views of the leading writers in the field. He felt able to rebut in print the views of Friedrich Max Müller, Professor of Comparative Philology at Oxford from 1868. Gladstone's library was also well stocked with English literature. He appreciated Shakespeare in the normal manner of an educated gentleman, though he had little time for Milton, who was suspect as a revolutionary Puritan. Gladstone read Charles Dickens and many other contemporary novelists, but his favorite writer of fiction continued to be Sir Walter Scott. George Eliot found a place in his literary pantheon, though a

126

subordinate one. Gladstone laughingly chided Lord Acton for exaggerating Eliot's greatness. He was angry with Acton, he told him in 1885, "for lifting her above Walter Scott (even this, I think, your Titanic audacity has attempted), or putting her on his level, yet I freely own she was a great woman." Authors were welcomed to literary breakfasts at the home of the Gladstones during the London season, and they were frequent dinner guests, too. Even Disraeli's leading biographer has concluded that, for all Disraeli's wit, anyone would prefer Gladstone to his rival as a dinner companion. The stock of anecdotal information derived from his vast and eclectic reading was far greater.

Gladstone was concerned with the proper organization of libraries. He acted, for instance, as a trustee of the British Museum and in that capacity helped secure the appointment of Anthony Panizzi as chief librarian in 1856. It was Panizzi who created the round reading room at the heart of the British Museum. Much later, in 1890, Gladstone arranged for the preservation of Acton's magnificent library when it was threatened by its owner's bankruptcy. Gladstone persuaded the American philanthropist Andrew Carnegie to contribute funds sufficient to allow Acton to keep his books. In the same year, Gladstone published a paper entitled "On Books and the Housing of Them." The guiding principles of library care, he characteristically explained, were "economy, good arrangement, and accessibility with the smallest possible expenditure of time." He took a particular interest in the Bodleian, the university library at Oxford. Realizing that its stock was exceeding the available room, Gladstone invented movable shelving to minimize the amount of space occupied. During the closing years of his life, he visited many libraries with the purpose of gathering information about how best to create a permanent home for his own books. As early as 1860, he had added an extra wing to Hawarden Castle to hold his growing library. By the 1890s, he concluded with regret that 10 percent of his books were duplicates, purchased inadvertently. But he intended to ensure that his collection, properly arranged and endowed, should be of lasting value. He erected St. Deiniol's Library in the village of Hawarden and had his books moved there shortly before his death. He asked that scholars and clergymen should be encouraged to spend a period of residence there to profit from the collection. Gladstone's books, complete with his marginal annotations, are still in regular use at Hawarden as the core of a research library. Many have had cause to be grateful for the statesman's foresight.

DANTE STUDIES

In the vast range of postclassical literature, Gladstone's favorite was Dante. The Florentine poet of the turn of the fourteenth century captured Gladstone's imagination in the mid-1830s. The politician admired what he called the "intensity" of Dante's verse. Of the three books of the *Divine Comedy*, the poet's greatest achievement, Gladstone most enjoyed the third, the *Paradiso*, which depicts the state of those pure enough to inhabit the celestial regions. That was to break with the received taste of the recent past. The literary world had preferred the *Inferno*, the vision of hell, or sometimes the *Purgatorio*, the picture of the intermediate state in which souls are being purified. To judge from his allusions, Disraeli's choice was the *Inferno*. Gladstone's literary taste, however, had been formed largely by Arthur Hallam, his closest friend at Eton. It was Hallam who, more than any other critic, led the way in the appreciation of Beatrice, the lost love of the poet who appears in the *Paradiso* as the guide through the heavens. Hallam died young, in 1833, but his collected works, to which Gladstone contributed, helped to foster a Victorian cult of Beatrice. Gladstone retained a strong and affectionate admiration for Hallam and, under the influence of his memory, he came to revere the *Paradiso*. He particularly treasured the words uttered about the will of God by a nun in the lowest sphere of the heavens: "In his will is our peace." The line consoled him in his disappointed loves of the 1830s, and, when his courtship of Catherine proved more successful, he soon drew her attention to the beauty of the phrase. The *Paradiso* became meat and drink for his inward life.

Dante was also woven into the web of his thought. In the conflicts that ravaged Italy in the years round 1300, the poet had been a partisan of the Holy Roman Emperor against the pope, and as a result he had been exiled from his native Florence. Consequently he was taken up as a hero by early nineteenth-century partisans of an Italy free from papal influence. Gabriele Rossetti, father of the more famous poet, wrote a study that claimed to lay bare intricate anti-Catholic messages encoded in Dante's verse. Although Hallam rightly dismissed such speculation, Gladstone persisted in regarding Dante as a leading opponent of the temporal power of the papacy. The poet's political thought, embodied in his *De Monarchia*, appealed to the statesman. He saw it as an eloquent statement of the equal rights of church and state represented by pope and emperor. Each was supreme in his own sphere. "Denying to the Church the right or capacity of property," Gladstone wrote in an article published in 1887, Dante "gave spiritual power to the Pope, and temporal power to the Emperor, each in theory independent of the other, each universal." The balance attracted Gladstone because it matched his own wishes for the modern world. The state should not interfere in the life of the church; the church (and especially the pope) should not meddle in affairs of state. Driven by his aversion to contemporary papal claims, Gladstone even toyed with Dante's idea that because the election of a pope in 1294 was invalid, all subsequent popes held no title to their office. Dante was a faithful Catholic of his day, but he showed great hostility to the papacy — a combination that suited Gladstone precisely. In Dante he saw Catholic doctrine without Roman tyranny.

Gladstone valued Dante most as a "Christian philosopher." The poet accepted the scholastic synthesis of Christian theology and ancient philosophy newly forged in the thirteenth century. Dante revered Aristotle, a man he called "il Maestro" or "il Filosofo." In writing of Dante, Gladstone recognized that "the intellect of that extraordinary man was trained under Aristotelian influences, and imbued, nay saturated, with Aristotelian doctrine." Dante's teaching consisted of Aristotle Christianized, a blend that once more was exactly what Gladstone sought. He, too, had been nurtured on Aristotle, but he was eager to transpose the philosopher into Christian terms. Dante had already achieved the feat by taking over, for example, Aristotle's classification of virtues and vices. Consequently Gladstone felt able to assume the correctness of Dante's moral judgments. Thus, in discussing vanity he is careful to insist, following Dante, that this negative quality should be seen not as a vice, but only as a defect. Gladstone respected those who similarly took Dante as a guide. Esteem for Dante was a trait of A. P. Forbes, whom Gladstone recommended for selection as Bishop of Brechin in 1847. Equally it cemented a friendship with R. W. Church, whom Gladstone appointed Dean of St. Paul's Cathedral in 1871. Gladstone eagerly assisted Dante scholars, published translations of passages from Dante into English, and even wrote a fanciful article that strained the evidence to bring together two of his foremost loves, Dante and Oxford. Allusions in his verse, Gladstone suggested, show that the poet must have traveled to attend the university. Dante, alongside Aristotle, Augustine, and Bishop Butler, was Gladstone's mentor.

MODERN LITERATURE

Dante cemented Gladstone's love of Italy long before he became a champion of Italian national aspirations. Afterward it seemed to him all the more deplorable that the Italian language and the country's literature were neglected in Britain. He took relatively little interest in recent French literature. Although German writing fared rather better — he quite often alluded to the works of Goethe and published translations from Schiller — his preference was for Italian literature. The early nineteenth-century poet Giacomo Leopardi was the writer he rated most highly. Leopardi, after all, had translated Homer and had composed verse in *terza rima*, Dante's characteristic style. There was the drawback that Leopardi was an unbeliever, but, as Gladstone noted, it is for others to take heed to themselves rather than to be inquisitive in judging such men. So fully had Leopardi's writings entered the fabric of the politician's mind that he would quote the poet with casual ease when discussing entirely different topics. Second to Leopardi among modern Italian men of letters in Gladstone's estimation was Alessandro Manzoni, a dramatist and novelist and also a loyal Catholic. His novel *I Promessi Sposi* (1825-26) had gained him a European reputation. Gladstone visited the author near Milan in 1838, their conversation dealing chiefly with questions surrounding the apostolic succession, and wrote to him in 1859 with appreciation for "the seeds sown by your hand both of Faith and of civilization." Gladstone's Italian policies were undergirded by a sympathetic acquaintance with the nation's modern literature.

The recent poetry of his own land was equally dear to him. Gladstone took Wordsworth as a sound guide, though not as an authority like Dante. Shelley, who had re-read Homer each year and had loved the *Paradiso*, gained the politician's respect. Gladstone persuaded himself, though few others, that Shelley's *Prometheus Unbound* should be read as a Christian poem. But among modern poets, in Gladstone's view, Alfred Tennyson had no rival. According to Gladstone, Tennyson's *Idylls of the King*, a reworking of the legends of King Arthur, brilliantly blended the national with the universal, the human with the Christian. In drawing on nature for his illustrations, Gladstone claimed, Tennyson could bear comparison with any poet, ancient or modern. Gladstone wrote a review of the first installment of *Idylls of the King* (1859) celebrating the poem's "essential and profound though not didactic Christianity." He quoted another of Tennyson's compositions, *Locksley Hall*, as an affirmation of belief in providence:

> Yet I doubt not through the ages one increasing
> purpose runs,
> And the thoughts of men are widened with the
> process of the suns.

The poet's periodic expressions of "honest doubt" Gladstone chose to ignore. As early as 1844, he urged Peel, unsuccessfully, to grant Tennyson a special government pension on account of the quality of his verse. From the 1860s onward, the two men met frequently, and in 1883, on Gladstone's recommendation, Tennyson was raised to the peerage. Their mutual esteem was strained by only one factor, a rivalry over guarding the reputation of Arthur Hallam. Each considered himself Hallam's best friend. From time to time, as over the publication of Hallam's letters to Gladstone in the 1880s, jealousy flared up between them. Yet Gladstone's delight in Tennyson's verse never dimmed, for he regarded the poet as a distinctly religious author.

THE VISUAL ARTS

Gladstone believed that the law of the beautiful varies in the different arts. He held that whereas poetry is judged by the mind, painting appeals to the eye. Gladstone had much less confidence in his eye than in his mind. On his first visit to Italy, he felt at a loss when confronted by the various schools of art. Yet by 1843, his judgment had matured sufficiently for him to make able critical comments on the collection of paintings he was beginning to assemble. He was eclectic in his taste but held firm preferences nevertheless. He disliked the floridity of the high Renaissance style, especially as expressed in Leonardo da Vinci. Instead, he admired the so-called "Primitives," the art of Italy from the thirteenth to the fifteenth centuries, the age of Dante. Gladstone appreciated the simplicity, the purity, and supremely the piety of artists such as Giotto. Gladstone was by no means unusual in enjoying what contemporaries called "early Christian art." John Ruskin, the art critic whose word was law, held very similar views. Nevertheless Gladstone was in the vanguard of the advancing taste of the times. He commissioned several Pre-Raphaelites in the mid-century years when they were avant-garde. He especially favored William Dyce, a painter on the fringe of the Pre-Raphaelites, who was also a Scottish Episcopalian enthusiast for choral music and had helped with the planning of Trinity College, Glenalmond.

Perhaps Gladstone's greatest aesthetic achievement was the assembling of the finest collection of Wedgwood pottery made during the nineteenth century. Wedgwood, with its classical designs, had a particular appeal. Among his favorites was a jasper-ware dinner service. Yet all the items except the most strictly useful were disposed of, together with the bulk of the paintings, at a sale in 1875, when the statesman's finances were at a low ebb after the heavy expense of his first premiership. In his artistic taste, as in so many other spheres, Gladstone won proficiency through application. He was no mere dilettante.

CATHERINE GLADSTONE

A secure home life at Hawarden made possible the range of Gladstone's pursuits. His wife Catherine, two years younger than William, was to survive him by two years. She lightened family conversation, stimulating William's rather ponderous humor. "Oh, William dear," she once remarked, "if you weren't such a great man you would be a terrible bore." She delighted in the special language made up by her original family, "Glynnese." Words were adapted or applied to fresh contexts so that "null and void," for example, became "vull" in Glynnese. Her life was a cheerful harum-scarum affair. Letters would be left for days on the drawing room floor, though early in their married life Catherine promised William that his correspondence would not be treated so absent-mindedly. Apart from her husband, she was habitually unpunctual. She neglected the orderly Victorian social round of morning calls, and she forgot to send out dinner invitations. Yet she compensated for it all by great personal warmth. She maintained a reservoir of sympathy for all in distress. When her sister Mary died in 1857, she became a virtual stepmother to Mary's twelve children. Much of Catherine's time was spent in charitable work. She opened orphanages at Clapton in London and at Hawarden itself. She was also responsible for "Mrs Gladstone's Free Convalescent Home for the Poor" at Woodford in Essex. There can be no doubt that she complemented Gladstone admirably. One of their sons records that at exciting moments William and Catherine, with arms round each other's waists, would sing together:

> A ragamuffin husband and a rantipoling wife,
> We fiddle it and scrape it through the ups and
> downs of life.

They had a happy home.

Gladstone once wrote, as Prime Minister in 1869, that "my country is my first wife." During the long parliamentary sessions in London, Catherine was often neglected, and even at Hawarden by the 1860s there was little time for walks together. Catherine rarely complained, for she admired her husband and identified closely with his political career. Nothing delighted her more than the appreciation of his efforts expressed in outbursts of popular acclaim. She enjoyed watching him in the House of Commons or joining him at public meetings. Catherine regarded such events as treats: "hearing you," she told him, "is ever to me like listening to beautiful, sweet music." More could hardly have been hoped for in a wife. In one respect, however, Catherine did not take pains to further William's prospects. She did not enjoy acting as a political hostess, and when Gladstone's prominent supporters were denied an expected invitation, they sometimes felt themselves slighted. Yet Catherine was careful to protect her husband from intrusive callers, since she believed his time was too precious for interruptions. When he was considering retirement in the 1870s and again in the 1880s, Catherine pleaded that he should remain at the center of affairs. She was reluctant to see him leave the leadership of the Liberal Party partly because she believed his services were invaluable for the country, but there was also a more personal reason. She loved, according to their daughter Mary, "being inside the mainspring of history." Catherine was a buttress to Gladstone's work.

THE GLADSTONE FAMILY

Gladstone's four sons were limited in access to their father but greatly enjoyed his company when they were small. "We had teaspoonfuls of black coffee," one of them recalled, "and rides on his foot slung over his knee while he sang 'Ride a cock-horse to Banbury Cross'." He measured their height, played card games with them, and once carried four children simultaneously on his back. On another occasion the boys surreptitiously cut the top off a tree in the grounds of Hawarden to make their own Christmas decoration. Their father asked what they were doing. "Nothing," they answered. On the following morning they were summoned to see Gladstone. There was no mention of the tree, but their father spoke of the importance of telling the truth even in small matters before dismissing them with a twinkle in his eye. The incident was remembered as wise and kindly guidance.

School for the boys meant going away at about the age of seven and enduring repeated floggings. Each survived to go on to Eton and university. The oldest, William, became the owner of Hawarden on his marriage in 1875. It was he who organized the selling of wood chips to Liberal trippers inquiring after the tree-cutting feats of his father. The younger William entered parliament in 1865, sitting successively for Chester, Whitby, and East Worcestershire. Although he held minor government office from 1869 to 1874, he made little mark in politics and died before his father, in 1891. Stephen, the second, was a retiring personality who found satisfaction as the parish clergyman of Hawarden. Henry was a successful jute merchant in India before returning to England in 1890. Eventually, in 1932, he was to become a peer as Lord Gladstone of Hawarden. Herbert, the youngest, was the closest to his father. He gained a first-class degree and was appointed lecturer in history at Oxford. In 1880, however, he turned to politics under his father's patronage. He was to become Liberal chief whip, Home Secretary, and, in 1910 as Viscount Gladstone, Governor-General of South Africa.

The three surviving girls were given the customary perfunctory education of the day by governesses at home. At twenty-nine, Agnes, the oldest, announced that she intended to take up nursing, but Catherine dissuaded her. Two years later she married E. C. Wickham, a clergyman who was then Headmaster of Wellington College, a prominent independent school, and who later became Dean of Lincoln. The other two girls remained within the Hawarden orbit. Mary and Helen had quick minds and followed politics closely. "Helen and I nearly died of excitement," Mary recorded in her diary of a visit to the House of Commons to hear their father speak in 1866. She revered her father as a figure of heroic proportions. "I think Papa is rather like Shakespeare," she noted four years later. In 1880 she became his private secretary, taking charge of much of his correspondence and calming irritated members of the government. Although in 1886 she married a clergyman, Harry Drew, nine years her junior, she did not leave Hawarden. Harry succeeded Stephen Gladstone as the village clergyman there in 1904. Helen went to Newnham College, Cambridge, as a mature undergraduate in 1877, and in 1882 she was appointed its Vice-Principal. Following her sister's marriage, she took over the primary responsibility for her parents, and in the last two years of Gladstone's life she left Newnham in order to be able to care for him full-time. As an unmarried daughter, she was expected to take on the role. Both Mary and Helen sacrificed their prospects for the sake of their father, but, with no evident resentment, they showed every sign of appreciating the chance of serving him. Their admiration was matched by their love.

Gladstone's relations with his sister Helen continued in later years to be much less satisfactory. They met infrequently. In 1878, when she had failed to repay a loan, he refused to open a Christmas parcel of gifts for the family and wrote to tell her why. He could not understand her inability to do battle with her weaknesses any more than he could fathom her Roman Catholic allegiance. On her death, at Cologne in 1880, William hurried to her hotel to investigate her affairs. He calculated that there were more books of devotion beside her bed from before the First Vatican Council than from after it. Helen's piety, Gladstone concluded, must have been of a pre–Vatican Council variety. Gladstone believed that the representatives of that tradition were not the Roman Catholics but the Old Catholics who had rejected the Council's innovations. Since in Britain there were no organized Old Catholics, Helen must be buried according to the rites of the nearest equivalent. It was therefore proper that she should be interred in the family vault at Fasque as a Scottish Episcopalian. Gladstone plainly wished to regard his sister as being one in religion with the rest of the family. It is a sign of his unwillingness to come to terms with her conversion to the Roman Catholic Church nearly forty years before. If the incident reveals Gladstone's capacity for casuistry, it also illustrates the strength of Gladstone's attachment to the Anglican communion. Even more it lays bare his failure to sympathize with the wishes of one of his closest relatives.

DIVORCE AND TEMPTATION

Gladstone was particularly insistent on the Church's teaching about marriage. He was prepared to go to great lengths to defend the sacred institution. In 1849 he traveled from England to Italy in pursuit of the wife of his Oxford and parliamentary friend Lord Lincoln, the heir of the Duke of Newcastle. Lady Lincoln had long shown a liking for other men, and at last had gone off with Lord Walpole to the Continent. Gladstone determined on a quixotic attempt to persuade her to return. It was wasted effort, for the couple eluded him, and soon a divorce went through. Gladstone recognized that the aggrieved party in a marriage broken by adultery had the right of divorce. Even in those circumstances, however, he felt that the best course was to maintain the marriage in hope of repentance. With such a high doctrine of the married state, Gladstone was dismayed by a bill of 1857 designed to permit easier divorce. Previously the dissolution of a marriage had required a private act of parliament, a troublesome and expensive method available only for the few. A Royal Commission of 1853 had recommended that in cases of cruelty, divorce should be possible through the courts, and now the government proposed to implement its report. Gladstone made twenty-nine interventions in debate against the bill during a single day. Yet resistance was forlorn: his only success lay in securing the rejection of a proposal to compel clergymen to marry divorcees. In his opposition to the bill, Gladstone was not trying to ensure the subjection of women. On the contrary, he strongly objected to the provision that husbands but not wives should be allowed to initiate divorce proceedings. He declared that he was defending "the equality of the sexes under the Christian law." Women, he held, should not be victimized by men.

Gladstone's work for prostitutes had long been an expression of the same principle. He kept up his rescue efforts even when in high office, and by 1854 he had been involved in eighty to ninety cases. In no instance, he ruefully recorded, had a girl's way of life been changed solely through his help. Some had exercised a fascination over Gladstone. One, Miss Summerhayes, was so striking that he had her painted in 1859 by William Dyce as Dante's Beatrice. Gladstone's diary reveals that dealings with certain other prostitutes became a source of sexual temptation. It was almost as though he courted moral danger in order to reassure himself that he had the strength to resist. The worst entanglement, however, came with a woman of higher station, Mrs. Laura Thistlethwayte. Possessing great beauty and charm, she had led a life of sexual immorality before being converted to evangelical Christianity, and in the 1860s she was the most prominent of a whole regiment of women who acted as popular evangelists. Laura Thistlethwayte was still capable of casting a feminine spell over men of her acquaintance, and in the autumn of 1869, while Gladstone was overtired from his duties as Prime Minister, he fell under her influence. By sending him batches of her manuscript autobiography for comment, she drew him into greater intimacy. Coquettishly, she accused him in a letter of laughing at a passage in her book. "Dear 'Broken Reed' and 'Wounded Spirit', he replied, "send me the naughty letter back." It was the vocabulary of making up after a lover's tiff. Shortly afterward Laura Thistlethwayte seems to have used the word "love" in a letter that has not survived and then to have proposed burning their correspondence. Gladstone declined, explaining that burning removes a bridle. He realized, perhaps just in time, that his guard was down. If his word can be trusted, there was no question of infidelity, but Gladstone was nevertheless subject to acute temptation. He recognized that his powerful emotions had to be reined in.

Gladstone's private life was as many-sided as his public career. It is astonishing that a man so immersed in political affairs should find time for scholarship, yet his study of Homer and Dante was detailed and sustained. During a long lifetime, he repeatedly returned to these authors for intellectual stimulus and spiritual nourishment. In both cases he was eager to relate them to the Christian faith. The place of ancient Greece in the providential order was the theme of more than one university address. Dante was valued most of all because he integrated the classical legacy with Christian teaching. Gladstone collected books in abundance to fill out his understanding of the world even more than to provide the background for policy decisions.

He appreciated the verse of Leopardi, Manzoni, and Tennyson and he collected paintings and china because a liberal education had given him a taste for everything human. For Gladstone the family was so central a social unit that it was worth defending in parliament to the last ditch. In his own family, relations with his sister Helen were strained, but his children respected him for his domestic qualities as well as for his public virtues. He was drawn into testing times, especially by Laura Thistlethwayte, but his love for his wife was not in the end compromised. Catherine's high spirits and profound devotion were essential resources for William throughout his married life. With her at his side, he was able to fulfill the duties of the highest office of state.

8 Gladstone's First Government, 1868-1874

When Gladstone entered office as Prime Minister in December 1868, the country held high expectations of his administration. He had just won the first general election under the reformed franchise of 1867. Although still only about a quarter of the male population could vote, there was much talk of a decisive shift toward democracy. Would the government, spurred on by the electors, make drastic changes in national life? Gladstone had announced a program of intended reforms in December 1867. It was his judgment that the nation had passed "from a stationary into a progressive period." The administration, he argued, was bound to reflect the wishes of the country, but the shift was in any case congenial to Gladstone. He had been taught by Peel that it was the responsibility of government to manage change from above, and in office as Chancellor, Gladstone had ripened into a constructive statesman of great skill. His government would not shy away from undertaking fresh schemes. Whig administrations of mid-century had normally preferred, at least in domestic affairs, to respond to issues as they arose, but Gladstone's government would initiate. The alteration of style marked the transition from Whiggery to Liberalism on the progressive side of British politics. Whigs were normally reactive; Liberals were essentially proactive. Despite all his respect for Whig aristocrats, Gladstone was far more inclined by his energetic temperament to align himself with the Liberal demand for action. With a heavy program of legislation, the burden on the Prime Minister was enormous. Already in January 1869, before parliament was in session, Gladstone reported completing at least ten hours' work on public business each day at Hawarden. When in London, he was assisted by a staff of only three private secretaries. There was no time for newspaper reading, let alone for the study of Homer. Gladstone, already nearly sixty years old at the start of his premiership, expected that it would be his only term of office, and so he was determined to press through a range of measures while he had the chance. He threw himself wholeheartedly into the task of government.

THE CABINET

Gladstone's authority as Prime Minister was unchallenged. During his first ministry from 1868 to 1874, no one considered the idea that he should be supplanted. He acted himself as Leader of the House of Commons, managing the passage of government legislation. There were fourteen other members of the cabinet. Six were Whigs, five of them peers. Three, apart from Gladstone himself, were Peelites in origin. Three were plain Liberals, reflecting much of the parliamentary party. Another, John Bright, represented the popular Radical current in the party. As the first Nonconformist to serve in a cabinet, Bright held an important symbolic role, and Gladstone took pains, though in the end unsuccessfully, to keep him in office. The other member, Robert Lowe, the Chancellor of the Exchequer, was the chief problem for Gladstone. Lowe, in 1866

142

the leading rebel against Gladstone's abortive Reform Bill, was an intellectual Radical. He was capable, according to the Prime Minister, "of tearing anything to pieces, but of constructing nothing." Another advanced Liberal, James Stansfeld, was to join the cabinet in 1871. Stansfeld later recalled that Gladstone's procedure was not what he expected. "I naturally thought that his position was so commanding, that he would be able to say, 'This is my policy; accept it or not as you like'. But he did not. He was always profuse in his expressions of respect for the cabinet." Gladstone had valued his own liberty of action as a minister in earlier administrations, and so as Prime Minister he gave individual ministers their head. Even the troublesome Lowe, holding Gladstone's former office as Chancellor, was allowed to formulate his own policies. Yet in collective decision making, Gladstone's views normally prevailed by dint of argument. He prepared carefully, as his surviving agendas testify, and his stamina carried him through the fifty or so cabinet meetings held each year. Gladstone believed in the cabinet as an instrument of government, and operated it efficiently.

In retrospect, and after experience of later administrations, Gladstone described the 1868 cabinet as "easily handled." Its smooth operation was partly attributable to the fact that he faced no concerted opposition. The Whig members, with whom he commonly felt less sympathy on questions of policy, were in no sense a political faction pressing distinctive views; rather, they were independent landowners of refined manners who placed affability high on the scale of virtues. Gladstone found Lord Clarendon, Foreign Secretary until his death in 1870, "a most lovable and genial man." Clarendon's experience of cabinet office, reaching back to 1840, proved invaluable in the early stages of the ministry. Lord Granville, Clarendon's successor at the Foreign Office, played an even more crucial role. Since he was the son of the British ambassador to France and he had been brought up in Paris, diplomatic technique and social skills came naturally to him. "People think that I am a very idle man,"

Granville once remarked; "I am sorry to say it is quite true." He was admired for his combination of a languid style with acute intelligence. He had worked with Prince Albert in planning the Great Exhibition of 1851, and he retained an influence over Queen Victoria. Granville cooperated closely with Gladstone in shaping foreign policy, a subject that will be discussed further in Chapter 9. Profoundly loyal to the Prime Minister, he compensated for some of Gladstone's weaker points. Gladstone might cause offense with his penchant for concentrating on issues and ignoring the need to develop rapport with individuals, but Granville sensed how people were feeling. He hastened to mend fences even before the Prime Minister was aware that damage had been done. Without Granville, the cabinet would have been much harder to guide.

THE PARLIAMENTARY PARTY

If Whiggish skills served Gladstone well in the cabinet, Whiggish attitudes constituted one of his greatest problems in parliament. More than half of Gladstone's party in the House of Commons were landowners; all those in the House of Lords were substantial landed proprietors. The traditional views of the upper classes were well entrenched among them. They were wedded to the defense of property rights, and they tended to look down on the common people. Since they believed that government existed to uphold the rule of law rather than to pursue fresh policies, their natural instinct was to act as a brake on reform. Furthermore, many of them shared a Broad Church theology according to which religion was primarily a spur to moral endeavor for a better world, a sanction for the idea of progress. Their ideal was a common Christianity free from dogmatism and superstition. Their pet hate was clericalism, the assertion of special privileges for the clergy. There must be, as one of those who moved in Whig-Liberal circles put it, no "cowardly resignation to priestly authority." Such men were suspicious of Gladstone's preoccupation with dogma and the interests of the Church of England. Whigs assumed that the state had the responsibility of encouraging virtue and restraining passions among the mass of the people. Gladstone, on the contrary, saw these tasks as belonging to the church. When the state took on such duties, he believed, it exceeded its proper powers and infringed on the sphere of the church. The characteristic Whig attitude verged on the Erastian belief that the state should control the church; as his reaction to the Gorham Judgment had shown, Gladstone hated Erastianism. The divergence repeatedly created difficulties during his ministry.

There was also restiveness among more advanced sections of opinion within the party. Gladstone's supporters in the House of Commons did not form a coherent bloc. They were united by little more than belief in free trade and efficiency. Voting with the opposition was common; abstention from voting was commoner; absence from the House was commonest of all. Most M.P.s had business interests to pursue outside parliament. When they were present, the most likely rebels against government policy were found among the more advanced Liberals. This grouping was itself fragmented. It did not, as yet, include a working-class component (the first working-class Liberal M.P.s were not elected until 1874). It did, however, embrace a large number of Scottish representatives, always concerned that the separate legislative claims of their country should be remembered. It also included a body of Irish M.P.s, some Protestant but more of them Roman Catholic. They could be relied on to adopt a distinctive line, as when, in 1870, one of them wrote to Gladstone demanding government efforts to restore the temporal power of the pope. No proposal could have been less welcome to the Prime Minister. Another large section, over fifty strong, consisted of Nonconformists. Their special aim was disestablishment of the Church of England. Behind each section was a sizable body of public opinion that needed to be placated if it was not to grow disaffected. Management of the government majority in the House of Commons was therefore a delicate task. Gladstone rarely took up such work himself, but almost daily he was in contact with the Liberal chief whip, G. G. Glyn, who relayed party feeling to him. The Prime Minister and chief whip became fast friends. When Glyn had to give up the whip's post in 1873 because he succeeded his father as Lord Wolverton, Gladstone was deprived of a strong support. "Rely upon it," Gladstone wrote to him, "that I am truly & deeply grateful to you for all you have been to me & done for me." Glyn performed in the House of Commons a role similar to Granville's in the cabinet — that of keeping Gladstone's followers in line behind their leader.

THE IRISH QUESTION

The first measure of the administration was the disestablishment of the Church of Ireland. Gladstone's early political thought had revolved around the defense of this branch of the Anglican Communion: *The State in Its Relations with the Church* had been written so as to provide a rationale for resisting precisely what Gladstone was now proposing. Over the intervening years he had become convinced that the continued recognition of Anglicanism as the official religion was a legitimate grievance of the people of Ireland. The great majority of the Irish population were Roman Catholics, but a Protestant Church received state patronage. In 1865 Gladstone had spoken of Irish disestablishment as a "question of the future" that would eventually need to be taken up, but only when the time was suitable. An event in December 1867 convinced him that the hour had come. In that month a group of Irish Fenians attempted to free some colleagues being held at Clerkenwell Prison in London, and twelve people were killed. The outrage showed that the Fenian terrorists, committed to securing Irish independence, could mount a major operation in England. The great bulwark against mass support for the Fenians in Ireland was the Roman Catholic Church, which regularly condemned their secret oaths and violent methods. Gladstone believed that unless the Roman Catholic population were shown that the British government wished to do them justice, there might be a further strengthening of terrorism. Accordingly, in March 1868, before the general election that brought him to power, Gladstone carried a series of resolutions in the House of Commons in favor of Irish disestablishment. He was fiercely attacked for inconsistency. How could the erstwhile champion of the Church of Ireland now call for its separation from the state? Gladstone wrote *A Chapter of Autobiography* in self-vindication. He pointed out that his youthful book *The State in Its Relations with the Church* had defended the Irish Church on the ground that the state should recognize the truth of the Church's teaching. In modern conditions of religious pluralism, that ground was untenable. Once that contention could not be maintained, the case for establishment fell, since justice demanded that the Irish majority should not chafe under an alien Church. Disestablishment should go ahead.

Although Gladstone was passionately assailed by anti-Catholic zealots for deserting the Protestant cause, his policy proved popular at the general election of 1868. The new parliament contained 382 Liberals and only 276 Conservatives. Irish disestablishment had been well chosen to rally the Liberal Party. A few dissidents, usually men with a Church of Ireland background, fell away, but the great sections of opinion within the party were all pleased. The Roman Catholic Irish naturally appreciated the concession of one of their main demands. While the Whigs saw the proposal as calculated to bring peace to society and security to property in Ireland, their antiecclesiastical prejudices made them deaf to clerical cries that a sister church was being ruined. The Scots, largely Presbyterian in religion, were unmoved by appeals from Irish Episcopalians. And the Nonconformists of England and Wales rejoiced as much as the Catholics of Ireland. Their pressure group, the Liberation Society, had long been advocating the separation of church and state, and now the Liberal leader had taken up the cause. Gladstone had been carefully courting Nonconformist leaders at private soirées since 1864. In 1868 he had carried through the Commons a bill to abolish compulsory church rates, the local taxation for maintaining parish churches that fell on all property owners, whether Anglican or not, and so had dealt with another long-standing Nonconformist grievance. The chapel-goers had high hopes that before long he would propose disestablishment in England itself. And so Gladstone was praised throughout the Liberal ranks. The issue that he had chosen unified the party during the general election and the early months of the administration, lifting morale and smoothing the path of the Prime Minister. It is a good example of Gladstone's skills as a politician dealing with a mass public.

The main business of the 1869 session was the passage of the Irish Disestablishment Bill. Gladstone personally took charge of the measure, replying to the debate on the second reading in a particularly masterly way. Every objection to the case for disestablishment was met and refuted. "It is for the interest of us all," he contended, "that we should not keep this Establishment of religion in a prolonged agony." The principle of the bill could hardly be resisted thereafter, but what could still be challenged were the practical arrangements for the finances of the disestablished Church. Many Whigs who normally supported the administration, including the former Prime Minister Earl Russell, favored "concurrent endowment." The assets of the Church of Ireland, they argued, should be allocated between the various Christian denominations of the land so that all the religious communities would feel an obligation to the British state. The Conservative opposition prudently decided to adopt the same ground in the House of Lords, where, with the assistance of forty-nine Whig peers, the bill was amended so as to include concurrent endowment. Gladstone, however, refused to have any truck with the Erastian notion of controlling churches through state patronage. He resolved to resist concurrent endowment to the uttermost, knowing that he had the firm backing of the Irish Catholics and the English Nonconformists in the House of Commons. There was therefore a confrontation between the two Houses of Parliament: the Commons sent the unamended bill a second time to the Lords; the Lords again made their amendments. Now Gladstone wanted to abandon the whole bill in the confidence that there would be popular agitation in favor of the government, which had received a mandate for the measure less than a year before. He was prepared to precipitate a crisis in order to avoid infringing his own deeply felt views about the relations of church and state. Granville, by contrast, persisted in delicate negotiations with the Conservatives and secured a compromise that did not surrender to concurrent endowment. He attained Gladstone's objectives without provoking a constitutional struggle. The Church of Ireland was duly severed from the state on 1 January 1871. It was an episode in which, as a government colleague Lord Kimberley noted, Gladstone showed a lack of "cool judgment."

Gladstone did not suppose that disestablishment by itself would settle Ireland, for he recognized that unrest in the Irish countryside was a symptom of deep-laid resentments. The mass of the Irish peasantry believed, with some justice, that long ago their ancestors had been deprived of their land by conquerors from England. The landlords of Ireland, they were convinced, had no right to their property. Every undue exaction of rent, every eviction, was salt in an old wound. The extent of the alienation of the people from their natural leaders horrified Gladstone, who still upheld his youthful belief in the importance of the aristocracy. Only through closer bonds between the landlords and the peasants on their estates could the social peace of Ireland be achieved. He never entertained anything like the idea of overturning the aristocracy, but he did think that tensions might be eased by eliminating acts of oppression by irresponsible landlords. It was his desire to strengthen good custom with the force of law so that tenants could be guaranteed their "historical and traditional rights." In 1866, he had backed a bill with this objective, but it had been withdrawn

because of lack of time. In 1870, he made an Irish Land Bill on
these lines the main legislation of the session. It was very much
Gladstone's personal measure, the result of a close study of
Irish custom. In cabinet, Lord Clarendon, himself a great land-
owner, resisted tampering with existing rights of property, and
Gladstone was fortunate that once again Lord Granville was
prepared to act as mediator. The bill had a long passage
through the Commons, spending sixteen days in committee,
but the Conservative majority in the House of Lords gave the
bill an unopposed second reading. They feared that if they
offered resistance to a popular measure, as they had done in
the previous year, they might suffer legislation against their
powers. So the bill passed into law. Its most drastic provision,
inserted by John Bright, allowed tenants to borrow from the
state to buy their land. In the main, however, it was far less
revolutionary, confirming existing good practice in exactly the
way that Gladstone had intended. Although it did not prevent
further Irish unrest, the act did demonstrate Gladstone's conviction that Ireland must be treated justly.

EDUCATION, THE NONCONFORMISTS, AND THE CHURCH OF ENGLAND

The other major bill of 1870 was concerned with education.
England did not yet enjoy a national education system supported by the state. Elementary instruction was still provided
in schools run by individuals or societies, only some of which
received government grants. During the late 1860s, it had become apparent that existing arrangements were entirely un-
satisfactory: the provision of elementary schools by voluntary
agencies was steadily falling behind population growth. Parliamentary reform had given a share in political power to many
working men, and yet they had in some cases received no
education. England was woefully behind her Continental
neighbors, particularly Prussia, and a remedy seemed overdue.

Gladstone's administration took up the challenge by proposing to set up local elected boards that would erect and manage new schools. The controversial question was what type of religious instruction should be given in the schools. Gladstone had no doubt that ideally education should be the responsibility of the Church of England, whose National Society had sponsored denominational teaching for many years in a high proportion of the voluntary schools. He wanted the new school boards to be free to provide such definite Anglican instruction. Religious teaching had to be denominational, Gladstone believed, or else there would be no guarantee of its doctrinal content. Rather than allow the instruction to be undenominational, he preferred to have no religious teaching at all. His view was unusual. W. E. Forster, his education minister, favored the undenominational solution, and so did the majority of the parliamentary Liberal Party. Many feared clerical influence in the schools if distinctive Anglican teaching were to be given. Eventually, after extensive parliamentary debate, the cabinet agreed to accept undenominational teaching, and Gladstone acquiesced reluctantly. His defense of the educational mission of the Church of England had failed. Yet the Education Act of 1870, together with a similar bill for Scotland two years later, was unusually significant, for it ensured a sharp rise in literacy levels in the later nineteenth century. For the first time, elementary education became general throughout England.

The Education Act nevertheless created a political problem for the administration. The Nonconformists in the Liberal ranks were dismayed that the act gave extra money for new buildings to the National Society of the Church of England and even to Roman Catholics. The state, in their view, was promoting soul-destroying error. Their irritation increased when, early in 1871, they began to realize that the act would continue to finance Anglican and Catholic instruction over the long term. Clause 25, allowing denominational teaching for certain poor children, became a symbol of discrimination against Nonconformists. Like Gladstone, most of the Nonconformists wanted no public interference in religious instruction, since the state, they feared, might tamper with authentic Bible teaching. Consequently there was a "Nonconformist Revolt" against the government. Further policies worsened the relationship. In 1871, religious tests preventing non-Anglicans from graduating at the universities of Oxford, Cambridge, and Durham were abolished, a change that in itself was welcome to Nonconformists, but Gladstone wanted to ensure that the universities nevertheless maintained their traditional role of training the ministry of the Church of England. Nothing could alter Gladstone's allegiance to Oxford tradition. When it became clear that many college fellowships would still be restricted to Anglican clergy, Nonconformists were dismayed. They were further shocked when Gladstone resisted parliamentary motions calling for English disestablishment, claiming that he had thrown into the debate "a gratuitous and flippant sneer at the Nonconformists." As a result of their various grievances, they announced that they would no longer give active support to the administration. Gladstone shared the Nonconformist attachment to biblical truth, but he differed sharply with their belief that all religious denominations should be equal. For all his evolution toward Liberal opinions, he remained in his later years a champion of the interests of the Church of England.

When in office, Gladstone was able to promote the welfare of the established Church by his exercise of ecclesiastical patronage. Many leading posts in the Church of England, including all the diocesan bishoprics, lay in the gift of the crown, which acted on the advice of the Prime Minister. Gladstone took a deep interest in this dimension of his public work, never showing so much excitement as when there was a vacant see to fill. He compiled a formidable list of the qualities he looked for in a potential bishop:

> Piety. Learning (sacred). Eloquence. Administrative power. Faithful allegiance to the Church and to the church of England. Activity. Tact and courtesy in dealings with men: knowledge of the world. Accomplishments and

literature. An equitable spirit. Faculty of working with brother bishops. Some legal habit of mind. Circumspection. Courage. Maturity of age and character. Corporal vigour. Liberal sentiments on public affairs. A representative character with reference to shades of opinion fairly allowable in the Church.

Gladstone's record on the last score was challenged. It was claimed that he was making too many High Church appointments to suit his own preferences, but he staunchly defended himself. Of his thirty major selections up to 1883, he pointed out, only eleven were High Churchmen, and nineteen came from other schools. But he admitted that far more of the nineteen were Broad Churchmen than were evangelicals. The problem in promoting evangelicals was largely political. Gladstone did not wish to advance men, especially to seats in the House of Lords as bishops, if they would turn out to be active political opponents, and evangelical clergymen were nearly all Conservatives. Even if the evangelical party was neglected while Gladstone was in office, he went out of his way to inquire about the suitability of men for particular posts. In 1870, when the see of St. Asaph in north Wales fell vacant, he spent a great deal of time discovering a suitable candidate who could speak Welsh, the language of the people. Gladstone was eager that the Church of England should have effective leaders, sound in the substance of the faith and popular in their dioceses. As Prime Minister, he was able to work toward that goal.

QUEEN VICTORIA

Gladstone's loyalty to the monarchy was almost as powerful a sentiment as his attachment to the Church of England. The premiership brought him into regular contact with Queen Victoria, whom he wished to serve as diligently as he was able. During his first administration, however, the relationship went sour. There had for some years been signs of strain. Victoria was an emotional woman who expected sensitivity to her feelings from other people. Gladstone, immensely conscious of the respect due to the throne, treated her with unwelcome formality. All had been well in the days of Prince Albert, himself a rather stiff personality. Albert had valued Gladstone's contribution in the planning of the Great Exhibition of 1851 and admired his work as Chancellor. When Albert died in 1861, however, Gladstone did not comfort the queen as adequately as she would have wished. Victoria appreciated his review of her husband's biography, but as she retired into a self-indulgent widowhood, she must have sensed that Gladstone was not entirely sympathetic. In 1869 there was an unfortunate incident. While staying at Balmoral Castle, the queen's residence in the Scottish Highlands, Gladstone disregarded Victoria's strongly felt preferences about Sunday morning worship. The queen, following the constitutional principle that in Scotland she conformed to the Church of Scotland, attended the local Presbyterian service. Gladstone insisted on traveling some distance to the nearest Episcopal church and, to the queen's annoyance, ordered a royal carriage for the purpose. Victoria was still helpful to the government in composing the differences between Lords and Commons over Irish disestablishment, but a certain coolness was in the air between the queen and her Prime Minister.

During 1871, a political issue further poisoned the atmosphere. Army reform was a government priority, not least because Gladstone recalled only too vividly the blunders of the Crimean War. The process of reform had begun in 1870 with a closer definition of the powers of the commander-in-chief, a post held by a cousin of the queen, the Duke of Cambridge. With the Franco-Prussian War of 1870 underlining the importance of military efficiency in the modern world, the cabinet determined to press on despite the evaporation of the duke's goodwill. The chief structural change planned for the army was the equivalent of civil service reform. Just as the Northcote-Trevelyan proposals, which Gladstone put into operation in

1870, were designed to ensure recruitment to the civil service by merit, so it was proposed to introduce meritocracy into the army. An Army Regulation Bill was introduced in 1871 to stop the traditional practice of buying and selling officer's commissions. At first the Duke of Cambridge gave vague assurances of support, but when the bill reached the House of Lords, he refused to vote for it. Amid much bitterness, the Lords rejected the measure, viewing it as a slur on the reputation of the armed forces. But the cabinet had another option, since the purchase of commissions was possible only because of a royal warrant dating from the reign of George III. Accordingly, another royal warrant abolishing purchase was issued by a reluctant Queen Victoria on the advice of her government. The Lords were outraged, and, although they passed the bill, they went to the length of carrying a vote of censure against the government. "Nothing," wrote Lord Kimberley, "which this Govt. has yet done has cost so great an effort." The idea of proceeding by royal warrant came from Edward Cardwell, the Secretary for War, but the incident gave Gladstone a reputation for high-handedness and abusing the prerogative of the crown. The queen took offense at how she, her cousin, and her officer corps had been treated.

From the beginning of his administration, Gladstone had been trying to bring the royal family more into the public eye. The monarchy, he believed, should not only be valued for its own sake but should also act as a focus of social cohesion. The increased electorate after 1867 needed to be bound together by a common allegiance to the crown, but if this was to be the case, royalty would have to play a more obvious and admirable part in national life. Yet Victoria, still mourning her husband, tried to avoid public engagements, and her son, the Prince of Wales, was becoming notorious for profligacy. By 1871, a swelling chorus of criticism of the throne was even leading to talk of republicanism. In June of that year, Gladstone put to the queen a plan that would simultaneously give the Prince of Wales definite responsibilities and encourage the Irish population to identify with the crown. There should be a royal residence in Ireland, and the prince should act as viceroy. The queen, Gladstone noted sadly, showed "some apparent disinclination to the subject." The reason was that Victoria was beginning to feel hounded by her Prime Minister. At that juncture, the controversy about army purchase reached its climax, and then Gladstone began demanding that the queen should postpone traveling north to Balmoral so as to be able to complete parliamentary business. It was a hot August, and Victoria's self-control snapped. "It really is abominable," she wrote to the Lord Chancellor, "that a woman, a Queen, loaded with cares & anxieties, public & domestic which are daily increasing should be unable to make people understand that there are limits to her powers. What killed her beloved Husband? Overwork & worry." She insisted on going north before the Prime Minister wished. Gladstone told his wife that Victoria's behavior weighed on him "like a nightmare." Their relationship was irreparably damaged.

Gladstone nevertheless persevered in his efforts to make the monarchy more popular. When at the end of the year the Prince of Wales fell ill with typhoid fever, there were fears for his life, and a wave of public sympathy swept across the country. The Prime Minister determined to seize the opportunity of his recovery by holding a thanksgiving service in St. Paul's Cathedral in the heart of the capital. The queen disliked the idea, and, when she had been forced to concede the principle of holding a thanksgiving, she tried to limit its length. Gladstone, however, was at his most dogged, insisting on a full order of service. The occasion in February 1872 proved a great public success, the first in the sequence of public celebrations of family events in the royal household that has continued down to the present day. Yet republicanism would not go away. In the following month a Radical M.P., Sir Charles Dilke, proposed a Commons motion calling for returns of the expenditure of the royal family. How much, for instance, had the royal yachts cost during the last ten years? Gladstone made a powerful but conciliatory speech in reply, and the motion gathered only two votes. Nevertheless, the appearance of republican sentiment on the Liberal benches confirmed Victoria's growing aversion to Gladstone's party. By the following year he was aware of a distinct preference for Disraeli and the Conservatives on the part of the queen. With his easy manner and whimsical turn of phrase, Disraeli was much more welcome at court. He flattered the queen unstintingly. When she published some very unliterary extracts from her diary about travels in the Highlands, Disraeli the novelist knew how to win her heart. "We authors, Ma'am," he remarked on one occasion. Gladstone, by contrast, found it hard not to be brusque with the queen. He was at once the most loyal of Victoria's subjects and an object of her suspicion. It was a position that he found hard to bear.

FRUSTRATIONS OF OFFICE

Meanwhile the government undertook another swath of legislation. Working men were given legal security for their trade unions by an act of 1871, but another alienated them by making picketing during strikes an offense. H. A. Bruce, the Home Secretary in charge of these measures, also carried a Licensing Act in the following year. Although the act did not satisfy temperance advocates in the Liberal ranks, it broke new ground by introducing restrictions on the opening times of public houses. In 1872, the government introduced the secret ballot. Previously voting for parliament had involved making a public declaration; now it was to be by marking a piece of paper in private. Gladstone personally regretted a change that, in his opinion, tended to decrease a voter's responsibility for his choice, but he acquiesced in a long-standing Liberal demand. In 1873, the Lord Chancellor, now Lord Selborne, restructured the upper echelons of the English legal system. All these measures were signs of the pressure on a newly reformed parliament to introduce further reforms elsewhere in national life. For Gladstone it meant "constant tumult of business," and for parliament it meant congestion. Since government measures were supplemented by a plethora of private member's bills and Commons procedure was still cumbersome, many bills had to be abandoned each session, and demoralization spread in the parliamentary Liberal Party. Gladstone knew that a large program of legislation was essential for keeping the diverse sections of the party together and that frustration mounted whenever a favorite proposal had to be dropped for lack of time. Outside the House of Commons, pressure groups began to despair of seeing their particular schemes carried. By 1873 the Liberals were in disarray.

Gladstone hoped to rally them by mounting a reform of the Irish universities, a project that would attract support equally from Whigs who longed for order in Ireland and from Radicals who wanted to abolish traditional abuses. A new examining university was to be created, based on the former University of Dublin. Colleges in different parts of Ireland could affiliate with it whether they belonged to a single denomination or were undenominational. It was a bold attempt to overcome the antipathies between Protestants and Catholics in Ireland. Gladstone hoped that the new institutions would train a single social elite well disposed toward Britain. But the plan foundered on the divisions of Irish society. Several Protestant M.P.s from Ireland objected to the removal of part of the endowments of Trinity College, Dublin, an old Anglican foundation, while most Catholic M.P.s heeded their hierarchy's condemnation of the scheme. When the bill was narrowly defeated in the Commons, Gladstone's cabinet decided to resign. There followed a week of elaborate negotiation in which Disraeli tried to create maximum embarrassment for the Liberal leaders without committing himself to forming a government before he was ready for office. When eventually pinned down to a definite decision, he declined to serve. Gladstone resumed office, but, with the chief legislation of the session rejected, the prospects for the government were bleak. Party morale slumped to fresh depths. What was to be done?

With typical willingness to shoulder responsibility, Gladstone determined to resume his old office as Chancellor of the Exchequer. Since he continued as Prime Minister, the change entailed assuming a far greater burden of work. As Chancellor, he could return to the program of fiscal reform that had earned him popular support a decade before and frame lower taxation to attract votes at the next election. The specific proposal that emerged was the abolition of income tax. Because it was easy to collect, Gladstone believed, the tax encouraged governments to spend money unnecessarily, and so to rescind it would be to strike a major blow for economy in the nation's finances. Gladstone was forced to bring the issue before the public earlier than he intended because the army and navy were demanding far higher departmental budgets than the Chancellor was willing to concede. And so he decided to call a general election on the question of ending the income tax. He went to the country confidently expecting the old slogan of retrenchment to win the day, but he was acutely disappointed. In the election of February 1874, the Liberals won only 300 seats, the Conservatives 352. The defeat was not the result of a loss of votes among the Nonconformists or the working classes, even though both groups nursed grievances against the previous administration, but rather the result of defections on the right wing. Prosperous middle-class voters disliked the torrent of reforms that had swept through parliament in the previous five years, and they also resented the failure of the Liberals to reduce the rates they had to pay for local services. Gladstone's party was beginning to lose the very voters in the suburbs that he had hoped to woo by the abolition of income tax. With Disraeli restored to office as Prime Minister, Gladstone looked forward to an early retirement from the leadership of his party.

During 1872, Disraeli described the Liberal front bench as a line of "exhausted volcanoes." It was an apt taunt, but it also implied a certain grudging admiration. Gladstone's ministers had been immensely active during the early years of his administration, pouring forth a volume of measures that had no precedent in nineteenth-century government. The congestion of public business so irritating to the Radical cohorts was a symptom of a huge legislative output. Education, army purchase, liquor licensing, secret ballot, trade union reform — these and many lesser issues had been dealt with. Gladstone himself had carried disestablishment and land reform in Ireland. Government had moved decisively away from the eighteenth-century stance of responding to events toward the twentieth-century approach of inaugurating change by legislation. The alteration was partly dictated by circumstances, since after the Reform Act of 1867 there was an enlarged electorate expecting great things of government. Each grouping in the Liberal coalition looked for its own pet scheme to be pressed forward. Yet the alteration was also the result of Gladstone's personal contribution. Believing that government existed to initiate, not just to administer, he possessed an enormous fund of energy that fitted him for the task of leading a government dedicated to reform. He would have liked far more changes than were actually achieved. It is therefore no wonder that he encountered opposition from defenders of the existing order — from Queen Victoria, the Conservative majority in the House of Lords, and even the Whigs within his own party. He also faced problems on account of his loyalty to Church principles, whether over individual ecclesiastical appointments or over the place of the Church in elementary and higher education. His hearty dislike of Erastian tendencies was particularly troublesome. It could be said that such difficulties were of his own making, but in reality they arose from the same source as his strengths in the role of reforming Prime Minister. He was committed in conscience to certain convictions. He was ready to modify them in the light of changing circumstances, as his willingness to disestablish the Church of Ireland revealed, but when principles seemed to dictate a particular course of action, he did not flinch from it. He fought tenaciously for his goals. Because a Christian moral sense manifestly shaped his conduct of government, it can be said that Gladstone's faith lay behind the reforming achievements of his first administration. It enabled him to redefine the role of government in British society.

9   Gladstone's Foreign and Imperial Policies, 1868-1898

Much of Gladstone's energy in his later years was channeled into overseas issues. A British Prime Minister or opposition leader was necessarily involved in questions covering half the globe, but Europe remained Gladstone's primary concern. The Continent was transformed in the later nineteenth century by the policies of Prussia. From 1862, when Count Otto von Bismarck became chief minister, the north German state asserted itself far more emphatically in international affairs. In 1864, Prussia, backed by Austria, seized the province of Schleswig-Holstein from Denmark, and then two years later turned to trounce Austria. There was talk during the Schleswig-Holstein crisis of British intervention in defense of Denmark, but Gladstone, seeing no effective way of punishing Prussia, was among the cabinet majority who upheld the traditional British policy of nonintervention on the Continent. In 1870, Bismarck's strategy of blood and iron was crowned with triumph in the Franco-Prussian War, and in the following year the king he served became the Emperor of Germany. From then on, the Prussian minister set about consolidating the position of the new united Germany through intensive diplomacy. Secret bargaining was used to divide the other great powers. Alliances, open or unannounced, bound the states of Continental Europe in a pattern of international relations that was to prevail up to the First World War. Gladstone, like other European liberals, was sympathetic to the growth of German nationhood, for he believed that a united Germany as much as a united Italy was a natural unit on the map of Europe. Yet the network of alliances created to bolster German power was to be ruinous for Gladstone's vision of international cooperation in the cause of peace. The rise of Bismarck meant the undermining of the concert of Europe.

THE FIRST ADMINISTRATION

Gladstone's reaction as Prime Minister to the Franco-Prussian War is instructive. His first effort was to secure treaties with both sides, signed in August 1870, that guaranteed the neutrality of Belgium. It was evidence of the view he shared with Lord Granville, his Foreign Secretary, that the rights of small states must be preserved. The collapse of France came so soon that the next major issue claiming Gladstone's attention surrounded the terms of peace. He believed that France was bound to make territorial concessions to the Prussians, but he was strongly opposed to the proposed transfer of the whole of the provinces of Alsace and Lorraine to the victors. Since the people of Alsace-Lorraine were French through and through, the transfer would infringe the principle of national self-determination that Gladstone held so dear. He therefore proposed a formal remonstrance against Prussia, but Lord Granville, ever more cautious, successfully resisted him in cabinet. It was pointless, Granville believed, to alienate the Prussians in their hour of triumph. But Gladstone felt so strongly about the matter that he took the extraordinary step of publishing an anonymous article against the majority view in his own cabinet. It was wrong, he argued, to suppose that the

Germans had before them "a career of universal conquest or absolute predominance, and that the European family is not strong enough to correct the eccentricities of its peccant and obstreperous members." Interference was legitimate on behalf of "the general judgment of civilised mankind." Gladstone knew as well as his colleagues that it would be impossible to back British opinion by force of arms, yet he believed that moral force would have an effect. In this he misread Bismarck's views of such arguments. Gladstone believed that international affairs formed a branch of Christian morality, but Bismarck had no difficulty in separating politics from ethics. No mere remonstrance would make him cede any ground.

During the early years of his ministry, Gladstone was eager for Britain to exert moral authority on another issue — the work of the First Vatican Council. It was feared that the Council would declare that Roman Catholics must uphold the infallibility of the pope, a proposal that aroused all Gladstone's old vehemence against the papacy. In 1869 the Bavarians and in 1870 the French tried to rally European opposition to any decree of infallibility. Gladstone dearly wanted Britain to participate, but the experienced Lord Clarendon, the Foreign Secretary until his death in mid-1870, felt it was foolish to meddle in such ecclesiastical questions. He prevented Britain from expressing all but a minimum of support for the French initiative. Gladstone was thwarted, and his strong convictions on the subject were pent up until he had retired as Prime Minister. At the start of the administration, foreign policy was framed much more by Clarendon than by Gladstone.

The Prime Minister played a larger role when Clarendon was succeeded by Lord Granville, a younger man to whom Gladstone was less inclined to defer. Gladstone typically laid down the basic principles of policy, and Granville then executed it. Gladstone contributed the ideals of joint European action and the observance of international treaties. Granville brought the diplomatic skills that were so valuable in cabinet discussion of domestic affairs. Together they handled the crisis caused when, in 1870, Russia announced that her warships would enter the Black Sea in defiance of the Treaty of Paris that had ended the Crimean War. As on the eve of that war, Russia was trying to intimidate Turkey. Gladstone and Granville insisted that the treaty was still valid, they initiated consultations with the other powers, and they guided negotiations toward a conclusion that met Russian demands but also guaranteed Turkish interests. It is a good example of a partnership in foreign affairs that worked smoothly and effectively.

An overseas issue that occupied a great deal of the government's time was negotiation with the United States about the *Alabama* claim. The Americans contended that they were due large damages for the havoc wrought by the *Alabama*, a ship constructed in Britain for the South during the Civil War. Other British-built ships had also preyed on Northern vessels. The Americans argued that as a result the Civil War had been unnecessarily drawn out, and so they made so-called "indirect claims" for immense sums in compensation. Anglo-American relations had been poisoned by the affair since the close of the war in 1865. When Gladstone assumed office, the British position had already been undermined by a Conservative offer of arbitration, and so there was no choice but to enter elaborate negotiations. Gladstone wisely ensured that other Anglo-American difficulties would also be discussed — disputes about the Canadian boundary, dissension over fisheries, and claims for compensation for Irish Fenian raids into Canada. Eventually, in May 1871, the Treaty of Washington was signed, establishing a mechanism for arbitration. The United States then pressed its indirect claims, and several members of the government lost patience. There had already been, according to Lord Kimberley, "concession upon concession." Gladstone persevered even when the prospects for a settlement seemed bleak. Eventually the indirect claims were dropped, and British compensation to America was fixed at the high figure of £3 million. The public saw the whole process as a symptom of British weakness, and as a result the government undoubtedly lost a measure of popular support, but Gladstone took a broader view. He recognized that the termination of all existing disputes with America would open the way for closer cooperation in time to come, and he viewed the definition in the Treaty of Washington of the role of neutrals during civil wars as a contribution to the growing body of international law. When similar circumstances arose in the future, there would be much less scope for dissension.

COLONIAL POLICY

Gladstone's colonial policy remained what it had been in earlier years: the encouragement of self-financing alongside self-government. Self-financing would save money for the mother country, while self-government would promote resourcefulness. Gladstone also believed that a relaxation of controls offered the best guarantee for the long-term loyalty of a colony. He told Lord Granville in 1869 that his previous policy toward Canada had been "that we did not *impose* British connection upon the Colony, but regarded its goodwill and desire as an essential condition of the connection." Accordingly Granville, Colonial Secretary up to mid-1870, set about withdrawing troops from Canada, New Zealand, and southern Africa, with the result that military expenditure on the colonies was reduced from £3,388,000 in 1868 to £1,906,000 in 1870. Although the process had to be reversed in Canada when rebellion broke out in 1869, there was a clear overall tendency to decrease the burden of overseas possessions on the imperial exchequer. The start of Gladstone's first ministry has therefore been seen as the culmination of an anticolonial phase in British history. Gladstone certainly disliked the exercise of British rule over peoples of different races, believing it to be contrary to the principle of self-determination, and he took little interest in India. When, in 1873, the queen wished to be declared Empress of India in order to secure a higher standing among European monarchs,

Gladstone declined to take up the necessary legislation. The contrast with Disraeli's policies, both before, during, and after Gladstone's administration, seems striking. Disraeli had dispatched troops to Abyssinia in 1867 amid much beating of the imperial drums; in 1872 he proclaimed in a speech at the Crystal Palace that the Conservatives, unlike the Liberals, were champions of the empire; and in 1876 he fulfilled the queen's wish by making her Empress of India. Gladstone's government does appear anticolonial in comparison.

Nevertheless, that assessment is not accurate. Gladstone was dismayed in 1871 when Australia started a trend for the colonies to impose protective tariffs. He hoped to be able to prevent this infringement of free trade but discovered that the home government lacked the authority. The ideal of colonial autonomy in Gladstone's mind evidently had limits. Furthermore, the administration presided over a number of colonial adventures in the tropics. Edward Knatchbull-Hugesson, Under-Secretary to Lord Kimberley at the Colonial Office, was full of imperialist bluster, later becoming a Conservative. Africa attracted popular attention when, in 1872, H. M. Stanley found David Livingstone in the heart of the "dark continent," and in the following year the government sent a military expedition to the Gold Coast. Toward the end of the administration, Kimberley was making plans for the annexation of Fiji, and the succeeding Conservative government simply implemented his scheme. All this amounted to early participation in the "new imperialism," the drive to carve up the world into empires that seized most European powers at about this time. Gladstone was not an enthusiast for this dimension of his own administration's policies (he was reluctant to sanction either the Gold Coast expedition or the plans for Fiji), but he was not opposed in principle to British rule abroad. In 1878 he wrote that "the sentiment of empire may be called innate in every Briton." What he disliked was unnecessary expense, gratuitous conflict, and the oppression of less powerful peoples. He was content to retain existing overseas responsibilities but not to add to them. He could not wholly restrain the rising tide of opinion in favor of colonial expansion, even among his colleagues. If his government was not anticolonial, Gladstone himself respected other nations too much to wish to lord it over them.

THE EASTERN QUESTION

Gladstone's concern for the fate of small nations is best illustrated by his part in the debate over the Eastern Question in the later 1870s. In 1874 he had been defeated in the general election, and in the following year he had resigned as Liberal leader. In 1876, however, he was stung into action by the situation in southeastern Europe. The Ottoman Empire of the Turks continued to control the territories bounded by Austria-Hungary, Romania, and Greece, but its chaotic administration provoked frequent local revolts. Roused by Christian resentment against Muslim domination and by incipient national feeling, the peoples of the Balkans periodically tried to imitate the Greeks in throwing off Turkish rule altogether. In 1870 the Ottoman authorities permitted the organization of a Bulgarian Church separate from the Greek Orthodox Church. Why, thought the Bulgarians, should political freedom not follow in the wake of ecclesiastical freedom? Soon there was a widespread Bulgarian uprising, but during 1876 it was suppressed by the Turks with great brutality. Russia, Austria-Hungary, and Germany, always ready to fish in the troubled waters of the Balkans, called for Turkey to introduce reforms. France and Italy accepted an invitation to join in making the demand, but Britain, though invited, demurred. Disraeli, now Prime Minister, did not wish to take sides against Turkey. He was adhering to the Crimean War policy of shoring up the Ottoman Empire as a bulwark against Russian expansion. Disraeli refused to join in concerted European action for the defense of the oppressed Bulgarians.

Gladstone was horrified. The Crimean War had loaded

him with a personal sense of responsibility for southeastern Europe. He had also developed a strong affinity for Eastern Orthodoxy, and he was dismayed that the disturbances in the region prevented Orthodox delegates from attending a conference on Christian reunion on which he had pinned high hopes. People were being massacred while Disraeli, his old rival, was protecting the assassins. Yet Gladstone did not take the lead in denouncing the atrocities among the Bulgarians. During July 1876, the Liberal press stirred up popular outrage at the rape, murder, and pillage allowed by the Turkish authorities, but it was not until 6 September that Gladstone was forced out of silence by the enormity of events. On that date he published *The Bulgarian Horrors and the Question of the East*. The pamphlet, which he followed up with speech-making, was an immediate best-seller. It was filled with passion:

> Let the Turks now carry away their abuses in the only possible manner, namely by carrying off themselves. Their Zaptiehs and their Mudirs, their Bimbashis and their Yuzbashis, their Kaimakams and their Pashas, one and all, bag and baggage, shall I hope clear out from the province they have desolated and profaned.

Gladstone called on the British government to reverse its policy, to "concur with the other states of Europe in obtaining the extinction of the Turkish executive power in Bulgaria." The call was embarrassing for the official leader of the Liberal Party, Lord Hartington, who was supporting government policy, but Gladstone's denunciation put him at the head of rank-and-file Liberal opinion in the country. The Nonconformists in particular had only a few years earlier become disillusioned with his administration, but now they were mobilized on behalf of the Bulgarians, and he acted as their mouthpiece. His moral protest reforged an alliance between Gladstone and the Liberal voters that was never subsequently broken.

During a campaign against the government stance on the Eastern Question that lasted nearly four years, Gladstone showed astonishing physical resilience for a man in his late sixties. He delivered speech after speech up and down the country, and he carried the offensive into parliament. In the spring of 1877, with war clearly imminent between Russia and Turkey, Gladstone proposed a Commons motion censuring the administration's pro-Turkish policy. He appealed to "a tradition not which disregards British interests, but which teaches you to seek the promotion of those interests in obeying the dictates of honour and of justice." Britain, in association with the other European powers, should try to achieve "local liberty and practical self-government" in the Balkan region. He was arguing that the policy he favored for British colonies should be extended to the peoples of Bulgaria, Montenegro, Bosnia, and Herzegovina. Events, however, gathered their own momentum, and the threatened war between Russia and Turkey broke out later in 1877. Disraeli feared Russia would seize Constantinople, and he prepared for hostilities, but Russia rapidly imposed a peace settlement on Turkey without British involvement. A European Congress at Berlin was convened to modify the terms. Disraeli (now Lord Beaconsfield) returned proclaiming that he had secured "peace with honour," and public opinion veered in his favor. Yet Gladstone maintained his onslaught. Why had the government stationed Indian troops in Malta? Did it have sinister designs? Why had Britain taken Cyprus from Turkey at the Congress of Berlin? Why spend money on an unnecessary acquisition? Through exertions worthy of his Homeric warriors, Gladstone put the government once more on the defensive.

The world outlook that informed his rhetoric was in some ways typical of the times. Gladstone dealt in stereotypes. European freedom was contrasted with Asiatic oppression, and he assumed that awareness of the responsibilities of citizens did not exist in the East. Without civic individuality, he had written earlier, "the European type becomes politically debased to the Mahometan and Oriental model." During the debates on the Eastern Question in the late 1870s, he praised the insurgents of Montenegro as "a band of heroes such as the world has rarely seen." The Turks, by contrast, were "the one great anti-human specimen of humanity." There had been a transformation in his views since the time when revolutionaries were by definition wrong and the authorities automatically in the right. The change was partly the result of his growing Liberalism, but it was also a consequence of the rise of racial thinking that marked the later nineteenth century. By 1887, Gladstone could write of "the great English-speaking race" comprising Americans and Englishmen alike. He criticized the transfer of Indian troops to Malta in 1878 essentially on the constitutional grounds that they were supposed to serve only in the East, yet he was also fanning suspicions of an alien race. There can be little doubt that Gladstone's mistrust of Disraeli, a Jew by birth though not by faith, strengthened his wariness of orientals. Affinities of blood, he often said, counted for much. This strand in his thinking, if not very attractive, was extremely common at the time. Lord Salisbury, Disraeli's successor as Conservative leader, spoke airily of "inferior races." Gladstone believed that in the struggles over the Eastern Question he was defending a race as well as a civilization.

THE MIDLOTHIAN SPEECHES

Gladstone's campaign against the government's foreign policy was no less than a crusade. It bore the marks, he recorded in his diary at the end of 1878, of the will of God.

> For when have I seen so strongly the relation between my public duties and the primary purposes for which God made and Christ redeemed the world? Seen it to be not real only but so close and immediate that the lines of the holy and the unholy were drawn as in fire before my eyes.

During 1879 there were further causes for moral protest when British troops on the Northwest Frontier of India invaded

Afghanistan and other forces were drawn into a war against the Zulus in southern Africa. Both conflicts were consequences of decisions by local officials, but both seemed part of Beaconsfield's endless quest for national prestige. The Prime Minister was guilty, in Gladstone's eyes, of fomenting popular enthusiasm for aggressive wars, a "jingoism" that he denounced unsparingly. The culmination of his assault on the government was the Midlothian Campaign of November and December 1879. Knowing that an election could not be far away, Gladstone agreed to stand as a candidate in the county constituency of Midlothian surrounding Edinburgh. His sitting Conservative opponent was the Earl of Dalkeith, heir of the Duke of Buccleuch, a leading Scottish peer. Gladstone could count on growing Liberal strength in the area, but he wished to rouse the country as well as the constituency. In a series of speeches delivered on consecutive days in and around Midlothian, he mounted a devastating onslaught on every aspect of Beaconsfield's conduct of affairs. Vast crowds hung on his words, and for days the newspapers were full of reports. It was an oratorical triumph, unparalleled before or since in British politics.

Overseas relations were central to the indictment, and in the third Midlothian speech, Gladstone formulated a succinct statement of "the right principles of foreign policy." His first principle, characteristically, was to pursue "just legislation and economy at home." If domestic policy produced a contented people and saved money, he argued, selective intervention could more easily be undertaken in international affairs. The second principle was simply to aim for peace, a fundamental objective at all times. Third, Britain should participate in the concert of Europe. By maintaining common action, he claimed, the selfish aims of each separate power would be neutralized. In the fourth place, the country "should avoid needless and entangling engagements," for unnecessary overseas responsibilities were nothing but a handicap in times of difficulty. The fifth principle was to recognize that all nations possessed equal rights. Only if nations agreed to accord each other the same respect they

172

demanded for themselves could an informal system of public law be created. Finally, Gladstone declared, "the foreign policy of England should always be inspired by a love of liberty." So far as it was compatible with the other principles, this one implied that the country should exert its influence on the side of small nations struggling to be free. The six principles form an impressive catalogue. They show, if evidence were called for, that Gladstone was doing more than pursuing a vendetta against Beaconsfield. Rather, he was complaining that the government was ignoring the axioms that should guide a civilized European power. The Midlothian principles were widely recognized at the time, and have been since, as a classic exposition of the values of Christendom in international relations.

THE SECOND ADMINISTRATION

The Midlothian Campaign, more than any other single factor, won the general election of April 1880 for the Liberals. Party morale had been lifted to new heights by Gladstone's oratory, and Conservative strength had been sapped. "The downfall of Beaconsfield," wrote Gladstone, "is like the vanishing of some vast magnificent castle in an Italian romance." Yet Gladstone had not been the official leader of the party before or during the election campaign, and Queen Victoria ardently hoped to keep him out of office. "The Queen," she wrote to her secretary, "will sooner *abdicate* than have anything to do with that *half-mad firebrand* who will soon ruin everything and be a *Dictator*." Nevertheless, Gladstone's personal ascendancy over the party ruled out the appointment of any other Prime Minister. In the second administration that he now formed, Granville and Kimberley were installed once more at the Foreign and Colonial Offices. Not surprisingly, the overseas policy of the new ministry in some areas adhered closely to the principles of Midlothian. On the Northwest Frontier of India a forward base was abandoned, and in southern Africa the Dutch settlers whose republic of the Transvaal had been annexed under Beaconsfield were given their independence in 1881. Yet Gladstone did not insist on a wholesale reversal of Conservative strategy. On the Eastern Question, his government tried to find common ground with the opposition in enforcing the Treaty of Berlin that Beaconsfield had signed, and Cyprus was retained. There was now a new framework of international agreement within which Gladstone and Granville felt bound to operate. Although the Liberals had been elected in reaction to Conservative foreign policy, in practice there was a high degree of continuity.

It was hardest, as Gladstone himself was aware, to square his government's Egyptian policy with the Midlothian platform. Egypt was in theory part of the Ottoman Empire, but the local ruler, the khedive, enjoyed virtual autonomy. France had traditionally exerted the greatest foreign influence in the country, but British trading interests were expanding. Beginning in 1875, when the Egyptian government declared bankruptcy for the third time, France and Britain imposed a system of "dual control" over its financial affairs. In the same year, Disraeli obtained for Britain a majority holding in the recently constructed Suez Canal, the shortest route from Europe to India. When, during 1881, public order broke down in a seminationalist rising, Britain felt bound to become involved in order to protect the interests of overseas investors. Gladstone tried to ensure joint action with France, and a combined naval force was stationed offshore. The French decided that the venture might become too expensive, however, and so withdrew their vessels. At this point the powder keg ignited. Egyptians fired on the Royal Navy. The British admiral demanded the removal of the Egyptian cannon. When no action was taken, he bombarded Alexandria on 11 July 1882. John Bright, the Quaker champion of peace, immediately resigned from the cabinet. Gladstone hoped, as he told Bright, that the bombardment "*might* be found effectually to serve the end of peace," but he was severely disappointed. It was soon necessary to send in the army to restore order, and Egypt was effectively occupied. The international repercussions were serious. France was deeply offended by Britain's unilateral action, and Anglo-French relations were to remain icy for the next two decades. Although Gladstone repeatedly insisted that the occupation of Egypt was only temporary, British control was to last until the 1950s. The Prime Minister was actually among the bondholders whose investments had been threatened by chaos in Egypt, but he had been profoundly reluctant to act. The decision to intervene was taken at a time when, weary from the demands of handling the Irish issue, he was outnumbered in cabinet. Britain had been sucked into Egypt against Gladstone's better judgment.

Worse was to follow. Egypt claimed an imprecise suzerainty over the Sudan to the south, but Sudanese patriots, fired with a form of Muslim millenarianism, were resisting Egyptian attempts to exert authority. In November 1883, an army sent by the khedive of Egypt met disaster, and British forces were drawn into the Sudan. Since the government had no intention of keeping troops there, it sent an agent to report on the best means of evacuation. The choice of official representative was unfortunate. General Charles Gordon was an impetuous spirit, admired by the public for heroic deeds in China during the 1860s, who arbitrarily extended his own terms of reference and planned to consolidate the British presence. When Gordon was trapped by the Sudanese in Khartoum, Gladstone was extremely reluctant to send a fresh expedition to rescue him. There were complaints in the Commons that too little was being done to help a man who was surrounded in the city by enemy forces. Gladstone, in a typical but unhappy equivocation, denied that Gordon was *surrounded*. There were merely, he claimed, "bodies of hostile troops in the neighbourhood, forming more or less of a chain around it." When eventually a relief column was dispatched to Khartoum and it was found that Gordon and his remaining men had been killed only two days before, there was a public outcry against the Prime Minister. The death of Gordon was a severe blow to Gladstone's standing in the country, and among military men it earned him enduring ignominy. But Gordon had exceeded his orders, and Gladstone's overriding motive had been to avoid yet another unnecessary entanglement. The Sudan was abandoned, but the flame of popular imperialism was fanned.

Gladstone's second ministry was much more thoroughly involved than his first in the new imperialism. Fresh annexations were far from his intention, for all he desired, as in the past, was that the nation should retain the affections of colonists of British stock. "While we are opposed to imperialism," he said in 1881, "we are devoted to empire." Events, however, proved inexorable. It has been suggested that economic rivalry was behind the new imperialism. Although it is true that chambers of commerce urged territorial extensions at this time, they had no discernible effect on Gladstone. Nor was he aiming, as Bismarck undoubtedly was, to divert the populace from domestic ills by acquisitions overseas. Competition in land-grabbing between the great powers was equally remote from Gladstone's way of thinking. The primary reason for the growth of the empire in his second administration was that pragmatic responses had to be made to problems on the periphery of empire. That is why Egypt was occupied and that is also why, in 1884, a protectorate was declared in West Africa. A similar pragmatism guided the British response to the imperial adventures of other powers. A series of annexations by Bismarck in 1884 and 1885 had to be accepted or else he would have stirred up trouble about the British presence in Egypt. Likewise, in 1885 Britain tolerated the advance of Russia into northern Afghan lands for the sake of peace. In these international developments, Gladstone was little involved, at least initially, and Lord Granville allowed himself to be outmaneuvered. With advancing years, Granville was losing his grip on affairs, and Gladstone, under pressure from other issues, exercised inadequate supervision over foreign relations. There can be no doubt that the record of his second administration in foreign and colonial matters was much less satisfactory than that of his first. The ambitions of the other powers were too strong.

THE THIRD AND FOURTH ADMINISTRATIONS

The third administration in 1886 lasted less than six months. By this time Granville, in Gladstone's opinion, was definitely too infirm to serve as Foreign Secretary. Age had taken its toll, even though he was six years younger than the Prime Minister. Granville was given the Colonial Office, and Lord Rosebery, a man still in his thirties, took Granville's old place. Rosebery was intelligent and charming, and he enjoyed the queen's favor, but he was moody and thin-skinned. The Irish Question was coming to the fore, and so Gladstone left Rosebery to conduct foreign relations by himself. "No other important issue of a disturbing character should be raised," Gladstone cautioned him, "while we have this big Irish business on hand." Rosebery determined to follow in the tracks of Lord Salisbury, his Conservative predecessor, who, unlike Beaconsfield, was not given to showiness in foreign affairs. Salisbury was a skillful realist, trying to steer clear of crises and entangling alliances, and so his example could be grafted onto the Gladstonian tradition. Rosebery veered toward the Conservative policy of trying to protect Turkey against Russia, but his method was thoroughly Gladstonian. He favored building up the small state of Bulgaria against Russian ambitions, and he also tried to resurrect the concert of Europe. Gladstone found much to praise in his policy.

Rosebery was therefore the natural choice as Foreign Secretary when Gladstone formed his fourth ministry in 1892. But grief over the recent loss of his wife accentuated Rosebery's pricklier side. He allowed himself to be persuaded to take office, but in return he expected absolute control over the conduct of foreign affairs. He had announced in advance that the government would undertake "the experiment of having a continuous Foreign Policy." That meant following Salisbury's strategy more consistently than before, an approach that entailed diverging from Gladstone. The Prime Minister, still chafing over the occupation of Egypt, wanted moves toward withdrawal, but Rosebery would have none of it. He successfully resisted Gladstone by threatening to resign. Gladstone also wished to avoid permanent involvement in Uganda, but again Rosebery thwarted him, eventually declaring a protectorate over the country in 1895. Gladstone continued to hold that undertaking such responsibilities wasted men and money. He was even more strongly averse to increased spending on the Royal Navy, his old battleground with Palmerston. Although in 1894 the rest of the cabinet believed a stronger navy was essential, Gladstone was totally opposed. This was the issue that precipitated his final resignation as Prime Minister. In his last administration, the elderly Gladstone found himself with little power over foreign affairs.

CLOSING YEARS

Nevertheless, even after he had retired from parliament, Gladstone was still stirred by the sufferings of oppressed peoples. The Armenians, the first nation to embrace Christianity, were scattered about the region that is now eastern Turkey. Like so many others, they were subjects of the Ottoman Empire who suffered from its incompetent administration. They were periodically punished for resisting taxation, and sometimes the punishment turned into massacre. When that happened to the Armenians in 1895 and 1896, Gladstone addressed two public meetings to draw attention to their sufferings. "Had I the years of 1876 upon me," he told one of his sons, "gladly would I start another campaign, even if as long as that." As it was, the Nonconformists once more responded warmly to his appeals. Yet the policy that Gladstone recommended differed significantly from what he had urged in the past, when his remedy had been joint remonstrance by the European powers. Now he recognized that the need for concerted action was being used as an excuse for inactivity by individual states. If necessary, he argued, Britain must act independently to protect those who were suffering under Turkish rule. He took the same line when, in 1897, Crete rose in rebellion against the Turks. Gladstone again believed that delays imposed by the quest for coordinated action were preventing assistance for a just cause. In the last years of his life, he still cherished the ideal of a united Christendom, but when individual powers were exploiting the concert of Europe as an instrument of their separate ambitions, he concluded that Britain must break free of it. Gladstone's support for small nations struggling for liberty emerged in the end as his strongest commitment in overseas affairs.

The Midlothian speeches of 1879 form a landmark in the history of Liberal internationalism. They expounded ideals inherited from the Conservative Lord Aberdeen but modified by growing experience of a world of shifting power structures. The six principles of Midlothian were not rigid positions: for one thing, they had to be balanced against each other; for another, Gladstone's mind was always in motion, so that the passage of time transformed them. In particular, it became increasingly apparent that the concert of Europe as Gladstone originally envisaged it was unworkable because in the era molded by Bismarck, hard political interests counted for more than common cultural traditions. Nevertheless, Gladstone's internationalist convictions enabled him and his fellow ministers to achieve a great deal in foreign affairs. The *Alabama* arbitration is a good example of the way in which Gladstone tried to transform his ideal vision into a binding structure of public law. Gladstone's record in imperial affairs was less happy. Contrary to his wishes, there were advances of empire during his first administration and the more serious entanglement in Egypt during his second. Yet in imperial and foreign affairs alike, Gladstone staunchly resisted the boastful spirit of national self-aggrandizement. His was a Christian vision of world order in which nations should aim to do to others what they wished to have done to them. Consequently, he showed particular sympathy for the aspirations of small groups such as the inhabitants of Alsace-Lorraine, the Bulgarians, and the

Armenians. "Remember," he declared in his second Midlothian address, "that the sanctity of life in the hill villages of Afghanistan, among the winter snows, is as inviolable in the eye of Almighty God as can be your own." Equal justice for all nations was Gladstone's lodestar in international affairs.

10 Gladstone and the Liberal Party, 1874-1894

During the later nineteenth century, authority in Britain remained to a remarkable extent in the hands of the aristocracy and gentry. The upper middle classes — financiers, businessmen, and professionals — were increasingly joining them in positions of power, but the country was still ruled by a landed elite. When at the time of the 1867 Reform Act people had spoken of the arrival of "the democracy," all they meant was that skilled working men who were urban householders now possessed a parliamentary vote. Even after the next Reform Act, passed in 1884, about one-third of the male population and all women were still excluded from the franchise. The men who could not vote — many lodgers, those who had changed households within the previous twelve months and those receiving poor relief — were drawn chiefly from the lower ranks of the working classes. Even if a number of agricultural laborers and city slum-dwellers had been enfranchised, the right to vote still seemed a matter of status. In the final years of Gladstone's political career, with the vote esteemed a prized possession, men prided themselves on their capacity to cast it judiciously. They were hungry for information about political controversies, and the newspapers were full of lengthy reports of parliamentary debates and party meetings. Circumstances were right for any politician who treated voters as responsible agents, capable of evaluating arguments and coming to reasoned conclusions. Gladstone knew that he could expect a favorable response from his hearers when he appealed to their sense of civic duty. His exhortations to vote Liberal fell on willing ears.

RELIGION AND CLASS

It does not follow, however, that the outcome of elections was determined by a rational assessment of the issues. Instead of weighing up the pros and cons of Liberal and Conservative policies for the national good, individual voters normally cast their ballots in accordance with the preferences dominant in their social group. For many working men, the wishes of their employer came first, with the expectations of family, friends, and neighbors running them a close second. Usually the various pressures reinforced each other, so that whole streets voted almost unanimously and elections took on the air of community carnivals. The focus of loyalties was frequently the place of worship: attenders of the Church of England usually voted Conservative, while chapel-goers were normally Liberals. Since the Church of England was identified with the royal family, the House of Lords, and the well-to-do, its worshipers naturally wanted to conserve. Since Nonconformist chapels were associated with the manufacturers who had paid for them and the small shopkeepers who ran them, their adherents admired enterprise and progress. The rule was not absolute: in Lancashire as many mill owners were Anglican as were Nonconformist. Yet it is clear that, down to the First World War, religion was the factor most likely to predict political allegiance, so that the line between Church and chapel corresponded closely with the line between Conservative and Liberal. The social base of Gladstone's Liberal Party consisted primarily of Nonconformists. The chapel-goers, he remarked in 1877, formed "the backbone of British Liberalism."

If religion created the sharpest political cleavage during the period, class was steadily becoming more divisive. There were signs in the later nineteenth century that the middle classes and the working classes were beginning to polarize politically. As early as 1868 in certain outer London constituencies, middle-class voters were combining to support Conservative candidates. The wave of reform in Gladstone's first administration, as we have seen, frightened more of the well-to-do into imitating them. A crucial stage in the process was the redistribution of seats following the 1884 Reform Act. Constituencies returning a single M.P. to Westminster were carved out of the suburbs in the growing cities. In each of them a majority of the electors occupied substantial houses in leafy streets and found the Conservative defense of property rights very much to their taste. It was the phenomenon of "villa Toryism." As the Conservative leaders increasingly targeted the middle classes in their speeches, the party started to turn from a bastion of the landed elite into a vehicle of bourgeois interests. Conversely, the Liberals benefited from a rising tide of class consciousness among the working people. It is true that eventually this development would be channeled away from Liberalism into the twentieth-century Labour Party, and already in the 1890s the Liberal Party was troubled by a number of Independent Labour candidates thrown up by industrial grievances, but for the most part the Liberals kept the support of working-class voters, who hoped for legislation to improve their lot. There was genuine enthusiasm among trade unionists for the Liberal cause; a growing body of miners, for instance, looked to the party to enforce an eight-hour workday. Virtually all miners were Liberals. It is clear that class was beginning to shape how people voted.

NONCONFORMISTS AND THE WORKING CLASSES

Gladstone showed a full realization of these social realities from the later 1870s onward. After the Nonconformists rallied to his side in the battles surrounding the Eastern Question, he paid them particular attention, writing articles in their journals, addressing conferences they sponsored, and occasionally attending their chapels. A close bond developed between the Liberal leader and the mass of chapel-goers. They recalled with gratitude his record of abolishing compulsory church rates and disestablishing the Church of Ireland. Despite his High Churchmanship, Nonconformists recognized that he shared their personal faith. Gladstone's religion, commented a Baptist periodical at his death, was part of himself: his home was pure, he rigidly observed the Lord's Day (an overgenerous view), and he was constant in attendance at worship. Samuel Morley, a wealthy Congregational M.P., could not praise him sufficiently. "I regard Mr. Gladstone," declared Morley, "as the greatest, purest, and ablest statesman of the present age, and of all ages or any age." Members of the prohibitionist lobby, largely Nonconformist in its support, were equally flattering, even though Gladstone had done nothing to promote their cause. Although he disapproved of drinking to excess, his strongest recorded view on alcohol was the displeasure he expressed when no Sauternes was provided at a parliamentary dinner. Yet he was careful not to alienate the prohibitionists, and in return they gave him adulation. One of their leaders told the House of Commons in 1883 that temperance reformers had confidence in Gladstone. "Confidence!" he went on. "They have more than confidence, they have a passionate faith in him that nothing can shake." The devotion that Gladstone attracted was in fact beyond reason, an almost religious faith. Respect for the statesman became an unwritten article in the Nonconformist creed.

Gladstone's appeal to the Nonconformists meant that he attracted significant numbers from the working classes, for the chapels retained their hold on a large section of the artisan community. Nevertheless, Gladstone had not always courted the support of working-class electors as a distinct group. In the 1860s, he had praised the restraint of Lancashire millworkers during the cotton famine, but in the early 1870s, as M.P. for the predominantly working-class seat of Greenwich in Kent, he had markedly neglected his constituents. There was little enthusiasm for him among the dockyard workers of Greenwich. Yet he well knew that the 1884 Reform Act, for which he was responsible, expanded the working-class electorate so much that it became imperative to mobilize its potential in the Liberal cause. The 1886 election campaign was the first in which he publicly described the party struggle as one of the classes against the masses. The classes — the landed and the moneyed — were ranged on the Conservative side; the masses — the common people — were identified with the Liberals. It was a tactic that his opponents resented, since it savored of stirring up class hatred. And in truth, Gladstone himself did not think it healthy that parties should be divided horizontally according to class rather than vertically according to principle. With his deep-seated deference to the nobility, he coveted the allegiance of the aristocrats for Liberalism. But he recognized the direction of social change, and, like the wise politician he was, he determined to turn it to the advantage of his party. In the last years of his career he showed special sympathy for trade unionists, even when on strike, and he gave parliamentary time during his fourth administration for discussion of the miners' Eight Hours Bill. He wanted to demonstrate that labor interests were Liberal interests. Gladstone made full use of his sensitive antennae for detecting changes in the electorate.

PUBLIC SPEAKING

The chief technique Gladstone used for drumming up popular support was public speaking. He enjoyed immense natural advantages as an orator. As early as the 1830s, it was noticed that he possessed excellent elocution, together with a graceful manner, and that speaking apparently cost him no effort. His voice, as one of his private secretaries described it, was a "deep, melodious baritone, wielded with incomparable although unconscious skill, and capable of every variety of inflexion." A regional accent added a dash of piquancy to the effect. To the end of his life Gladstone pronounced certain words in the manner of his native Liverpool: "prefer" became "prefurr" and "garden" almost "gyarden." Although he was skilled at improvising, he normally prepared with great care. He worked out a logical structure in advance and followed it from brief notes. There were, admittedly, defects in his style. Critics poured scorn on his tendency to use twenty words where a couple would have served. He could be imprecise in his conclusion so that the effect of the speech was weakened. And, like most orators, he occasionally lapsed into bathos. He once encouraged farmers to raise chickens, adding the words "and, if I may say so, from eggs." Yet each speech was a powerful performance that made demands on the audience. Gladstone refused to speak down to his listeners; the intellectual content always demanded mental effort. The moral tone was an even more marked feature. Gladstone believed that ordinary hearers, while unable to judge finer points of policy, could always respond to an analysis cast in terms of right and wrong. So he gave free rein to the moral view of politics that came naturally to him. It proved an effective formula for rousing an audience to a white-hot pitch of enthusiasm.

There is ample testimony to the impression made by Gladstone's oratory. He was frequently interrupted by spontaneous applause, his speeches would be followed by an uproar of approval, and in some cases groups of men hitched themselves to his carriage to draw him in triumph from the public hall to the railway station. Individuals were profoundly moved. Laura Tennant, a sophisticated young woman, listened to Gladstone speaking on finance at Edinburgh in 1879 or 1880. "I felt," she recalled, "as if I were in Church and tempted to kneel down and pray." John Clifford, a leading Baptist minister, heard him talk about the Irish question at a private lunch in 1887. "His manner most earnest," he wrote in his diary.

> The trend of his mind majestic, penetrating, victorious and irresistible. He is a commander of men. Plain of speech and simple, clear and aggressive. The moral momentum immense. It was a contest. The hearer felt he was witnessing a fight for righteousness, for humanity, for God. He speaks with what seems slow and sustained deliberation, but with immense mental and moral force.

Gladstone's oratory revealed the inner man — combative, passionate, and religious. Occasionally the religious allusions landed him in trouble. During the 1892 election campaign, for example, he was persistently heckled by a questioner who spoke of his own understanding of the position. Gladstone, by now eighty-two years old and perhaps off his guard, was stung into replying that he could not be responsible for the understanding that it had pleased the Almighty to place in his adversary's skull. It was a retort that a hostile press found "rude and commonplace." In this instance a reference that came naturally to Gladstone's lips did no good at all. Normally, however, it was the Christian undergirding of his speeches that guaranteed their impact on a sermon-habituated public. Since most of the electors were in church on a Sunday, they could be roused in conscience by exhortations on a weekday. The Midlothian campaign, Gladstone's greatest rhetorical achievement, created such a stir because the speaker was addressing a like-minded audience.

POPULAR IMAGE

Another explanation of the impact of Gladstone on the electorate lies in the publicity he received. During the 1870s, it became normal for reporters to telegraph news of a politician's evening meeting for publication in the newspapers the following morning. Gladstone's speeches were usually reported word for word in the press, and so he was able to reach a mass audience immediately through the printed page. The more important speeches were also reissued in booklet form for a further batch of readers to enjoy at their leisure. In addition, Gladstone composed pamphlets such as *The Bulgarian Horrors* for separate publication and wrote a wide range of articles for the periodicals. Many had no explicit political bearing, and yet they helped to consolidate Gladstone's hold on the public. After their introduction in 1870, postcards offered another means of contact with the people. Gladstone wrote vast quantities in answer to inquiries and even requested — successfully — that the Post Office should introduce a thicker postcard for his convenience. Typical was the response to a letter from Thomas Rowe, a Liberal market gardener of Rusholme near Manchester, who announced in 1880 that he had just read *Juventus Mundi*. By return of post came a card inscribed, "With Mr Gladstone's compliments and cordial good wishes to Mr Thomas Rowe," together with several pamphlets on Homer. Four days later came a copy of Gladstone's *Homeric Synchronism*. "What enhanced the value of the gift in Mr. Rowe's eyes," according to a memoir of the market gardener, "was the fact that on the very day before [Gladstone] was summoned by the Queen to form a new ministry, he found time to send off his book and his autograph to an unknown admirer in Rusholme." Despite his responsibilities for high affairs of state, Gladstone did not lose the common touch.

That was the kernel of Gladstone's popular image. To the end, he remained plain "Mr Gladstone" — not a peer or even a knight, for he refused all the honors offered him. The Bristol Operatives' Liberal Association felt no embarrassment at sending him a gift of a goblet and six tankards such as its members would have liked to receive. His feats of chopping down trees, a hobby begun for exercise relatively late in life, had the effect of bringing him close to the working people. Tree-felling served not merely as a metaphor for clearing away the antiquated lumber of the state but also as a sign that he shared the experience of physical labor. Once while staying at a country house in Peebles-shire he was discovered holding an animated discussion with the head gardener on the qualities of a new American axe. Visitors to Hawarden were keen to view the latest tree stumps. In 1878, a Clay Cross grocer even challenged him to face a local champion in a tree-felling competition, an occasion on which Gladstone declined by postcard for "age and other reasons." His efforts fostered an attractive folk myth — the leader as worker. And the image of Gladstone was propagated in many other forms. Dinner plates and cream jugs were adorned with his portrait; Gladstone busts were manufactured in abundance; his picture was sold for hanging on the parlor wall or in the committee room of the Liberal Club. Veneration came close to idolatry. A rough Northumbrian miner, on first hearing Gladstone address a meeting, broke down with emotion. His handkerchief, saturated from wiping his eyes, was never used again since, he declared, it was forever sacred with "Gladstone's tears." The great Liberal leader enjoyed a cult following.

LIBERAL DIVISIONS

Gladstone's heroic standing was a powerful weapon in dealing with the party in the years after 1880. He drew a personal loyalty from ordinary Liberals that no other politician could hope to equal. That was just as well, for the party sectionalism that had troubled the first administration continued to be a problem thereafter. Various groupings jostled each other as everyone wanted priority in the legislative program. Labor was demanding more attention for industrial grievances. The Trades Union Congress was voicing the requirements of working people across all the crafts, and especially from the end of the 1880s, individual trade unions were giving more time to political affairs. A proportion of Irish M.P.s formed an independent parliamentary party in 1880, which meant that even while they voiced greater demands, they had less scope for disturbing Liberal unity from within. Many Scottish M.P.s within the party, however, were more assertive in the 1880s than they had been in the past. Some called for the separation of the Church of Scotland from the state, while others, particularly from the Highlands, wanted relief for the crofters who were struggling with high rents and poor harvests. Welsh M.P.s were almost unanimous in pressing for the disestablishment of the Church of England in Wales. A rising tide of Welsh national feeling in the later 1880s strengthened their influence so that Gladstone declared in favor of disestablishment for Wales in 1889. English Nonconformists, on the other hand, tended to be more loyal to the party than in the past. They remembered that their revolt in the early 1870s had brought them no benefits, and now, in response to Gladstone's appeals, they saw themselves as the party's backbone. Yet some among them, especially temperance reformers, still believed in pushing forward their particular schemes. Gladstone had the enormous task of welding these diverse sections into a single fighting force.

The task was complicated by the emergence of a new party organization. In the early 1870s, the Radicals had usually been at odds with each other. Sectional rivalry, aggravated by different local allegiances and serious personality clashes, had weakened all their chances. In 1877, however, a National Liberal Federation was created to link the various towns in which Radicals were strong and to hold an annual conference to publicize their objectives. The purpose of the Federation was to put the energy of all the Radical sections behind chosen causes and so to exert stronger pressure on the Liberal leadership. It was the brainchild of Joseph Chamberlain, an able and energetic Birmingham Unitarian who had retired from screw manufacturing to devote his time to politics. In the Federation, Gladstone faced an organization that was simultaneously a tool for Chamberlain's ambitions and a body that could claim to represent popular Liberal opinion. At the same time, there was a growing reaction on the other wing of the party, for traditionalist Whigs disliked Chamberlain as an upstart and deplored the creation of a Federation designed to initiate reform after reform. The Whigs would have preferred to administer the country quietly, without constant legislative turmoil. At their head was Lord Hartington, the languid but dogged heir of the Duke of Devonshire who had led the party during Gladstone's period of retirement from 1875 to 1880 and was ready to do so again. Behind Hartington were several younger Whigs with a relish for the political game. Although they were relatively few, they continued to regard power as their natural prerogative, and, since landowners still outnumbered businessmen in the House of Commons, they could drum up a powerful force in the parliamentary Liberal Party. In the early 1880s, the party was torn between Radicals and Whigs, the friends of Chamberlain and the supporters of Hartington. It was a hard party for Gladstone to lead.

LEADERSHIP SKILLS

Both sides, however, needed Gladstone. The Radicals knew that once he was convinced of the merits of a case, he could still throw immense energy into a campaign. The Whigs were aware of the continuing conservative instincts that made him eager to retain peers and their relations in the party and so willing to do his utmost to conciliate them. Consequently, Gladstone functioned as a focus of unity in the party, a bond between the two divergent groups. Although he alienated each side from time to time by veering in the opposite direction, members of both sides recognized that he was their best hope of exerting leverage on the other body of opinion and so clung to him as an ally. Furthermore, Gladstone pursued a strategy designed to achieve unity. In retirement he reflected that, if he had a striking political gift, it was knowing when public opinion could be harnessed to achieve a particular goal. He would cast about for an issue that would raise enthusiasm in all sections of the party and use it to mobilize them for success. "There is now no *cause*," he had noted down in 1873. "No great public object on wh. the Liberal party are agreed & combined." The assault on Beaconsfieldism in foreign policy, though not originally intended as such, had proved to be a uniting cause of precisely this type. Home Rule for Ireland, a subject we shall consider in Chapter 11, was to have the same binding effect on the bulk of the party after 1886. The strategy was not always successful: parliamentary reform, taken up in 1883, aroused Whig suspicions, and Home Rule cost Gladstone the support of both Hartington and Chamberlain. Yet the moral fervor Gladstone brought to his campaigns ensured that they gained widespread support in the country. Coteries of politicians withdrew from his chosen cause at their peril. They risked isolating themselves from the mainstream of party opinion that Gladstone could divert into fresh channels, apparently at will. His popularity greatly enhanced his authority as party leader.

Gladstone's ascendancy over the parliamentary party was not achieved by management skills. In the second administration of 1880-1885, he summoned only five meetings of the party, and he neglected individual M.P.s. When supporters were brought up to him in the lobby of the House of Commons, he would decline to be introduced and continue writing letters. Looking after party morale was left to the chief whip and his team. Yet Gladstone was devoted to the Commons and its ways, once describing himself as an "Old Parliamentary Hand." His opponents taunted him with the phrase because it seemed to smack of deviousness, but it well expressed his expertise in the byways of procedure. It was Gladstone who in 1881 asked that questions put down for answer by ministers should be consolidated in separate blocs. The resulting institution of Prime Minister's Question Time became one of the most celebrated of British parliamentary practices, a device for calling a wayward executive to heel. It cost Gladstone much pain in the same year to propose a method for curtailing debate as a remedy for Irish obstruction of business. Nowhere was his conservatism more apparent than in his adherence to parliamentary custom. On one occasion he sternly rebuked a new member who had the temerity to put his feet on a Commons bench. Parliament was a world of its own, and Gladstone was its master. Already by 1860 he had been acknowledged the greatest orator in the Commons, and after the departure of Disraeli for the House of Lords in 1876, he had no rival. Younger Conservatives might badger him, but that was merely testimony to his centrality in the parliamentary arena. Despite being in his seventies during the 1880s, he was still capable of brilliant performances. Principles were laid down, qualifications made, implications drawn out — all with admirable dexterity and riveting moments of vehemence. It was said that the despatch box where front bench spokesmen stood to deliver their speeches bore indentations made by his rings as he brought his hand down to emphasize a point. Gladstone dominated the House of Commons even more than the country at large by the spoken word.

A speech of 1883 may be taken as an example. The underlying question was whether or not Charles Bradlaugh, a self-professed atheist who had been returned as M.P. for Northampton, should be allowed to take his seat in the Commons. The controversy had disrupted each session since 1880, and now, three years later, Gladstone's government was proposing to settle the issue by allowing M.P.s to make a nonreligious affirmation instead of an oath implying belief in God. The bill was eventually to fail by a narrow margin because of fears of explicit secularism in parliament, but on the second reading of the bill Gladstone expounded a masterly case. Although initially he suffered from a great deal of interruption, he was able to answer each criticism adeptly, pointing, for example, to a procedural precedent in 1854, nearly thirty years before but well within his memory. When he took up the central case, he did so by formulating his opponents' view as a proposition:

"that the main question for the State is not what religion a man professes, but whether he professes some religion or not." He showed that a number of Conservatives had taken the view summarized in the proposition. Then he specified the various reasons why the proposition was untenable. It was a breach in the principle that there should be a divorce between religious profession and civil privilege; it was not a defense of the full Christian faith, since all it asserted was the need for some religious belief; and it drew the line at an unsuitable place: if bare belief in God were to be the criterion, opponents of Christianity such as Voltaire could have taken a seat. Then came the climax. "I have no fear of Atheism in this House," he declared. "Truth is the expression of the Divine mind; and however little our feeble vision may be able to discern the means by which God will provide for its preservation, we may leave the matter in His hands, and we may be quite sure that a firm and courageous application of every principle of justice and of equity is the best method we can adopt for the preservation and influence of truth." Gladstone was seizing the highest ground in the debate and obviously felt deeply about every word he uttered. Many M.P.s recalled the speech as a high point of parliamentary oratory.

CABINET GOVERNMENT

Gladstone was less successful in cabinet than in parliament during the 1880s. As during the first administration, his lack of camaraderie was a handicap. The Foreign Secretary, Lord Granville, who always sat immediately on Gladstone's right, helped once more to compensate for the Prime Minister's insensitivity. But there were greater obstacles to overcome in the second administration than in the first, since positions were more entrenched. It is true that most of the fifty or so cabinet meetings held each year passed harmoniously, but an increasing proportion did not. Of the twenty men who served in

Gladstone's second cabinet, nine were Whigs or of Whiggish inclination. They did not form an organized bloc, but they did tend to sympathize with Lord Hartington on most issues. Hartington — as might be expected of an heir to vast acres — feared for the security of landed property, particularly in Ireland, and he often acted as a brake on legislative proposals. The Radicals in the party were represented by John Bright until 1882, but more significantly by the rising Joseph Chamberlain. After the appointment of the two men, Gladstone received a sharp note, written in the third person, from the queen: "she thinks that there are now enough radicals in the Ministry and trusts that no more may be admitted." Gladstone had no wish for more, and though he was glad of Chamberlain's energy in cabinet, he never became cordial with the Birmingham Radical. Chamberlain, with Sir Charles Dilke as an ally from 1882, constantly wanted to press forward with legislation that would attract the popular vote. He also saw to it, when convenient, that the press heard about ideas floated in cabinet. Chamberlain was a restless force, often running athwart the wishes of Hartington and the other Whigs. As tensions multiplied, hammering out policies became burdensome work.

It is hardly surprising that Gladstone shrank from the task. He was conscious of his age and, from time to time, of ill health. In January 1883 he compiled a "sleep register," woefully recording five hours, four hours, or even just one hour a night before reaching Cannes in the south of France for a holiday. His physician sometimes recommended rest, although it is also true that on at least one occasion he urged that the excitement of politics was essential to Gladstone's health. The Prime Minister himself longed to retire. It was not just that the demands of office were becoming excessive even for a man of his stamina. It was also that he wished for a period of leisure in which he could prepare himself spiritually for death. Although politics was a Christian calling, he believed that responsibility for the state of his soul came first. He spoke frequently to colleagues about retirement at some point before the end of the

195

1880 parliament, holding that he had been thrust into power only by extraordinary circumstances, by a popular reaction against Conservative policy. Once government had been settled on a sounder basis, he argued, it was time for him to leave the premiership. It has been pointed out that it was tactically useful for Gladstone to be able to say he would soon resign office. When he hinted at retirement, the Whigs and the Radicals both rallied to his side, each wanting his continuing support against the other faction. Virtually nobody other than Gladstone himself wished him to go. The consequence of physical weakness and the urge to retire, however, was often a lack of strategic planning. Gladstone was reluctant to summon the cabinet, and so there was inadequate preparation for the legislative programs of 1882 and 1883. Although unforeseeable crises played their part in disrupting the government's work, poor coordination was equally responsible. The Prime Minister must bear a share of the blame for the small number of significant measures carried by his second administration.

Nevertheless, the record is far from empty. Apart from the Irish legislation, there were a number of reforms that dealt with long-standing grievances. Gladstone abolished the Malt Tax that had penalized barley growers and home brewers of beer. Death duties were also revamped during his tenure of the Exchequer up to 1882. The statute book was cleared of acts making ground game the property of landowners: country folk had deeply resented the fact that catching a rabbit was a criminal offense. The last major disability of the Nonconformists was removed when, in 1880, they were allowed to hold their own services in parish graveyards. But reform of local government proved a fiasco. Each year from 1881, the ministry prepared a measure setting up local authorities outside the boroughs where they already existed. Each year the bill — whether for London, the English counties, or Ireland — had to be abandoned for lack of time. Consequently, the only major reform relating to Britain was the extension of the parliamentary franchise to rural householders. The Reform Act of 1884 was planned and steered through by Gladstone himself. For the first time, it established identical qualifications for the vote in every part of the United Kingdom. In order to carry the bill, Gladstone had to overcome resistance from many Whigs within his own party as well as an initial rejection by the Conservative majority in the House of Lords. The new franchise was won only by conceding a redistribution of parliamentary seats that favored the Conservatives. Yet the Reform Act was a sound measure, allowing Liberalism to put down roots in parts of the countryside for the first time. It settled the voting arrangements in Britain until the end of the First World War.

Gladstone's second administration collapsed in the spring of 1885. The cabinet had been demoralized by internal dissension and was happy to resign following a minor defeat in the Commons. When Gladstone returned to power in February the following year, the government was so embroiled with the Irish question that it achieved very little. The Prime Minister found cabinet relations severely strained by his new Irish policy, and the third administration lasted a mere six months before it was defeated at the polls. With Home Rule for Ireland now entrenched as Gladstone's central preoccupation, retirement as Liberal leader was postponed indefinitely. For a while he seemed to enjoy a new lease of life, but by the time he formed his fourth and final ministry in August 1892, he was very old indeed. The queen dismissed him as "a wild, incomprehensible man of 82½." Because he was increasingly deaf, the table was removed from the cabinet room so that his colleagues sat closer and he could hear. There were only forty-seven cabinet meetings over the nineteen months of his premiership. While Mrs. Gladstone protected him from all but essential duties, decisions were postponed and ministers became restive. Lord Granville, who had died in 1891, was no longer available to act as go-between and peacemaker. Gladstone was still capable of spirited performances in the Commons, but in March 1894 he reluctantly acquiesced when his colleagues explained to him that the time had now come to retire. Although disagreement over naval estimates was equally the precipitant, failing eyesight was given as the public reason. At their last interview, Queen Victoria pointedly did not thank him for his services, an incident that Gladstone found deeply painful. His final months in government had not been his best, but it is remarkable that a man well into his eighties should be capable of acting as Prime Minister at all. It is equally remarkable that able colleagues should accept him in that role. They realized that Gladstone was irreplaceable.

POLITICAL THEORY

In his years as leader of the Liberal Party, Gladstone did not shed his early social theories but remained deeply conservative to the end. On a visit to Oxford in 1890, he confounded the Liberal dons by arguing that the constitution had been ideal in 1830, before the first Reform Act. The control then exercised by peers over entry to the House of Commons, he assured them, was a thoroughly good thing. He still thought in the final years of his career that the aristocracy was the natural governing class, and he tried hard to coax additional peers into his last administration. He was an ardent monarchist — which made the queen's treatment of him the more galling — and he had no time for egalitarianism. One of his private secretaries put it to him in 1891 that he was the only real surviving Conservative. "Yes," he said, "I hate all the radical ideas of the present Tory Government." Gladstone was constantly aiming to preserve: corruption and inefficiency must be shorn away so that traditional institutions could become more secure. Just like Sir Robert Peel, Gladstone wanted to secure a fair balance between the privileged and the underprivileged, to guarantee public order and to make government respected. The great change in his views since his Peelite days was not about ends but about means. He had come to recognize that the mass of ordinary people desired similar goals, and so he could have confidence in their willingness to endorse wise measures of reform. Gladstone believed that there were limits to popular participation in public life. The shiftless population who sought help from the poor law could not be expected to play a part as active citizens, and so it was just that they should remain outside the franchise. On the other hand, solid householders, however slender their means, deserved full political rights. When mobilized, they formed a salutary check on the rampant self-interest of the well-to-do. Gladstone now trusted the people.

Gladstonian Liberalism was therefore a distinctive version of the creed. It was not a typical European form, repudiating authority in the name of freedom. It owed virtually nothing to the ideas unleashed by the French Revolution, and unlike the predominant Liberalism of nineteenth-century Germany, it had no place for an enlarged state. On the contrary, except on rare occasions, Gladstone was the apostle of a minimal state, always insisting that government expenditure should be pared to the bone. Measures designed to create additional public agencies — what Gladstone called "constructive" legislation — were anathema to him, and state socialism was beyond the pale. The needy should be helped by individuals and voluntary organizations, he insisted, not by the state, which would only sap self-reliance. Thrift, foresight, and enterprise were the keys to social progress: "it is the individual character," he once declared, "on which mainly human happiness or human misery depends." Commercial firms and local communities, like nations, should be given every opportunity to determine their own futures. Liberty, Gladstone held, was the greatest qualification for more liberty. Freedom became his central principle. "I was brought up to distrust and dislike liberty," he told a friend in 1891; "I learned to believe in it." That is why he thought George Washington a greater man than Oliver Cromwell and in the 1890s advised young men to study the history of America, the embodiment of liberty. He maintained that the party he led should unshackle people to enjoy freedom, and so its objectives should be peace, retrenchment, and reform. Apart from being desirable in itself, peace would foster trade and reduce public expenditure on armaments. Retrenchment would save money and, by putting it back in people's pockets, promote prosperity. Reform would allow voters to take control of their own destinies. Another age might prefer a different hierarchy of values, but in Gladstone's day the package was an attractive one.

A school of historians has suggested that Gladstone was careful to keep his religion apart from his politics. They do not deny his devout temper, but they argue that, like everybody else in public affairs, he was motivated simply by ambition for power. He had no fixed ideology or guiding principles, they claim, but constantly maneuvered for advantage on the shifting political terrain. His moralistic justifications for policies that differed only by a hair's breadth from what he had previously condemned were no more than adroit techniques for harnessing the masses and outflanking his opponents. How is this view to be assessed? There can be no doubt that Gladstone enjoyed the exercise of power: people do normally find fulfillment in areas where they have skills. Nor did he lack the tactical sense of an able politician, for he had accumulated a vast experience about ways of achieving his goals. Nevertheless, those goals were part of an elaborate vision of society. From the earliest period of his career, he had inherited convictions about the monarchy, the aristocracy, and the constitution, and over the years he had gradually modified without abandoning them as his eyes were opened to the importance of liberty. Gladstonian Liberalism was a coherent ideology, not a smokescreen for self-seeking. And it was closely blended with the Christian faith. Self-help, he believed, gave people the moral responsibility which, if used aright, would lead them to heaven; money was a divine trust, not to be squandered; public affairs formed an arena in which conscience must be obeyed. Church-goers, especially Nonconformists, recognized in Gladstone's calls to arms the same tones they heard in the pulpit. The late nineteenth-century electorate, saturated as it was by Christian teaching, formed a responsive audience. Gladstone's consequent standing with the public was in turn his greatest asset in dealings with M.P.s and cabinet colleagues. His titanic proportions rendered him indispensable as party leader and Prime Minister long — perhaps too long — into old age. It was because religion molded Gladstone's politics that his ascendancy over the Liberal Party was assured.

11 Gladstone and Irish Policy, 1880-1894

Ireland posed particularly acute problems for Gladstonian Liberalism. Britain's island neighbor was deeply divided because its landed elite had largely forfeited the affections of the people. The long-standing difficulty was that the main social cleavages reinforced each other. In much of Ireland, especially the west, smallholders and landless laborers worked tiny agricultural units on large estates. There was an economic gulf between the poor peasants and their rich landlords whom they rarely, if ever, saw. Although there was significant industrial development in the northeast and there was a growing middle class in Dublin and a few large towns, Ireland remained overwhelmingly rural, and in most of the countryside the landlords had grown extremely unpopular as a class. To the economic divide was added a cultural one, for the aristocracy and gentry were thoroughly anglicized. Some of the landed proprietors were descended from the Norman invaders who had dispossessed the native Irish in the Middle Ages, and others who were of Irish stock had become assimilated to the English establishment. Since many spent their lives in England, the landlords seemed like an alien force of occupation. Furthermore, the main religious cleavage followed the same line. The bulk of the people were Roman Catholics; nearly all the landlords were Protestants. Presbyterians, mostly descendants of Scottish immigrants, were strong in the northern province of Ulster, and Methodism had also put down roots there. But in many parts of the north and nearly everywhere outside the north, the rural population was overwhelmingly Catholic. During the middle decades of the century, their faith had been transformed as new kinds of devotion strengthened the loyalty of the people to their Church. The landed elite, on the other hand, formed the core of those who worshiped in the Church of Ireland, the equivalent of the Church of England. Because class, culture, and religion all marked off the landlords from the mass of the people, Ireland seemed fated to be unstable.

It did not follow that the whole of the island was in constant turmoil. On the contrary, most of the people were resigned to a life of toil and hardship. Political issues, which in any case were the concern of a small minority, usually focused on local questions and the personalities of the area. But the raw materials did lie ready for agitation against the existing social order, against the government that sustained it, and against Britain. From time to time grievances came to a head. One instance was Daniel O'Connell's campaign against the Act of Union with Britain that in 1845 had induced Peel's government to bid for the allegiance of the Irish priesthood with the Maynooth grant. Resentments simmered near the surface of Irish society. Because of widespread rural crime that often seemed to be a form of protest, the ordinary law was suspended by a long series of coercion acts that gave special powers to the authorities. The impossibility of governing Ireland except by illiberal measures had induced Gladstone to take up Irish issues during his first administration. The Church of Ireland had been disestablished to meet a central grievance of the Roman Catholics, and tenant farmers had been given greater legal rights against their landlords. There had been a frustrated attempt, through the Irish Universities Bill, to provide facilities for the creation of an educated Catholic elite. Gladstone had declared in 1871 that he wanted to attach Ireland to Britain by "silken cords of love." Since he then believed that the Westminster parliament was capable of giving all that the Irish needed, he saw no need to grant separate institutions of state. Ireland was to be conciliated by British acts of generosity.

POLITICAL MOBILIZATION

The Irish question was insistent during Gladstone's first period as Prime Minister because nationalism was assuming new forms. The Fenians, a secret society with a doctrinaire commitment to revolution, had been launched in 1858 to struggle for an Irish republic. Their greatest strength came from the United States, where Irish emigrants raised money to support the national cause in their homeland, and in Ireland they recruited among the artisans, shop assistants, and schoolteachers of the small towns. The Fenians were responsible for a number of bombings, including the one in the London district of Clerkenwell in 1867. Although opposition from the Roman Catholic clergy helped minimize their influence, they were able to play a significant part in constituency politics. Since they backed several successful Nationalist candidates for parliament during Gladstone's first administration, the Fenian threat seemed to lurk behind aspirations for Home Rule, a separate parliament for Ireland. Yet the Home Rule M.P.s, organized from 1874 as a small party, wanted to remain strictly constitutionalist and to have nothing to do with revolution. They aimed for a federal solution: a legislature and executive possessing authority over Irish concerns, with imperial affairs still being controlled by Westminster. The Home Rule M.P.s were an indication that those who elected them, predominantly tenant farmers, were seeking a political remedy for their discontents. Ireland was being mobilized for change.

A crisis was precipitated by the state of agriculture. During the 1870s, grain from the North American prairies began to flood into the United Kingdom, drastically reducing the income of cereal growers. Their difficulties were aggravated by bad weather that caused poor harvests in Ireland in 1877, 1878, and 1879. With farmers going into debt and no longer able to pay rent to the landlords, evictions for nonpayment reached a new peak in 1880. Acute shortages of food suffered by the mass of the people provoked young men to lash out in desperation. As cases of cattle maiming, threatening letters, and arson multiplied, criminal outrage became more common than it had been in thirty years. The distress of the whole rural community presented a golden opportunity for agitators. In October 1879, a Land League was set up to represent the interests of farmers and laborers. It promised to defend those who refused to pay rent, and it encouraged demands for fuller tenant rights. Some of the Land Leaguers hoped eventually to supplant the landlords entirely and give the land to the farmers. Most significantly, a group of leaders framed what was called a "new departure." Previously, agrarian grievances, pressure for Home Rule, and revolutionary action had been largely separate, but now all three were to be welded together into a powerful mass movement. Agricultural distress was to be the motor for Irish independence.

GOVERNMENT RESPONSE

It was this situation that faced Gladstone when he assumed office in 1880. Since his information from Ireland was inadequate, he was unsure of the extent to which the withholding of rent was a result of simple distress and how far it was the fruit of criminal conspiracy by the Land League. Believing that distress must be at least part of the answer, he sponsored a Compensation for Disturbance Bill that would have given some relief to farmers who were evicted. The bill foundered in the

House of Lords. Yet Gladstone and his Chief Secretary for Ireland, W. E. Forster, also recognized that the League was encouraging wholesale defiance of the law. Ordinary legal processes were proving ineffectual because when League leaders were brought to trial for inciting breach of contract, Dublin juries would fail to convict. Consequently, in 1881, Forster had to resort to two new coercion measures to reinforce the fight against crime. But Gladstone characteristically wanted to get to the root of the problem, and so in the same year he determined to deal with the land question by another major act. Like its predecessor in 1870, the new measure was very much a one-man effort involving detailed preparatory study and resolute guidance through the House of Commons. Gladstone had to steer a careful course. On the one hand, Irish M.P.s were demanding the "three F's" — fixity of tenure (the right to remain on a particular farm), fair rent, and freedom of sale. On the other hand, landlords in Britain as well as Ireland were looking on anxiously to see how far property rights would be respected. Gladstone told the Commons that he was not offering the three F's with capital letters, but if the bill contained F's at all, they would be little f's. Neither the Irish M.P.s nor the landlords were wholly satisfied, but both sides acquiesced. The Irish Land Act of 1881 introduced an effective mechanism for helping distressed tenant farmers: Land Courts with the power to fix reasonable rents. As the courts went into action, the authority of the Land League was broken, and peace gradually returned to the Irish countryside. The act was at once a parliamentary triumph for Gladstone and a notable contribution to the well-being of Ireland.

Another part of the problem confronting Gladstone at the outset of his second ministry was the behavior of the Irish M.P.s. At their head was Charles Stewart Parnell, who was gradually turning into a national hero in Ireland. As a landlord and a Protestant, Parnell was an unlikely figure to be cast in that role. He even disliked green, the color of Irish nationhood. Yet Parnell became the focus of the new departure. He had traveled in America, forging links with the Irish community there, and though he did not join the Fenians, he made use of their support. From 1879, as president of the Land League, he became a frequent speaker on its platforms. Parnell was a dilatory man, often disappearing from public affairs to spend time with his mistress, Catherine O'Shea, the wife of another Irish M.P., but his very inactivity seemed to create a lofty grandeur that was part of his mystique. Gladstone found him remote and enigmatic, privately calling him "a Sphinx." On occasion all fifty-nine Nationalist M.P.s could be roused for the defense of Ireland in parliament, but it was Parnell's twenty-four close associates who constantly harried Gladstone's efforts to legislate on Irish topics. They had developed formidable techniques of obstruction, making interminable speeches to lengthen sessions and working the rules of the House of Commons to their advantage. On one occasion in 1881, a single day's session was drawn out for forty-one and a half hours. Gladstone responded by proposing a change in the standing orders of the House according to which debate on a given issue could be terminated by a vote in favor of closure. Further procedural alterations were hammered out in discussions with the opposition during the following year. Gladstone felt distaste for tampering with parliament, but it was the only way of dealing with the Parnellite challenge.

GLADSTONE AND PARNELL

In September 1881, with the Land Act just passed, Parnell recommended that his followers in the League should bring a small number of test cases under its auspices. He probably had no very sinister intention; he simply wanted the farmers to know how low the Land Court would fix rents before they all rushed to seek a hearing. Gladstone, however, interpreted his advice as a scheme to wreck an act on which he had pinned his hopes for the future of Ireland. In October Gladstone denounced Parnell as "an irreconcilable," trying to drive a wedge between him and the Irish people, and the Irish leader was sent to Kilmainham Gaol under the Coercion Act. Six months later, however, circumstances had changed. By the spring of 1882, the tenant farmers of Ireland were using the Land Courts, crime was falling, and calls by Land League spokesmen to pay no rent had withered away. Convinced that a social revolution had been successfully averted, Gladstone believed that it was time for a symbolic gesture of goodwill. The cabinet established, through discreet contacts, that Parnell was now willing to wield his authority in favor of law and order. Parnell, in return, was given to understand that the government would legislate to help tenants in arrears with their rent. There was no formal negotiation, and Gladstone was scrupulous to distance himself from the proceedings, yet the agreement was to become known as the Kilmainham Treaty, and Gladstone was to be held responsible for what ensued. With sensible arrangements for the pacification of Ireland apparently in place, Parnell was released from Kilmainham Gaol on 2 May 1882.

On 6 May, Lord Frederick Cavendish, Forster's replacement in the government as Chief Secretary for Ireland, together with a prominent civil servant, was brutally assassinated by Fenians in Dublin's Phoenix Park. Cavendish was the younger brother of Lord Hartington, the leading Whig in the cabinet, and his wife was Catherine Gladstone's niece, whom the Gladstones had long treated as a daughter. "This grief," wrote Gladstone in his diary the following day, "lay heavy & stunning upon us." The Phoenix Park murders precipitated a reaction in British public opinion in favor of harsher treatment for Ireland. The recent government accord with Parnell seemed an act of treachery, and the Conservatives, capitalizing on the new atmosphere, called for a committee of inquiry into the discussions preceding his release from prison. The Prime Minister was charged with enhancing the status of a probable rebel whom he had denounced as a criminal only a few months before. The personal pain and public censure combined to create one of the most demanding periods in Gladstone's life. Yet he was not deflected from his course of conciliating the people of Ireland. Although a new Coercion Bill had to be introduced, an Arrears Bill for tenant farmers was also pressed through. Meanwhile, the fixing of rents under the Land Act served to calm the Irish, and the Home Rule M.P.s became much less assertive. As the Prime Minister had wished, Ireland was becoming more orderly.

THE BACKGROUND TO HOME RULE

Gladstone, however, was far from satisfied. Although he was prepared to enforce coercion vigorously, the suspension of the ordinary laws could not be tolerated forever. In a healthy society, he believed, the aristocracy and gentry should guarantee order through personal bonds with their tenants, but in Ireland there was no prospect of that solution working. The landlords often ignored the people on their estates and had done nothing effective to withstand the Land League. The 1881 Land Act, furthermore, had undermined the position of the landlords by sharing their rights with the tenant farmers. Accordingly the farmers, together with other middle-class groups, would have to be drawn into positions of greater public responsibility if Ireland was to enjoy sufficient social leadership. Self-reliance among such people, Gladstone had said in 1871, had been enfeebled over the years in Ireland, and now it seemed urgent to encourage the essential Liberal skill of self-government. In 1881, Gladstone toyed with giving Ireland the Home Rule that its Nationalist M.P.s wanted, in the hope that, by running their own affairs, the Irish would learn the arts of citizenship. He decided, however, to opt for the less drastic policy of establishing county councils, the creation of which could be combined with the local government measures planned for the rest of the United Kingdom. For a while preparations for the Reform Bill of 1884 pushed local government into the background, so that it was only in 1885 that the question of Irish local government came to the fore. There was agreement among Liberals that there should be county councils in Ireland, but Joseph Chamberlain proposed that in addition there should be a Central Board, consisting of county council representatives. It would go a long way, Chamberlain expected, toward meeting the demand for Home Rule, and he was in touch with Parnell, whom he hoped to bind by the scheme to his own Radical grouping. Gladstone gave his backing to the proposal for a Central Board, but the Whigs were resolutely against it. The Central Board was rejected by the cabinet in May 1885, shortly before the fall of the government. What measure would be put forward next?

The answer was dictated largely by political circumstances. The Conservative government that assumed office in June 1885 was in a minority and needed Parnellite help to survive, and so it was forced to be conciliatory toward Ireland. There were even discussions with Parnell about the possibility of the Conservatives taking up Home Rule. Lord Salisbury, the Conservative Prime Minister, would probably never have drawn his party into the Irish cause, but Parnell, thinking that he might, ordered his supporters in Britain to vote against Liberal candidates at the general election in November. Conservative interest in a Home Rule alliance meant that the Liberals could hardly offer Parnell less than their opponents. Furthermore, as Gladstone anticipated the election, he realized that, since the Irish electorate had been more than tripled by the 1884 Reform Act, the Home Rulers would do well in Ireland. They would be in a position to argue that Ireland had made clear its national demand for its own parliament. Gladstone therefore began to give practical consideration to Home Rule. During the autumn of 1885, he privately mooted the idea among close colleagues and sketched out schemes. It might be a drastic solution, something that British politicians had always unanimously rejected, but it would give the Irish the opportunity they needed of running their own affairs. A strong Liberal government, if it was returned by the electors, might seize the initiative and give the Irish what they wanted, but on terms acceptable to the whole United Kingdom. It was a characteristically bold step.

PARTY MANEUVERS

The electorate knew nothing of the way Gladstone's mind was working, but its verdict in November further complicated the situation. An overall majority eluded him: in the new House of Commons there were 334 Liberals (including their close allies), 250 Conservatives, and 86 Irish Nationalists. As the largest party, the Liberals might be expected to form a government, but if the Irish continued to support the Conservatives, the two smaller parties could combine to keep the Liberals out of office. Gladstone hoped the Conservatives, spurred on by the Irish, would take up Home Rule, and so he passed on messages to the Conservative leaders that they could be assured of Liberal support for the measure. At that point, however, the news broke that Gladstone was considering the concession of an Irish parliament himself. His son Herbert flew what was called the "Hawarden Kite," informing the press of his father's idea. Although it was supposed that Herbert was testing opinion to see which way the wind blew, in fact he was trying to ensure that Liberal newspapers did not prematurely lead the party into opposing Home Rule. The Conservatives saw their opportunity. Convinced that Home Rule would be intensely unpopular in Britain, they decided to have no more to do with Parnell and to leave the proposal to the Liberals. Gladstone could still have maneuvered to avoid the task, but he sensed that the time was ripe for leading the party into a Home Rule policy. Ireland was to be given its own legislative assembly.

Gladstone created his third administration in February 1886. The cabinet was formed on the understanding that it would merely consider the practicability of a measure of self-government for Ireland. Gladstone was proceeding cautiously because he realized that leading Liberals were yet to be convinced. He was, after all, proposing what he called "an absolute novelty," a reversal of the policy that Britain had pursued ever since the Act of Union in 1800. There was much dismay among the Whigs, many of whom saw the new policy as a betrayal of the cause of law and order to a pack of violent subversives. Hartington, whose intransigence on Irish questions had been strengthened by his brother's murder, led the Whiggish resistance, and, with four other peers who had been members of Gladstone's previous ministry, he refused to join the new cabinet. The Prime Minister tried to make the scheme more palatable for Whigs by preparing a Land Purchase Bill at the same time as the Home Rule Bill. The parallel measure would ensure that landlords alarmed by the prospect of an Irish legislature could sell their estates at a reasonable price. Despite this generous treatment for the landlords, there were serious misgivings among the more right-wing members of the party. More surprisingly, there was stiff criticism from the Radical wing too. At first Chamberlain, together with a Radical colleague, entered the cabinet, but, realizing that he had been outdone by Gladstone in the advocacy of drastic progressive legislation, he began to argue that the plan for Home Rule threatened the supremacy of the Westminster parliament. In March, again with his colleague, he resigned from the government and set about drumming up opposition to Home Rule in parliament and the country. Gladstone was clearly going to have difficulty in persuading his own party, let alone a larger public.

THE INTRODUCTION OF HOME RULE

Nevertheless, Gladstone's speech in April on the first reading of the Government of Ireland Bill was a masterpiece. He aimed to demonstrate that, since it had proved impossible to govern Ireland successfully from Westminster, it was necessary to create a separate legislature in Dublin. Westminster would retain its responsibility for United Kingdom functions such as defense, but Ireland would be given a subordinate assembly to take charge of domestic affairs. The Conservatives had recognized that there was a need for decisive action, yet they had opted for coercion instead of Home Rule. But Ireland had been without coercion for only two of the previous fifty-three years. If such a policy of repression was at last to be made effective, it would require autocratic government and secret methods — neither of which accorded with the British understanding of liberty. The solution was therefore to take another course, that of "stripping law of its foreign garb and investing it with a domestic character." Whereas England felt that her laws were English, and Scotland that hers were Scottish, Ireland did not feel that hers were Irish. The "just and generous sentiments of the two British nations" should be willing to concede to Ireland the ability to make her own laws. With one eye on the dissidents in his own party, Gladstone was careful to distance himself from the Irish, remarking at one point that he had no right to assume that Ireland would accept the boon through her representatives. He urged the advantages to Britain of the new arrangement, pointing out that it would remove the Irish M.P.s with their obstructive methods from the Westminster parliament and that it would also end the waste of public money on maintaining public order in Ireland. He hinted briefly at the peril of civil war if the legislation were rejected, but he hoped that M.P.s would wish to act on the principle that "the concession of local self-government is not the way to sap or impair, but the way to strengthen and consolidate unity." They would rely not on written stipulations, but on mutual affections. That was the way, he concluded, "by the decree of the Almighty, that we may be enabled to secure at once the social peace, the fame, the power, and the permanence of the Empire."

It was on dramatic occasions such as this that Gladstone

most needed his spiritual resources, and they served him well. "The message," he recorded in his diary on the day of his speech, "came to me this morning: 'Hold thou up my goings in thy paths that my footsteps slip not.'" He settled some final points of detail in the morning. "Reflected much. Took a short drive." Then he went to the House of Commons. "My speech, which I sometimes have thought could never end, lasted nearly 3½ hours. Voice & strength & freedom were granted me in a degree beyond what I could have hoped. But many a prayer had gone up for me & not I believe in vain." Gladstone's physical powers were heavily taxed. "Came home, & went early to bed: of course much tired. My legs felt as after a great amount of muscular motion, not without the weariness of standing." To deliver so long a speech, to expound so persuasive a case, was a remarkable feat for a seventy-six-year-old man. To do so when emotions were so powerfully aroused on all sides was astonishing. "Extraordinary scenes," he noted, "outside the House & in." The strain must have been enormous, but the performance had its effect. Several waverers in the parliamentary party were won over to the cause, and many more in the country were swayed by reading the reports in the press. John Morley, Gladstone's first biographer, was present on the occasion. "Few are the heroic moments in our parliamentary politics," he commented, "but this was one." The explanation lay not only in Gladstone's strength and virtuosity but also in his inner life.

THE DEFEAT OF HOME RULE

For the next two months the political atmosphere was electric. Would Gladstone carry Home Rule through the House of Commons? Hartington and his Whig circle were irreconcilable, and so the question was whether the Prime Minister would be able to rally sufficient Radicals to the cause. With their backing and Irish Nationalist support, the government could pass its bill.

But Chamberlain proved a major obstacle, mounting a series of powerful criticisms of the measure. The proposal was fundamentally flawed, he argued, by the provision that Irish M.P.s should no longer sit at Westminster. Without representation from Ireland, the supremacy of the imperial parliament would be at an end. Chamberlain was particularly eager to vote down the bill, since a defeat for Gladstone would be the best tactic for increasing his own influence as a left-wing leader. He played his cards with great skill. At a meeting of Radicals at the end of May, he produced a letter from John Bright, the veteran champion of an earlier generation of advanced reformers, announcing his intention of opposing the bill. Several M.P.s whose loyalties had been torn between Gladstone and the bill's opponents were persuaded to turn against it, probably sealing the fate of the proposal. When, on 8 June, the second reading debate took place, Gladstone called it "a golden moment" for settling the affairs of Ireland, but the bill was rejected by 343 votes to 313. He had lost the first contest over Home Rule.

Since the government had been defeated on a major item of legislation, a general election followed. In what was largely a referendum on Home Rule, the nation decided against Gladstone's scheme. The Liberals gained only 190 seats, whereas the Conservatives secured 316, and the Liberal Unionists (opponents of Home Rule on the Liberal side) 79. The triumphant Lord Salisbury duly formed a Conservative government that was to last until 1892. The Liberal Party suffered serious losses. Lord Hartington led away many Whig landlords fearful of drastic change in Ireland, and Chamberlain seceded with a knot of Radical Unionists, chiefly from his Birmingham power base. A small proportion of Nonconformists left because they were anxious about the possible fate of the Ulster Protestants under a predominantly Roman Catholic legislature, and a significant number of Liberal intellectuals abandoned the party because of worries about parliamentary sovereignty. Despite negotiations in 1887 with the Liberal Unionists, most of them did not return to the fold. Increasingly they cooperated with the Conservatives, whom Hartington and Chamberlain were to join in government from 1895.

Was Home Rule a mistake on Gladstone's part? Certainly he had hoped to avoid a rupture in the party, and he underestimated Chamberlain's willingness to resist. Yet there was no folly in making the attempt to carry Home Rule. Gladstone expected that it would take time to educate his party in the need for a fresh Irish policy. If the first Home Rule measure failed — and the Lords were virtually certain to reject it — another would be needed in due course. He had embarked on a campaign of attrition to persuade the country that only a major constitutional change would suffice to answer the Irish question. Home Rule was not a wild error of judgment but a long-term strategy.

A MORAL CRUSADE

Despite the losses in the crisis, Gladstone carried the bulk of his party with him. The parliamentary Liberal Party, though much smaller in the 1886 House of Commons than before, was similar in social composition to its 1885 predecessor. Gladstone's immense popularity with rank-and-file party workers guaranteed their continuing Liberalism. A newspaper hostile to Home Rule suggested that those who could not study national affairs closely were overawed by Gladstone and so lost their power of independent judgment. The analysis was not far from the truth. In Ireland, Gladstone earned the undying gratitude of Home Rulers. Their newspaper, *United Ireland,* sold not its usual 90,000 copies but 125,000 when it gave away a color portrait of Gladstone. Buoyed up by the fervent support he had kindled, Gladstone roundly condemned a Coercion Bill introduced by the Conservatives in 1887. In trying to swing public opinion at large behind Home Rule, he published an elementary exercise in voter analysis to show, as he put it, that "the flowing tide is with us." Gladstone wanted to imitate the great forward surge of Liberalism in the late 1870s, when ordinary voters, particularly the Nonconformists, had been mobilized against Beaconsfield's foreign policy. Now he hoped to rouse them in a similar way against Conservative repression in Ireland. During the late 1880s, Gladstone often singled out Nonconformist audiences to address. As Christian people, he told some of their leaders in 1887, they were trying to apply "the elementary principles of our duty which our Blessed Lord and Saviour came to proclaim upon the earth." He was putting himself at the head of a moral crusade.

It is often suggested that Gladstone became obsessed with the Irish question in these years. By focusing on one issue, it is held, he prevented the party from regaining general support from the nation. Certain other Liberal leaders who were only half-hearted in the cause pointed out the risk at the time. It is true that aiming for Home Rule was Gladstone's overriding preoccupation: "my politics," he commented privately late in 1886, "are now summed up in the word Ireland." One explanation is that he saw the settling of the Irish problem as the only justification for his continued presence in politics. Part of him still hankered after retirement, and only the exceptional issue of Home Rule that he had injected into British party strife lay between him and a quiet life of scholarship and spiritual recollection. Another reason for concentrating on the campaign to right Ireland's wrongs, however, was that Liberalism stood to benefit from having a single battle cry. With the defection of many Whigs in 1886, the party was even more in danger of being fragmented by rival Radical sections clamoring for temperance, disestablishment, and industrial and other reforms. Gladstone believed that if the Liberal Party as a whole took up Ireland, each group would have to put Home Rule before its own pet cause. The Irish crusade would prove a remedy for sectionalism, bringing cohesion to the party. Gladstone was not, in any case, concerned with Ireland to the exclusion of all else. He took a sympathetic interest in a variety

217

of issues, Welsh, Scottish, and labor questions among them. In the end, though, the redress of Irish grievances presented itself to Gladstone as a moral question that obliged him to press it forward. His crusading oratory was not merely an effective technique, though it certainly was that. Justice for Ireland was a vocation he felt bound to fulfill.

The moral tone that Gladstone adopted in his discussion of the Irish question was intensely irritating to his opponents. The Unionists judged that Home Rule was an unwise and wicked policy, since the Nationalist cause seemed to them a matter of crime, intimidation, and treachery against the crown. Yet Gladstone was recommending it on the grounds of Christian ethics. It is hardly surprising that interparty debate became fiercer than at any time within living memory. It was at this stage that porcelain manufacturers of Unionist sympathies produced chamber pots with Gladstone's portrait inside. Passions were further fanned by a judicial commission of inquiry into the activities of Parnell and his party that lasted more than twelve months during 1888 and 1889. *The Times* had published a letter, purportedly from Parnell, in which the writer vindicated the Phoenix Park murders. Parnell claimed it was a forgery and demanded an inquiry, but the commission was allowed to investigate the whole range of Parnellite links with agrarian unrest and republican conspiracy. Although associations with crime lingered around Parnell's party, the forger was discovered, and Parnell enjoyed his moment of triumph. But then, in 1890, a greater crisis broke over him. His relationship with Catherine O'Shea at last became public when her husband divorced her. Since the Liberals were in alliance with the Parnellites, the revelation posed a severe problem for Gladstone. The backbone of Liberalism, the Nonconformists, could not tolerate supporting a party with an adulterer at its head. Although he had long known of the relationship, Gladstone decided that he must now issue a letter urging that Parnell should go. The Irish Party had just re-elected Parnell as leader, but, under pressure from the

Roman Catholic Church, a section soon repudiated him. The Nationalists split into pro- and anti-Parnell sections that bitterly denounced each other. It was an unedifying business that undoubtedly damaged the prospects of carrying Home Rule to victory.

Gladstone found the episode a severe trial. "Personally," he wrote to a colleague, "I am hard hit." The fall of Parnell dictated a change of emphasis in Liberal policy away from the cause on which Gladstone had set his heart. Home Rule was not dropped, but other issues came forward. The Irish cause was set back further by the squabbles between the Nationalist factions that continued even after the death of Parnell in 1891. Morale among Liberal leaders had risen very little when a general election took place in July 1892, though Gladstone, as usual in a contest, was in a more optimistic mood. A typical incident took place just before he set off from Lord Rosebery's home in the Midlothian constituency to deliver a campaign speech in Glasgow. Gladstone called John Morley, the Liberal intellectual who was to be his biographer, to the library, where he was thumbing through a volume of the poet Horace, looking for a passage about Castor and Pollux. Morley thought it was in the Third Book. " 'No, no,' said Gladstone; 'I'm pretty sure it is in the First Book' — busily turning over the pages. 'Ah, here it is,' and then he read out the noble lines with animated modulation, shut the book with a bang, and rushed off exultant to the carriage." The passage was duly turned into the conclusion of the speech. Gladstone, still bookish, zestful, busy, had recovered his relish for combat. Ireland, at the insistence of the Unionists, was at the center of the election debate, but the cause proved less popular with the voters than Gladstone had hoped. The new House of Commons consisted of 273 Liberals, 82 Irish Home Rulers, 269 Conservatives, and 46 Liberal Unionists. As in 1886, the Liberals could not govern alone but had to rely on the Irish M.P.s for their majority. Even if Gladstone had not been committed to the proposal, it would have been forced on the new government as a priority.

WILLIAM EWART GLADSTONE

THE SECOND HOME RULE BILL

Gladstone faced a number of particular problems in 1892 as he took up Home Rule in his fourth ministry. One was the strength of opposition to the measure from within Ireland. The Protestants of Ulster were adamantly hostile to a proposal that seemed to threaten their prosperity and their religion. Gladstone underestimated the intensity of Ulster loyalism. Relying too much on history, he recalled that Ulster Presbyterians had been Irish patriots in the past and failed to understand their loathing for Catholic nationalism in the present. The Ulster Protestants maintained energetic propaganda against the Home Rule Bill, stirring fears of Catholic ambitions among some of Gladstone's Nonconformist followers. Another problem was apathy about the Irish cause in the cabinet. John Morley, the Irish Secretary, was an enthusiast for Home Rule, but Sir William Harcourt, at the Exchequer, was not. Harcourt was strongly Protestant in his attitudes and disliked the amount of attention being lavished on Irish Catholics. Many of his colleagues sympathized with his desire to press forward with legislation that would benefit Britain rather than Ireland. Gladstone, with Morley's help, was constantly having to rally a hesitant cabinet for the fight. The second Home Rule Bill proved exacting work.

The bill was introduced at the start of the 1893 session. It had been modified to meet Chamberlain's central objection in 1886 that the Westminster parliament would cease to be truly imperial if the Irish were no longer there. Now Irish M.P.s were to remain at Westminster, though they were not to vote on English or Scottish bills. Nevertheless the opposition parties argued that the bill was full of dangers, mounting vehement attacks and regularly organizing obstruction to demonstrate their patriotic wrath. Discussion of the bill was drawn out into eighty-two sittings. Gladstone contributed to the length of proceedings by making speeches that were sometimes so full that they encouraged young Tories to win their spurs by baiting him on trivial allusions he had made. Yet the "Grand Old Man," as he was popularly known, put on an astounding performance for a person of eighty-three. He was capable of improvising with great skill on minor technicalities. When the opposition proposed that Irish cabinet ministers should be excluded from the new legislature, Gladstone was reminded that the same arrangement had been in force from 1701 to 1705, and he immediately rose to dwell on the precedent with convincing authority. Although he was severely taxed by the interminable succession of fierce debates, his stamina enabled him to last out what became the longest session to that point in the history of parliament. Before its end, the fate of the Second Home Rule Bill had been decided. This time it was carried on its third reading in the Commons by 34 votes, but the peers turned out in force to reject the bill. Gladstone was not surprised that of the 560 members of the House of Lords who could have voted, 419 opposed it and a mere 41 supported it. The resistance of the upper house was one of the reasons why, just before his retirement early in 1894, he was trying to rouse his cabinet colleagues for a campaign against the Lords' veto on legislation. He had failed to carry the bill, but his fighting spirit was not quenched.

IRELAND AFTER GLADSTONE

For the next seventeen years, the Irish question faded from British politics. The Liberal Government under Gladstone's successor, Lord Rosebery, turned to other issues, and in 1895 the Conservatives, now in coalition with the Liberal Unionists, returned to power. They relied on a mixture of firm administration and selling off land to tenant farmers that for a while seemed to calm the affairs of Ireland. The Liberals meanwhile renounced their alliance with the Home Rulers. When at the 1895 election many Irishmen in Britain voted for the Conservatives as the party that would give public funds for Catholic

221

education, Liberals reacted in disgust. In 1896, while Gladstone was still alive, minor party spokesmen vied with each other in declaring the commitment to Home Rule dead and buried. Yet it was to come back to haunt the Liberal Party. At the general election of December 1910, the Liberals found themselves once more reliant on the Home Rulers if they were to form a government, and so they were compelled to take up the issue again. Home Rule passed the Commons and, because the Lords' veto had now been curtailed, the hostile majority in the upper house was set aside. Home Rule was due to become law in 1914, and only the outbreak of the First World War postponed it. It would probably have been resisted by a rebellion in Ulster, but as it was, the Nationalists were the first to take up arms in the Easter Rising of 1916. From that point events moved swiftly to the creation of an independent Ireland in 1921. If Gladstone had achieved a "union of hearts" by carrying Home Rule, the severance between Britain and Ireland with all its legacy of bitterness in Ulster might have been avoided. Had he managed to set up a legislature in Dublin, the history of twentieth-century Ireland might have been much happier.

Gladstone's strategy was therefore far-seeing. He was prepared to take initiatives for Ireland where others held back. It is true that, like all other British statesmen, he had his blind spots about the sister island. He tended to underestimate the extent of disaffection, whether of the Nationalists from Britain or of the Ulstermen from the Nationalists. He hoped that the two sides in Ireland were being superseded by what he once called "a more intelligent & less impassioned body." Nevertheless, he did recognize that behind Parnell there were the incipient forces of nationalism that could not simply be repressed but had to be met, conciliated, and redirected into fresh channels. Just as he showed practical sympathy for small nations struggling under the Turkish yoke, so he endeavored to meet the grievances of the Irish people, even though the rule under which they were suffering was British. The grand aim throughout was to encourage the Irish to fulfill their aspirations by taking responsibility for their own affairs. He hoped that following the 1870 Land Act they would do so spontaneously, but when a second Land Act proved necessary, he realized that there must also be fresh institutions through which the people could learn the arts of self-government. County councils or a Central Board would not suffice in the circumstances of 1885-1886, and so he went for Home Rule as a means of cultivating self-reliance. Gladstone's Irish policy was therefore of a piece with his economic or colonial policy: it was designed to set people free to be responsible. Trusting them to avoid too many pitfalls was part of his Liberalism. It was also related to his Christian belief. When he sometimes remarked that the course of events would be directed by a higher Power, he was giving expression not to a conventional platitude but to a deep-seated conviction. Gladstone held that the people of Ireland could be given authority over their own future because he believed that providence would watch over the outcome. As he showed by his language about the Home Rule campaign, he viewed justice for Ireland as a compelling religious concern. Irish policy was a branch of Christian ethics.

12 Gladstone and Victorian Christianity

From the beginning of Gladstone's public life to its close, Christianity colored all his activities. His faith entered his speeches, influenced his policies, and — as his diaries reveal — shaped his underlying spiritual discipline. Gladstone constantly aimed to preserve a devout spirit in the cut and thrust of politics — though that is not to say that he pressed his religious concerns on those around him. A cabinet colleague recalled that he talked little about his faith in general society. Gladstone spoke readily enough about "Church matters," the public affairs of the Christian bodies, but not about personal spiritual experiences. Yet, as another cabinet colleague, Lord Rosebery, put it in a tribute in the House of Lords, Gladstone's Christian allegiance was transparently real. "The faith of Mr. Gladstone," said Rosebery, "obviously to all who knew him, pervaded every act and every part of his life." Even as Prime Minister, Gladstone made a point of reading the more important religious publications. In 1881, for instance, he examined parts of the Revised Version of the New Testament as soon as it appeared and busily canvassed opinion about the quality of its translation on a visit to his old school at Eton. If such special events in the religious world excited him, the regular rhythm of churchgoing was also a pleasure. In later life, when in London he normally attended, twice a Sunday, the Chapel Royal, where he especially enjoyed the choral services. When Gladstone was at Hawarden, he made a habit of attending the daily service at 8 A.M., and at Sunday morning worship he read the lessons from time to time. At least once, while staying in Hawarden Rectory with his son Stephen, he went to church four times in a single Sunday — at 8 A.M., 11 A.M., 3 P.M., and 6:30 P.M. Even when confined to the house by illness, he kept up his pattern of worship. "Service for & by myself," he noted on one such occasion. His faith was sustained by regular praise of God.

HIGH CHURCHMANSHIP

Gladstone, who never went back on his early adoption of "Church principles," practiced a high form of churchmanship. Participation in holy communion was the heart of his devotional life. Although he did not attend the service weekly in later life, he still received communion more frequently than most Anglicans of his day. He was also willing to accept certain doctrines distinctive to the Anglo-Catholic school. He believed, for example, that there would be scope for moral progress in the future life and so accepted prayers for the dead. Gladstone's favorite theological authority remained William Palmer, whose treatise of 1838 had confirmed him as a High Churchman. In the 1880s, Gladstone wanted Palmer to compose a new work reasserting the claims of the visible church. It should set forth, Gladstone wrote, "the Civitas Dei, the City set on a hill, the pillar and ground of truth, the Catholic and Apostolic Church." He even considered editing Palmer's earlier work as a retirement task. Questions of liturgy and the setting of worship formed another subject that continued to fascinate Gladstone. He found it easy, for instance, to fall into conversation with William Butterfield, one of the leading ecclesiastical architects of Victorian England. Yet points of ceremonial never determined where he chose to worship. More advanced Anglo-Catholics might be attracted by a cross and lighted candlesticks on the altar, colored vestments, and even incense, but Gladstone cared for none of these things. His Catholic churchmanship was not dependent on ritual.

Nevertheless Gladstone did become a champion of the ritualists, those clergymen who were gradually introducing more elaborate ceremonial into the Church of England. By their imitation of Roman Catholic practice, these younger Anglo-Catholics provoked enormous hostility among Protestants in England. After prosecutions in the ecclesiastical courts had failed to stem the advance of ritualism, Archbishop Tait, mildly Broad Church but resolutely Protestant in his preferences, called for parliament to give the Church of England fresh powers to put down the nuisance. In 1874, Disraeli was happy to comply in order to yoke popular Protestantism firmly to the Conservative Party. When Disraeli's Public Worship Regulation Bill came before the House of Commons, Gladstone was its most vehement opponent. Although he moved a whole series of resolutions on the floor of the House, the measure was eventually carried. Gladstone opposed the bill so resolutely because he detested any attempt by the state to control the church. With his high doctrine of the church, he was horrified by Erastian interference in its life. Public worship, he believed, should not be "regulated" at all by parliament. The fact that Convocation, the collective voice of the Church of England, had not been consulted in advance only strengthened his hostility, and the fact that the bill had been sponsored by Disraeli no doubt added an edge to his criticisms. The legislation was intended, Gladstone told the Commons, to make the clergy "march, like the Guards, in the same uniform, with the same step, and to the same word of command." It aimed to quench liberty in the Church of England. Although Gladstone did not favor experiments in ritual himself, he nonetheless staunchly defended the freedom to experiment.

The range of Gladstone's ecclesiastical sympathies had always been wide, but from the 1870s his interest in other churches increased markedly. When the Nonconformists took the lead in the struggles surrounding the Eastern Question, Gladstone's appreciation rapidly ripened into admiration. He grew closer to some of their leaders. He read their most scholarly magazine, *The British Quarterly Review,* corresponded with its editor, and in 1879 contributed a sympathetic article about the evangelical movement. He helped the Congregationalist James Murray to compile *The Oxford English Dictionary.* And Gladstone's doctor during the last fourteen years of his life was a Baptist, Samuel Habershon. In 1877, he drew on his own experience of oratory to address a Nonconformist conference about preaching. Gladstone feared that Nonconformist ministers, like their Anglican contemporaries, were failing to preach about the duties of their hearers, but he made an exception for the Baptist Charles Haddon Spurgeon, the greatest of the Victorian preachers. In 1882, he arranged to attend evening service at the Metropolitan Tabernacle in order to hear Spurgeon. Despite these friendly contacts, respect for Nonconformists did not fit easily into Gladstone's High Church convictions. Protestants outside the Church of England were, on his principles, guilty of schism. Yet in an article published in 1894, he was able to resolve the conundrum. He granted that formally the Nonconformists were schismatics from the true Church, but he argued that their error was excusable inasmuch as they were born and bred in communities outside the Catholic Church and so did not realize what they were missing. Far more important, in Gladstone's view, was the orthodox faith they shared with Anglicans. For their part, Nonconformists did not like the article because they could not accept its premises. Some of them responded that they were Nonconformists by conviction rather than by nurture. Nevertheless, the article was kindly meant, and it allowed Gladstone to reconcile his experience of spiritual fellowship with his ecclesiastical theory.

In his 1840 book on Church principles, Gladstone had

treated the Church of England as a rallying point for Christian unity in the hope that other Christians might come to accept its formula of episcopal ministry without papal control. Because the Eastern Orthodox Churches shared this position, they were the most natural ecumenical partners of the Church of England. Gladstone read extensively about Eastern Orthodoxy and often met its representatives, lay and ordained. He formed the opinion that the Russian Orthodox were generally narrower in spirit than the Greek Orthodox, but he was willing to go a long way for reconciliation with all of the Eastern Churches. Since the eleventh century, a bone of contention between East and West had been the *Filioque* clause in the Nicene Creed. The Western Church had added the clause, thereby professing its belief that the Holy Spirit proceeds from the Father "and the Son." The Eastern Churches had insisted that the clause was not part of the original creed and so should be omitted. Gladstone was prepared to grant the substance of their case. He was delighted when an accommodation between the two views was hammered out by his friend Dr. Döllinger of Munich. Döllinger was the prime mover in reunion conferences held between representatives of East and West at Bonn in 1874 and 1875. The conferences, as Gladstone put it, considered "the terms on which theological controversy may be adjusted or narrowed in accordance with Scripture and Christian history." He had high hopes of progress toward this noble aim, only to be frustrated when the Conservative government's handling of the Eastern Question dissuaded the Orthodox from returning to another session. Gladstone was something of a pioneer in ecumenical relations.

THE VATICANISM CONTROVERSY

Throughout his career, Gladstone held that the great obstacle to rapprochement between the churches was the papacy. He had been received courteously in audience by Pope Pius IX in

1866, but it was the office rather than the man that posed the difficulties. Gladstone believed with all his heart that each nation should profess its own religious character. The international conformity of the Roman Church was unacceptable, especially since it was imposed by authority. Gladstone particularly disliked the ultramontane spirit that wished to centralize the church under the control of the Vatican and make extravagant claims for the papacy. When the pope summoned the First Vatican Council to meet in Rome in 1869, Gladstone was outraged that the ultramontane forces were dragooning the council toward a declaration of papal infallibility. Thereafter it would become an article of faith that when formally pronouncing from the chair of St. Peter, the pope was preserved from error. At the head of the ultramontanists was Gladstone's former friend Henry Manning, now a cardinal, who, in Gladstone's eyes, had betrayed the Church of England in order to go over to Rome. Behind those who opposed a declaration of infallibility were Dr. Döllinger and his former pupil Lord Acton, whom Gladstone had just elevated to the peerage. To Gladstone it seemed like a struggle between the children of darkness and the children of light. He tried unsuccessfully, as we noted in Chapter 9, to persuade the government he led to intervene on Döllinger's side, but all his fears were realized. Infallibility was carried by a large majority, the pope's authority scaled new heights, and, after some delay, Döllinger was excommunicated. Ultramontanism had triumphed.

Gladstone did not react until he was out of office. In September 1874, he visited Munich and in conversation with Döllinger he relived the pain of the Vatican Council. On his return he angrily dashed off a pamphlet denouncing the council's decisions. He hesitated before publishing so inflammatory a document but then issued it in November. *The Vatican Decrees* went through 110 editions and became by far the most popular of Gladstone's writings. The pamphlet was lapped up by those who hated the papacy and all its works, even though Gladstone was far more discriminating. His target was the exaggerated claims for the pope embodied in ultramontanism. He protested against the treatment of moderate Catholics such as Döllinger, he censured the power of the court of Rome, and he argued against the exaltation of the pope over the rest of the Church. The Vatican, he argued, had proved itself illiberal. He attacked "a policy which declines to acknowledge the high place assigned to liberty in the counsels of Providence." Most controversially, Gladstone pointed out the implications for the civil allegiance of English and Irish Roman Catholics. Papal directives, he pointed out, might touch on the political sphere. If the directives carried the stamp of infallibility, an Englishman or Irishman would be forced to put his religious loyalties before his duty to the crown. Hence the Vatican decrees infringed British sovereignty. Gladstone challenged Roman Catholics to state their position, and he was duly answered by a host of controversialists. Cardinal Newman wrote an able reply in which he showed how limited the principle of infallibility really was. It might cover general moral principles, but Catholics had to exercise their conscience in applying them. The question of infringing on national sovereignty did not arise. There can be no doubt that Newman was both more logical and more realistic than Gladstone. When Gladstone returned to the attack in February 1875 with a further pamphlet, he did not make good his charge about civil allegiance. The episode is perhaps an example of his impetuosity overcoming his judgment.

THE VICTORIAN CRISIS OF FAITH

Most of Gladstone's later controversial writings, however, were designed for the defense of the faith. "I am convinced," he told his wife in 1874, "that the welfare of mankind does not now depend on the State or the world of politics: the real battle is being fought in the world of thought, where a deadly attack is made with great tenacity of purpose & over a wide field ag[ainst] the greatest treasure of mankind, the belief in God,

and the Gospel of Christ." Part of Gladstone's purpose in retiring from politics in the following year was to play a part in
the developing struggle. He saw himself as a Christian apologist, defending the deposit of faith against the critics of the day.
Many members of the intellectual elite had become dissatisfied
with the standard case in favor of belief. Up to the 1850s, it had
been confidently argued that the universe showed signs of
purpose. It was inferred that an intelligent power — a God of
some sort — was responsible for creating it. The Bible, in turn,
showed signs of being an authentic revelation of the will of
God. Scripture was attested, for example, by the miracles it
recorded. The only rational course was to believe the Bible.
Such a case, depending on arguments framed during the eighteenth century, was beginning to appear dated in the mid-
nineteenth century. In an age that had learned from the Romantics to rate feeling above reason, it seemed increasingly odd
to try to argue people into Christianity with a chain of deduc-
tions. Younger people in particular were beginning to show
immunity to the traditional approach. Their doubts about the
validity of the Christian faith formed the kernel of the Victorian
crisis of faith.

The challenge to religion seemed to come primarily from
science. Research suggested that nature was governed by scientific principles that could properly be called laws. In a world
of that kind, there seemed no place for miracle. Why should
there be inexplicable breaches in the regular pattern of the
universe? Yet if miracles were inadmissible, a central prop of
Christian belief was knocked away. Gladstone did little more
than dabble in scientific questions, but he kept a watching brief
for their potential impact on religion. Laws about the operation
of the physical world did not trouble him, he told Lord Acton,
because the moral world was not subject to the type of laws
that science could investigate. Many other people, however,
failed to make Gladstone's distinction and maintained that
everything was open to scientific explanation. Charles Darwin's explication of the principle of natural selection appeared

to confirm their belief. Darwin's *Origin of Species*, published in 1859, suggested that evolution takes place by gradual automatic adaptation to the environment. It was easy to infer that there is no evidence in nature of a divine purpose, and this view undermined the defense of theism inherited from the eighteenth century. Darwin contributed to the decay of traditional apologetic, but, like most other Christians of the time, Gladstone was not dismayed. He saw no ground for supposing that evolution and revelation are at variance. Darwinism, he argued, does not exclude an act of creation. On the contrary, by binding together the various ranks in the created order, it actually enhances the argument from divine purpose. The complex process of adaptation is itself evidence for providential care of the world. Gladstone resisted any simplistic notion that Darwin had disproved the Bible. Although the theme did not occupy much space in his writings, its articulation was one of his services to the faith.

DEFENSE OF THE FAITH

During his later years, Gladstone was repeatedly drawn into debate on other issues surrounding Christian belief. Some of the discussion was face-to-face. From its foundation in 1869, Gladstone was a member of the Metaphysical Society, a group of intellectuals who gathered to consider papers on such topics as the immortality of the soul and the proof of miracles. The membership was diverse, including Catholic, Anglican, and Unitarian divines as well as various types of skeptics. After his retirement in 1875, Gladstone was a frequent attender, often taking the chair. Although he never read a paper to the society, he played a full part in discussion. Perhaps his most notable antagonist was T. H. Huxley, a distinguished man of science who ranged freely over biology, zoology, and geology. Huxley believed that scientific knowledge had made traditional religion untenable. He was the first to coin (at a Metaphysical Society meeting) the term *agnostic* to describe his own position. Religious truth, Huxley supposed, could not be known, and he saw it as his task to discredit all claims that it could. The debates of the Metaphysical Society spilled out into the periodicals, where there were several exchanges between Huxley and Gladstone over the creation narrative in Genesis. In 1891, Gladstone defended the Gospels against Huxley's claim that it was immoral for Jesus to have caused the destruction of a herd of swine. Gladstone habitually narrowed the debate to such points of detail. Huxley was irritated, suggesting on one occasion that Gladstone did not know the meaning of the term metaphysics. It is true that Gladstone's method seemed old-fashioned, though that was excusable in an elderly man. Nevertheless, he was right to oppose an exaggerated faith in science. A century later, very few scientists would maintain that science is the only path to knowledge, so that in the long run Gladstone turns out to have been the sounder metaphysician.

Another opponent in literary debate was Robert G. Ingersoll, an agnostic propagandist in America. Trained as a lawyer, Ingersoll became the best-known lecturer against religion of his day. Like Huxley, he looked to science for emancipation from thralldom to the superstitions of the past. "Science," he wrote, "destroys the dogmas that mislead the mind and waste the energies of man." In 1887, he had an exchange in *The North American Review* with a New York Presbyterian minister. Gladstone, who had just contributed an article on another topic to the *Review,* was persuaded to intervene. Ingersoll had cited the cases of Jephthah and Abraham, who were willing to offer their children as sacrifices, as instances of immoral behavior by biblical characters. There is nothing in the text, Gladstone suggested, to show that Jephthah's conduct should be approved. Likewise, the actions of Abraham, who lived at an early period, were contrary to later morality but not to that of his day. Gladstone went on to rebut the assumption that Darwinism is fatal to Christianity and to deal with a variety of lesser points, but his strongest criticism was reserved for Ingersoll's doctrine that people are not responsible for their thoughts. Belief, according to the agnostic, is an automatic effect of evidence on the mind. Gladstone pointed out that this view is incompatible with the existence of prejudice: bias — and not just the evidence — can create opinions that are mistaken. Gladstone was defending the principle that human beings are responsible for what they believe. He ranged a full battery of his intellectual heroes — Aristotle, Dante, Bishop Butler, even Cardinal Newman — against Ingersoll, and with their aid the statesman disposed of several popular fallacies. Perhaps he was using a hammer to crack a nut, but unless he had answered Ingersoll, the fallacies might have gained a wider circulation. Gladstone's apologetic was a worthwhile pursuit.

DOCTRINE AND BIBLE

As Gladstone looked about for allies in the conflict of belief with unbelief, he found some in the Broad Church school. In 1868, for instance, he wrote a favorable review of Sir John Seeley's *Ecce Homo,* a life of Christ which included no hint of his divinity. Gladstone also gave ecclesiastical appointments to Broad Churchmen. He twice promoted Charles Kingsley, perhaps best known for such novels as *Alton Locke* and *The Water Babies.* On the other hand, some Broad Churchmen traveled too far away from received Christian convictions for Gladstone's satisfaction. He suggested, for example, that in his critical writings on the Old Testament, Bishop Colenso had expressed a "destructive spirit." As long as there was no actual unorthodoxy in their teaching, however, Gladstone sympathized with their aim. "I profoundly believe," he told Manning in 1869, "in a reconciliation between Christianity and the conditions of modern thought, modern life, and modern society." That was essentially the Broad Church project. So it is not surprising to discover more liberal traits in Gladstone than among many of his High Church contemporaries. He disliked the Athanasian

Creed with its outspoken statements about the damnation of the unorthodox. He was willing, in a spirit of scientific inquiry, to attend two spiritualist séances. He was prepared to concede that the teaching of the apostle Paul about sin being the cause of death is mistaken: geology had shown that animals lived and died before the appearance of humanity in the world. And he was prepared to toy with the view, sometimes called "conditional immortality," that the soul will die unless it is granted eternal life as a special gift of God. He remained far from universalism, the belief that all human beings will ultimately be saved, but he eventually acknowledged that the Bible does not seem explicit about the fate of the lost. All this is simply evidence that Gladstone was prepared to consider objections to the normal Christian teaching of his time on their merits. He was not blinkered in his religious thinking.

Yet he was profoundly loyal to the Bible. In Gladstone's day, the so-called higher criticism was being introduced into Britain from Germany. When Gladstone read some of its ablest exponents, he found that he could not accept the Wellhausen thesis that the first five books of the Bible emerged at a late stage in the history of Israel. Gladstone insisted on the customary view that they were connected with Moses. Even if, for argument's sake, the critics' views on the age, text, and authorship of the books of the Bible were accepted, the authority of Scripture for the Christian life would remain. Gladstone was aware of the strong view of inspiration expounded by certain evangelical champions, but he was unable to accept it. We cannot judge in advance, he argued, whether the Scriptures should take an ideal form. The probability is that the Bible, like God's revelation in nature, will not be presented with mathematical precision. Although he rejected the idea of verbal inspiration, he warmly upheld the view that Scripture is uniquely inspired. In 1890, he contributed a series of articles on the Bible to the popular journal *Good Words* that were subsequently issued in book form as *The Impregnable Rock of Holy Scripture*. His advice to his fellow countrymen was to take their stand with him on that rock. The high sales of the book suggest that he was widely heeded.

BISHOP BUTLER AND THE INTELLECTUAL LEGACY

After Gladstone's final retirement from politics in 1894, he settled down to a major task he had long intended to fulfill: the production of an annotated edition of the works of Bishop Butler. His notes are, in fact, rather sparse and not particularly illuminating. Far more can be derived from a companion volume, *Studies Subsidiary to the Works of Bishop Butler* (1896), in which Gladstone collected a number of papers written over many years that were more or less connected with the teachings of Butler. The two publications drew attention to a writer who had been second to none in his influence over Gladstone. Butler, who had been bishop successively of Bristol and Durham between 1738 and 1752, had published a set of sermons that outlined a full ethical scheme and also a solid apologetic work, *The Analogy of Religion* (1736). *The Analogy* was directed against the Deists, a school of thinkers who accepted the existence of a God responsible for creating the world but denied that he continued to care for it by his providence. Butler's book contends that if it was reasonable to see evidences of God in creation, it was equally reasonable to see evidences of his activity in providence. Gladstone had read Butler at Oxford and then had absorbed his teachings more thoroughly in the 1840s. He was attracted by many correspondences, duly pointed out in his notes to the edition, between Butler and Aristotle. Gladstone was prepared to disagree with Butler over minor points but was far more concerned to vindicate him against his critics. When Butler warned against the abuse of the imagination, for instance, Gladstone hastened to explain that Butler was not entirely hostile to the imaginative faculty. In one or two respects, Gladstone actually misrepresented Butler in his zeal to defend him. He clearly venerated the bishop.

What aspects of Butler was Gladstone eager to transmit? There was in the first place the bishop's central teaching about providence. Gladstone admired Butler for encouraging his readers to refer all events to "a great governing agency" — that being Gladstone's own habit of mind. There was Butler's generosity to his opponents — again a quality that Gladstone had been careful to cultivate. There was the worth for the reader of grappling with the text of *The Analogy* as an intellectual exercise. "Butler," wrote Gladstone, "assuredly was not made for butterflies to flutter about." What Gladstone found most valuable, however, was Butler's principle that "probability is the very guide of life." God calls us, Gladstone argues, to a life of activity. How do we make decisions in the course of life? We cannot expect to achieve certainty before we act, but what we can work out is the balance of probabilities between alternatives. The "master gift" of Butler was an understanding that all we need is sufficient evidence to choose one course of action rather than another. Once probability points in a particular direction, we are obliged to act. Gladstone was especially keen to show how Butler's principle applied to politics, and it is clear that he formulated his own political practice in Butlerian terms. In order to make a policy decision, it was first necessary to amass information, then to weigh the probabilities, and finally, once a decision was taken, to pursue the policy with undeviating commitment. Others noticed that Gladstone would not reexamine his premises once his mind was made up. It was an approach that critics said made Gladstone stubborn. Because so much effort went into the original study of the evidence, however, a fairer estimate might be that it gave him force of character. Butler had taught him how to reconcile uncertainty with moral obligation, and Gladstone hoped others would gain equally from the bishop's instruction.

Gladstone had written another weighty statement for posterity a few years earlier. It appeared as "Universitas Hominum; or, The Unity of History" in *The North American Review* for 1887. The article contains Gladstone's view of the meaning of life, the chief contention being that the proper study of mankind is man. Despite the fallenness of human nature, Gladstone declares, mankind displays qualities "so beautiful, so good, so great" that the Creator could hardly do better. Homer, he goes on, depicts the totality of human life, and Dante does the same for the Christian dispensation. Both reveal something of mankind's sense of unity, which successive empires had tried to embody in political form. In Gladstone's own day the sense of unity found echoes in the concert of Europe, the law of nations, and the global bonds of the English-speaking nations. Writers had tried to represent the human ideal in the heroes of literature: Achilles in the ancient world, King Arthur in Christian times. Human fulfillment, however, lay in the future. A design was evident in history, a pattern of progress passing from the ancient Jews and Greeks through medieval and Renaissance Italy to the modern world. Now, with Christendom holding the mastery of the whole globe, Christian ideals for humanity were dominant. Any study we pursue, concluded the statesman, should fit into this perspective on the human condition. Gladstone's account, though rather disjointed (no doubt because of old age), is a powerful vision of the central preoccupations of his later years. He was eager to promote the welfare of humanity as a whole because that aim, as he saw it, corresponded with the divine purpose. The underlying concerns set out in the article emerged in his speeches, whether he was appealing to our common humanity with the villagers of Afghanistan or denouncing the inhumane treatment of the Irish. His political campaigns were of a piece with his Christian scholarship.

THE END

Gladstone's final years were sorely affected by ill health. After he had stepped down as Prime Minister in 1894, his eyesight was extremely poor, and he was put in the hands of a nurse.

He also caught influenza. "But," he recorded, "I am thoroughly content with my retirement; and I cast no longing, lingering look behind." Apart from his studies of Butler and a collection of his articles, he had a work on Olympian religion to keep him occupied. This last treatise, however, was never completed. He was forced to give up daily morning service because he did not rise until 10 A.M., but by way of compensation (a typical Gladstonian touch), he attended two evening services, at 5 P.M. and 7 P.M. He still maintained his custom of using up odds and ends of time. One day when he was planning to drive from Hawarden to Chester after lunch, his pudding was too hot, and so, while it cooled, he went away to change for the drive before returning to finish his meal. By this parsimony of time he contrived to save ten minutes. Gladstone's home was normally Hawarden, the owner of which, his oldest son William, had died in 1891 at the age of fifty-one. The younger William had written a number of hymn tunes, at least one of which is still in regular use. The other children were frequently with their father in his closing years. Stephen remained the parish clergyman, Henry had returned from India, and Herbert was rising in the Liberal Party. Agnes was usually with her husband in Lincoln, where he was dean of the cathedral, but Mary and Helen took turns in caring for their father. His wife, Catherine, was Gladstone's mainstay to the end — devoted, vigilant, and tolerant. He found great satisfaction in the family circle.

In 1897, Gladstone was twice taken to Cannes in the south of France to recoup his strength because he was gradually developing an acutely painful facial cancer. His suffering was sometimes eased by music, but it normally remained intense. His final travel, in February and March 1898, was to Bournemouth on the south coast of England, where, in the parish church, he received communion for the last time in public worship. From Bournemouth he returned to Hawarden to die. The end came on 19 May 1898, which was — appropriately — Ascension Day. Gladstone died peacefully among his family, with Stephen reading the prayers. It was a classic Victorian deathbed scene.

A state funeral was held at Westminster Abbey nine days later, by which time a variety of tributes had already been paid. Many thought that the one voiced by Lord Salisbury, the Conservative Prime Minister, was the most fitting. Gladstone would be remembered, said Salisbury, "not so much for the causes in which he was engaged or the political projects which he favoured, but as a great example, to which history hardly furnishes a parallel, of a great Christian man." Among the Nonconformists, a memorial sermon by the Baptist leader John Clifford was often interrupted by applause. Prizes were endowed at the ancient English universities in Gladstone's memory. At Oxford, a new chair of government was named after him. Four commemorative statues were erected in the major cities of the United Kingdom. The nation was swept by a powerful sense of loss.

Perhaps most representative of the public mood are the artless poems contributed to the provincial press when Gladstone's death became known. Charlotte Oates wrote in *The Cleckheaton Guardian,*

> We could but look and marvel, while we bowed
> Before his genius; his vast life-work showed
> The Statesman, Scholar, Author, was endowed
>   With gifts from Heaven.
> While on Fame's pinnacle in strength he stood,
> He did the world a great and glorious good;
> A central figure, kingly, whom we could
>   But venerate!

G. Hunt Jackson took up a more distinctive theme in *The Brighton Herald:*

> He moved among the forest trees,
>   The trusty axe within his hand;
> His fame was known across the seas, —
>   The Woodman of our England's strand.

Perhaps popular Liberal memories of Disraeli were in the mind of H. Simons as he wrote for *The Kettering Leader:*

No demagogue who strove to please,
No juggling mountebank was he,
But one who wrought by principles,
Born in a deep sincerity.

And *The Tiverton Gazette* carried an acrostic poem by James Merson:

Great and good was Gladstone,
Liberal to the end,
An orator great and author too,
Did and said what few could do.
Statesman, yes! indeed he was,
Titles he ignored,
One of England's greatest men,
None better able to defend
Empire, Empress, and Queen to the end.

National pride mingled with personal attachment and a certain open-mouthed admiration. The passing of Gladstone was marked by an outpouring of popular devotion.

PERSONAL QUALITIES

Behind the image was the man. What qualities enabled Gladstone to make such an impression? Prominent among them was the capacity, inherited from his father, for sheer hard work. Gladstone possessed enormous stamina that enabled him to sustain into old age a punishing program of reading, writing, meeting, and speaking. He was helped by a willingness to delegate to others, especially secretaries — a process he called "devolution." He was also well served by a quick intellect that had been thoroughly trained at Eton and Oxford. He was particularly skillful in drawing fine distinctions, an ability that came into its own in parliamentary debate. Gladstone possessed the power, in an unusual degree, of thinking on his feet. In the circumstances of the nineteenth century, a powerful voice was another great asset, enabling him to make impressive set-piece speeches in the House of Commons. It also allowed him to turn the platform into a powerful political tool: nothing touched the popular imagination more than the Midlothian addresses. Among more personal qualities, a sanguine temperament was an invaluable aid. In the hour of defeat, an unquenchable optimism would raise his own spirits and rally his followers. His remarkably generous judgments of others meant that, even when engaged in public controversy with them, he normally remained on good personal terms. There was also Gladstone's astonishing zeal — what a private secretary called "the extraordinary intensity and vehemence of all his impulses." This quality enabled him to direct the flow of his energy into particular channels, to exclude all distractions, and to press on to the goals he had set. It was not all gain, however, for his intensity sometimes verged on obsession. Opponents talked of him as mad, claiming that he would walk into a hatter's shop and order several dozen hats for himself. In fact he had once found a Brighton shop selling straw hats at bargain prices, and so his wife had bought two and a half dozen for her orphanage. The story was used to illustrate an impulsiveness that Gladstone himself regretted from time to time. Although he had to rein back his impetuosity, there is no doubt that his total commitment to a new cause could achieve great things in politics. It was the power behind the radical initiatives of his career.

One feature of Gladstone's personality was almost wholly a disadvantage. He lacked sensitivity. It was not a deficiency in sympathy for the obvious sufferings of others: Gladstone was often to be found relieving the distressed in a variety of ways. Rather, it was the absence of an instinct for knowing what another person was thinking. As his daughter Mary put it, he was "not exactly quick at understanding people's insides." Although he had a sure feeling for the mood of an audience, he was strangely inept at dealing with individuals. When a young relation came in from some unsuccessful cricket at the Lord's ground, Gladstone asked not about the day's play but about the acreage of Lord's. He had little facility for small talk; and to many he seemed to have no humor. That was unfair, for he delighted in puns. Shortly after the death of Archbishop Tait, Gladstone asked why the late archbishop was the laziest man on earth. It was because, Gladstone explained, he rose each day a Tait (at eight) and went to bed a Tait (at eight). Puns are often regarded as the lowest form of humor, and it is true that Gladstone's own jokes did not rise much higher in the scale. Although he appreciated the wit of others, he believed that serious topics should be treated seriously. Here was another reason why he failed to develop any personal rapport with most of his colleagues — a problem that greatly complicated his political relationships. Hartington confessed that, despite years of work together, he could not manage to understand Gladstone. Queen Victoria's resentment of Gladstone's apparent lack of interest in her personal concerns was an oppressive burden on his later years. The handicap ensured that he was less effective in the cabinet and the parliamentary party than he was in inspiring the Liberal Party at large. Gladstone had to rely on others to supply the skills he did not possess. That is why he depended so heavily on Lord Granville to smooth ruffled feathers in his first two cabinets. His secretaries and his family also had to cushion him against the peevishness of those who felt overlooked. He was fortunate in being so well served.

CHRISTIAN VALUES

Gladstone's political achievement was built not only on his personal qualities but also on values shaped by Christianity. He began with a structured set of Conservative principles. He entered his career intending to defend the monarchy, the House of Lords, and the established Church. The crown and the aristocracy, he held, derived their authority from the Almighty; the Church should remain united to the state because it taught the truth. Over time he revised his views. It is often suggested that the change was the result of experience, and that judgment, so far as it goes, is correct. Gladstone soon allowed his vision of the Church as the conscience of the state to fade because he recognized its impracticality. Yet the direction of the subsequent change was a consequence of learning the importance of other Christian values. He began to fear the interference of the state in the doctrine and discipline of the Church and so laid stress on ecclesiastical liberty. Through Sir Robert Peel and others he absorbed a Christian version of political economy and so wanted to remove economic restrictions on the free operation of providential laws. He believed that self-reliance would produce moral responsibility among the ordinary people and so moved toward the centrality of freedom as a political principle. Meanwhile, humanity also came to loom large among his guiding values. The doctrine of the incarnation showed that God had ennobled human nature. The Homeric poems, in which Gladstone discerned traces of revelation, depict human beings as possessing heroic stature. He increasingly conceived of mankind as forming a unity in God's plan, and this conviction led him to insist that all human beings, wherever they may be, should be treated justly. Small nations such as the Bulgarians should not be allowed to suffer under repression. The twin values of liberty and humanity formed the substance of Gladstone's Liberalism. The evolution of his political views took place for reasons that were conditioned by his Christian beliefs.

It could hardly have been otherwise. Gladstone absorbed numberless sermons, read weighty theological tomes, and meditated on Scripture. He often complained that politics became all-absorbing, but public life never turned into an end in itself. It remained a forum for service to the Almighty. Like Bishop Butler, Gladstone had a powerful sense of divine providence. Although we cannot necessarily discern the will of God in particular events, Gladstone wrote, we know that "the whole of life is providentially ordered on our behalf." Belief in providence explains why he expected Christian values to prevail. The Almighty would ensure that in due time his purposes were accomplished, but meanwhile it was for the believer to cooperate in the working out of the divine agenda. That calling could be fulfilled only through a life of spiritual discipline. The priority of discipleship showed in many features of Gladstone's life. He frequently read *The Imitation of Christ* by Thomas à Kempis. He thought the hymn "Hark, My Soul, It Is the Lord" too sacred for public worship, but he spent part of a Sunday during the Egyptian crisis of 1882 translating it into Italian. On the dressing table in his bedroom at Hawarden was the illuminated text, "Thou wilt keep him in perfect peace whose mind is stayed on Thee." In a many-sided career, a rich devotional life sustained him in all his activities. The Victorian crisis of faith was so disturbing to Gladstone because it struck at the foundation of his existence. Belief in God had to be defended because it was the root of all that was good for humanity: faith gave meaning to life. Gladstone was a great man because he was a sincere Christian.

A Note on the Sources

The materials available for the life of Gladstone are immense. Here some of the more important items are arranged in twelve sections that correspond to the topics of the chapters in this book. There are a number of background works as well as items by and about Gladstone. Section 1 contains a range of biographies and other books that relate to many aspects of the man and his times.

1. GLADSTONE AND VICTORIAN BRITAIN

After Gladstone's death, the family commissioned John Morley to write his biography. His three-volume *Life of William Ewart Gladstone* (London, 1903) is massive, lucid, and almost entirely reliable, although on the instructions of the family, Morley, who was an agnostic, did not examine the Christian foundations of Gladstone's achievements. An earlier study edited by Sir Wemyss Reid, *The Life of William Ewart Gladstone* (London,

1899), contains twenty essays on different aspects of the statesman by eight different hands. There is also D. C. Lathbury's *Mr. Gladstone* (London, 1907), which, as a volume in the Leaders of the Church, 1800-1900 series, sheds light on several religious issues that Morley left in obscurity. More recently, J. L. Hammond and M. R. D. Foot wrote a useful general account, *Gladstone and Liberalism* (London, 1952), and Sir Philip Magnus composed *Gladstone* (London, 1954), a witty and perceptive biography. Other lives are E. J. Feuchtwanger's *Gladstone* (London, 1975), which concentrates on politics; Peter Stansky's *Gladstone: A Progress in Politics* (New York, 1979), which quotes extensively from his speeches; Richard Shannon's detailed *Gladstone* (London, 1982), which is to be completed in a second volume; and Agatha Ramm's *William Ewart Gladstone* (Cardiff, 1989), a concise study in a series of political portraits. The most original perspective is to be found in H. C. G. Matthew's *Gladstone, 1809-1974* (Oxford, 1986). It consists of the introductions to the Gladstone diaries that Colin Matthew is editing and is to be followed by a second volume. Two valuable collections of essays were published almost simultaneously: *Gladstone, Politics and Religion* (London, 1985), edited by P. J. Jagger, and *The Gladstonian Turn of Mind* (Toronto, 1985), edited by B. L. Kinzer. Another helpful essay is D. M. Schreuder's "Gladstone and the Conscience of the State," in *The Conscience of the Victorian State,* edited by P. T. Marsh (New York, 1979).

The chief unpublished source for Gladstone is the vast collection of his papers, extending to 788 volumes in the British Library. The bulk of the collection is listed and indexed in the *British Museum Catalogue of Additions to the Manuscripts: The Gladstone Papers* (London, 1953). There is also a major deposit of family papers, running to some fifty thousand items, called the Glynne-Gladstone Manuscripts and housed in the Clwyd County Record Office at Hawarden. Also at Hawarden, in Gladstone's foundation of St. Deiniol's Library, is his collection of books, containing many annotated works. Correspondence from Gladstone is to be found in most of the main surviving collections of Victorian papers. Four volumes of manuscripts, consisting chiefly of political memoranda from the British Library, have been printed as *The Prime Ministers' Papers: W. E. Gladstone,* edited by John Brooke and Mary Sorensen (London, 1971-1981). Parts of Gladstone's correspondence have been published as follows: *Gladstone and Palmerston: Being the Correspondence of Lord Palmerston with Mr Gladstone, 1851-1865,* edited by Philip Guedalla (London, 1928); *The Queen and Mr Gladstone,* 2 vols., edited by Philip Guedalla (London, 1933); *Gladstone to His Wife,* edited by A. Tilney Bassett (London, 1936); *The Political Correspondence of Mr Gladstone and Lord Granville, 1868-1876,* edited by Agatha Ramm, vols. 81 and 82 of the Camden Third Series (London, 1952); and *The Political Correspondence of Mr Gladstone and Lord Granville, 1876-1886,* 2 vols., edited by Agatha Ramm (London, 1962). Of particular interest with regard to Gladstone's Christianity is *Letters on Church and Religion of William Ewart Gladstone,* edited by D. C. Lathbury, 2 vols. (London, 1910). There is an attempted full listing of Gladstone's speeches, together with the text of fourteen of the most important among them, in A. Tilney Bassett's *Gladstone's Speeches* (London, 1916). Gladstone himself assembled a selection of his published articles on a wide range of themes in *Gleanings of Past Years, 1843-1879,* 7 vols. (London, 1879). Another selection, devoted exclusively to theological and ecclesiastical subjects, appeared as *Later Gleanings* (London, 1898). Most useful of all is the published edition of *The Gladstone Diaries* (Oxford, 1968-), edited by M. R. D. Foot and H. C. G. Matthew, so far extending to eleven volumes and covering the years up to 1886. From 1868 onward, it contains a selection of Gladstone's correspondence as Prime Minister and his notes of cabinet meetings. Another useful tool will be *William Ewart Gladstone: A Bibliography,* edited by Nicholas Adams (Westport, Conn., forthcoming).

On the background to Gladstone's career, there are so many books that it is difficult to choose among them. Two general introductions are Eric Evans's *The Forging of the Modern State: Early Industrial Britain, 1783-1870* (London, 1983) and

Donald Read's *England, 1868-1914* (London, 1979). The economic development of Britain is clearly discussed in Peter Mathias's *The First Industrial Nation*, 2d ed. (London, 1983). An extremely intelligible analysis of social themes is to be found in Geoffrey Best's *Mid-Victorian Britain, 1851-1875*, 2d ed. (London, 1979). F. M. L. Thompson's *English Landed Society in the Nineteenth Century* (London, 1963) is an unsurpassed portrayal of its subject. There is more on the countryside in G. E. Mingay's *Rural Life in Victorian England* (London, 1977). Urban life is depicted by Asa Briggs in *Victorian Cities* (London, 1963) and, from a very different angle, by A. S. Wohl in *Endangered Lives: Public Health in Victorian Britain* (London, 1983). Keith Robbins considers the variations between England, Scotland, and Wales in *Nineteenth-Century Britain: England, Scotland and Wales — The Making of a Nation* (Oxford, 1988). For the Church of England, there is Owen Chadwick's masterly two-volume work *The Victorian Church* (London, 1966-1970), and for Nonconformity my introductory *Victorian Nonconformity* (Bangor, Gwynedd, 1992). There are helpful introductions to all aspects of the churches in *Religion in Victorian Britain*, 4 vols., edited by Gerald Parsons (Manchester, 1988).

2. GLADSTONE AND HIS UPBRINGING, 1809-1832

By far the most detailed study of Gladstone's family background is S. G. Checkland's *The Gladstones: A Family Biography* (London, 1971). Eton College figures prominently in John Chandos's *Boys Together: English Public Schools, 1800-1864* (London, 1984). Oxford is vividly depicted in V. H. H. Green's *History of Oxford University* (London, 1974). P. J. Jagger offers a detailed treatment of the evolution of Gladstone's spirituality in *Gladstone: The Making of a Christian Politician — The Personal Religious Life of William Ewart Gladstone, 1809-1832* (Allison Park, Pa., 1991). The tradition that formed Gladstone's early religious context is the subject of my *Evangelicalism in Modern Britain: A History from the 1730s to the 1980s* (London, 1989). And John Cannon provides an analysis of the circumstances leading to the political crisis of 1831-1832 in *Parliamentary Reform, 1640-1832* (Cambridge, 1973).

3. GLADSTONE AND THOUGHT, 1832-1841

The political context of the 1830s is illuminated in several books of high quality: two volumes by Norman Gash, *Politics in the Age of Peel* (London, 1953) and *Reaction and Reconstruction in English Politics, 1832-1852* (Oxford, 1965); G. I. T. Machin's *Politics and the Churches in Great Britain, 1832 to 1868* (Oxford, 1977); Richard Brent's *Liberal Anglican Politics: Whiggery, Religion and Reform, 1830-1841* (Oxford, 1987); B. I. Coleman's *Conservatism and the Conservative Party in Nineteenth-Century Britain* (London, 1988); and Ian Newbould's *Whiggery and Reform, 1830-41* (Basingstoke, 1990). Further analysis of the Whig political theory that Gladstone was challenging can be found in *That Noble Science of Politics*, by Stefan Collini et al. (Cambridge, 1983). E. R. Norman discusses currents of Anglican social thinking in *Church and Society in England, 1770-1970* (Oxford, 1976).

Gladstone's first book, *The State in Its Relations with the Church*, first appeared in 1838 but is most widely available in its fourth edition, published in two volumes in 1841. T. B. Macaulay's critique in *The Edinburgh Review* was reissued in his *Critical and Historical Essays* (London, 1850). The book is sympathetically considered by A. R. Vidler in *The Orb and the Cross: A Normative Study in the Relations of Church and State, with Reference to Gladstone's Early Writings* (London, 1945). R. J. Helmstadter provides an instructive analysis of the book in "Conscience and Politics: Gladstone's First Book," in *The Gladstonian Turn of Mind*, edited by B. L. Kinzer (Toronto, 1985). Gladstone's second book was *Church Principles Considered in Their Results* (London, 1840). Perry Butler offers a study of his religious evolution in *Gladstone: Church, State and Tractarianism* (Oxford, 1982). The thought of the Tractarians is expounded by Owen Chadwick in *The Spirit of the Oxford Movement* (Cambridge, 1990).

4. GLADSTONE AND CRISIS, 1841-1851

Worthy of note is the second volume of the standard biography of Robert Peel by Norman Gash, *Sir Robert Peel: The Life of Sir Robert Peel after 1830* (London, 1972). Its picture of a sober pragmatist is challenged by Boyd Hilton in "Peel: A Reappraisal," *Historical Journal* 22 (1979). In "Gladstone's Theological Politics," in *High and Low Politics in Modern Britain*, edited by Michael Bentley and John Stevenson (Oxford, 1983) and in *The Age of Atonement: The Influence of Evangelicalism on Social and Economic Thought, 1785-1865* (Oxford, 1988), Hilton argues that Peel transmitted to Gladstone a legacy of ideology and moral energy. For insights into the political crisis provoked by the Corn Laws controversy, see Norman McCord's *The Anti-Corn Law League, 1838-46* (London, 1958), Betty Kemp's "Reflections on the Repeal of the Corn Laws," *Victorian Studies* 5 (1962), and Donald Read's *Cobden and Bright: A Victorian Political Partnership* (London, 1967). The most useful studies of the Chartists are Asa Briggs's *Chartist Studies* (London, 1959) and Dorothy Thompson's *The Chartists* (London, 1984). D. A. Kerr treats the Irish question during this period in *Peel, Priests and Politics: Sir Robert Peel's Administration and the Roman Catholic Church in Ireland, 1841-1846* (Oxford, 1982). The two sections of the Conservative Party after 1846 are discussed in Robert Stewart's *The Politics of Protection: Lord Derby and the Protectionist Party, 1841-1852* (London, 1971) and in J. B. Conacher's *The Peelites and the Party System, 1846-52* (Newton Abbot, 1972).

Regarding Gladstone himself during this period, Matthew's biography carries unique authority. F. E. Hyde's *Mr Gladstone at the Board of Trade* (London, 1934), though old, is a helpful study of the young politician learning his craft. The Trinity College, Glenalmond, project is covered in Robert Ornsby's two-volume *Memoirs of James Robert Hope-Scott* (London, 1884). The household sermons compose three volumes of the Gladstone Papers at the British Library. For works about Gladstone's family life, see the references in section 7.

5. GLADSTONE AND REFORM, 1852-1868

H. C. G. Matthew provides a firm basis for understanding Gladstone's financial policies in "Disraeli, Gladstone and the Politics of Mid-Victorian Budgets," *Historical Journal* 22 (1979). A different perspective, minimizing the policy differences between Gladstone and Disraeli, is offered by P. R. Ghosh in "Disraelian Conservatism: A Financial Approach," *English Historical Review* 99 (1984). An older work, F. W. Hirst's *Gladstone as Financier and Economist* (London, 1931), gives a straightforward account of the fiscal policies. Gladstone set out his own financial principles in his budget speech of 1853, which is reprinted in *English Historical Documents, 1833-1874,* edited by G. M. Young and W. D. Handcock (London, 1956). A. B. Hawkins stresses Gladstone's frustrations at being excluded from office in "A Forgotten Crisis: Gladstone and the Politics of Finance during the 1850s," *Victorian Studies* 26 (1983) and in his book *Parliament, Party and the Art of Politics in Britain, 1855-59* (London, 1987). The Christian worldview encompassing Gladstonian finance is examined in Hilton's article listed in the previous section. Gladstone's reform of the civil service is treated by Henry Roseveare in *The Treasury* (London, 1969) and by M. G. Wright in *Treasury Control of the Civil Service, 1854-1874* (Oxford, 1969). W. R. Ward discusses Gladstone's Oxford reforms in *Victorian Oxford* (London, 1965).

The standard authority on parliamentary reform in the period is F. B. Smith, *The Making of the Second Reform Bill* (Cambridge, 1966). Gladstone's classic speech of 1864 in favor of reform is reprinted in *English Historical Documents, 1833-1874,* edited by G. M. Young and W. D. Handcock (London, 1956). J. R. Vincent provides a brilliant study of how the party coalesced as a reforming body around Gladstone in *The Formation of the Liberal Party* (London, 1966), but he exaggerates the statesman's willingness to maneuver for the sake of ambition. A much more pedestrian account of the same process is given in W. E. Williams's older work *The Rise of Gladstone to the Leader-*

ship of the Liberal Party, 1859-1868 (Cambridge, 1934). The nature of popular Liberalism is now perceptively analyzed by E. F. Biagini in *Liberty, Retrenchment and Reform: Popular Liberalism in the Age of Gladstone, 1860-1880* (Cambridge, 1992). Gladstone's great rival is well served in Lord Blake's *Disraeli* (London, 1966). Analyses of Gladstone's relationships with two other leading politicians can be found in John Prest's "Gladstone and Russell," *Transactions of the Royal Historical Society,* 5th series, 16 (1966) and E. D. Steele's "Gladstone and Palmerston, 1855-65," in *Gladstone, Politics and Religion,* edited by P. J. Jagger (London, 1985). In *Palmerston and Liberalism, 1855-1865* (Cambridge, 1991), E. D. Steele argues persuasively that Palmerston was a major influence over Gladstone's political evolution, especially by setting him an example of public speaking before popular audiences. Gladstone's relationship with the Nonconformists is examined in G. I. T. Machin's "Gladstone and Nonconformity in the 1860s: The Formation of an Alliance," *Historical Journal* 17 (1974) and Olive Anderson's "Gladstone's Abolition of Church Rates: A Minor Political Myth and Its Historiographical Career," *Journal of Ecclesiastical History* 25 (1974).

6. GLADSTONE AND OVERSEAS RELATIONS, 1835-1868

For background information on British imperial policy, see Bernard Porter's *The Lion's Share: A Short History of British Imperialism, 1850-1870* (London, 1975); C. C. Eldridge's *Victorian Imperialism* (London, 1978); and the essays in *British Imperialism in the Nineteenth Century,* edited by C. C. Eldridge (London, 1984). Paul Knaplund's *Gladstone and Britain's Imperial Policy* (London, 1927) has been justly criticized for concentrating too exclusively on Gladstone's wish to encourage existing colonies toward independence. See also A. G. L. Shaw's study entitled *Gladstone at the Colonial Office* (London, 1986). Bruce Knox discusses the Ionian Islands question in "British Policy and the

Ionian Islands, 1847-1864: Nationalism and Imperial Administration," *English Historical Review* 99 (1984).

For background on foreign policy, consult Kenneth Bourne's *The Foreign Policy of Victorian England, 1830-1901* (Oxford, 1970), and M. E. Chamberlain's *Pax Britannica? British Foreign Policy, 1789-1914* (London, 1988). M. E. Chamberlain has also written *Lord Aberdeen: A Political Biography* (London, 1983), a detailed study of Gladstone's mentor in the field. J. B. Conacher deals authoritatively with the politics of the Crimean War in *The Aberdeen Coalition, 1852-1855* (Cambridge, 1968). *Gladstone's Foreign Policy* (London, 1935), by Paul Knaplund, is a good book but inevitably shows its age. J. L. Hammond expounds Gladstone's vision of the concert of Europe in terms of interwar collective security in "Gladstone and the League of Nations Mind," in *Essays in Honour of Gilbert Murray*, edited by J. A. K. Thomson and A. J. Toynbee (London, 1936). Carsten Holbraad's *The Concert of Europe: A Study in German and British International Theory, 1815-1914* (London, 1970) is more thorough and more reliable. K. A. P. Sandiford's essay "Gladstone and Europe," in *The Gladstonian Turn of Mind*, edited by B. L. Kinzer (Toronto, 1985), provides a useful survey of Gladstone's attitudes toward the various powers. A. A. Iliasu examines a significant episode in "The Cobden-Chevalier Commercial Treaty of 1860," *Historical Journal* 14 (1971). For consideration of the turning point in British attitudes to Italian unification, see D. E. D. Beales's *England and Italy, 1859-1860* (London, 1961) and C. T. McIntire's *England against the Papacy, 1858-1861* (Cambridge, 1983). In "Gladstone and Italian Unification: The Making of a Liberal?" *English Historical Review* 85 (1970), D. M. Schreuder deals with the issue in relation to Gladstone over a longer period.

7. GLADSTONE AND PRIVATE LIFE, 1832-1898

W. E. Houghton describes the cultural atmosphere of the Gladstonian era in *The Victorian Frame of Mind, 1830-1870* (New

Haven, Conn., 1957). Other illuminating studies can be found in Richard Jenkyns's *The Victorians and Ancient Greece* (Oxford, 1980) and F. M. Turner's *The Greek Heritage in Victorian Britain* (New Haven, Conn., 1981). Sir Hugh Lloyd-Jones evaluates Gladstone's Homeric scholarship in "Gladstone and Homer," in *Blood for the Ghosts* (London, 1982). Gladstone's books on Homer were his three-volume *Studies on Homer and the Homeric Age* (Oxford, 1858); the summary work *Juventus Mundi: The Gods and Men of the Heroic Age* (London, 1869); the more special-ized work entitled *Homeric Synchronism: Enquiry into the Time and Place of Homer* (London, 1876); a primer called simply *Homer* (London, 1878); and a work of his old age entitled *Landmarks of Homeric Study* (London, 1890). A key to his approach can be found in a lecture entitled "On the Place of Ancient Greece in the Providential Order of the World," which is reprinted in *Rectorial Addresses delivered before the University of Edinburgh, 1859-1899,* edited by Archibald Stoddart-Walker (London, 1900), as well as in volume 7 of Gladstone's *Gleanings of Past Years, 1843-1879* (London, 1879). Gladstone's reverence for Dante is explained by Owen Chadwick in "Young Gladstone and Italy," *Journal of Ecclesiastical History* 30 (1979), which has been reprinted in *Gladstone, Politics and Religion,* edited by P. J. Jagger (London, 1985). There is an article by Barbara Reynolds entitled "W. E. Gladstone and Alessandro Manzoni" in *Italian Studies* 6 (1951). Marcia Pointon has contributed a comprehen-sive essay entitled "Gladstone as Art Patron and Collector" to *Victorian Studies* 19 (1975). On Gladstone's library, there are his daughter Mary Drew's essay "Mr Gladstone's Books" in her *Acton, Gladstone and Others* (London, 1924) and F. W. Ratcliffe's essay "Mr Gladstone, the Librarian, and St Deiniol's Library, Hawarden," in P. J. Jagger's collection *Gladstone, Politics and Religion.*

Mary Drew also wrote the first biography of her mother, *Catherine Gladstone* (London, 1930). It has been supplemented by Georgina Battiscombe's *Mrs Gladstone: The Portrait of a Marriage* (London, 1956) and Joyce Marlow's *The Oak and the*

Ivy: An Intimate Biography of William and Catherine Gladstone (New York, 1977). Penelope Gladstone, a descendant of the statesman, has written *Portrait of a Family: The Gladstones, 1839-1889* (Ormskirk, Lancashire, 1989). And see Pat Jalland's essay "Mr Gladstone's Daughters" in *The Gladstonian Turn of Mind,* edited by B. L. Kinzer (Toronto, 1985). Part of Mary Drew's correspondence has been published in the following volumes: *Letters of Lord Acton to Mary, Daughter of the Right Hon. W. E. Gladstone,* edited by Herbert Paul (London, 1904); *Some Hawarden Letters, 1878-1913,* edited by Lisle March-Phillipps and Bertram Christian (London, 1917); *A Forty-Year Friendship: Letters from the Late Henry Scott Holland to Mrs Drew,* edited by S. L. Ollard (London, 1919); and *Mary Gladstone (Mrs Drew): Her Diaries and Letters,* edited by Lucy Masterman (London, 1930). There have been biographies of two of Gladstone's sons — Henry by Ivor Thomas (*Gladstone of Hawarden* [London, 1936]) and Herbert by Sir Charles Mallet (*Herbert Gladstone: A Memoir* [London, 1932]). Herbert, by then Viscount Gladstone, also offered a vindication of his father's memory in *After Thirty Years* (London, 1928). Gladstone's embroiled relationship with his sister Helen is brought out by Colin Matthew in the introduction to volume 9 of *The Gladstone Diaries.*

Colin Matthew also provides the best discussion of the statesman's concern for rescuing prostitutes in *Gladstone, 1809-1874* (London, 1986). This theme is the subject of Richard Deacon's *The Private Life of Mr Gladstone* (London, 1965). Gladstone's quixotic quest for Lady Lincoln is recounted by F. D. Munsell in *The Unfortunate Duke: Henry Pelham, Fifth Duke of Newcastle* (Columbia, Mo., 1985) and by C. C. Eldridge in "The Lincoln Divorce Case: A Study in Victorian Morality," *Trivium* 2 (1967). The most significant correspondence with Laura Thistlethwayte is printed as an appendix to volume 8 of *The Gladstone Diaries.* There is an account of Gladstone's attitude toward women's rights in A. P. Robson's "A Bird's Eye View of Gladstone," in *The Gladstonian Turn of Mind,* edited by B. L. Kinzer.

8. GLADSTONE AND GOVERNMENT, 1868-1874

Volumes 7 and 8 of *The Gladstone Diaries* contain the most useful published material concerning the first administration. In "Gladstone and His First Ministry," *Historical Journal* 26 (1983), Derek Beales makes some useful correctives to Colin Matthew's introduction to these diaries, pointing out in particular that Gladstone was adopting a proactive stance. J. P. Parry offers the fullest analysis of divergent attitudes among government supporters in "Religion and the Collapse of Gladstone's First Government, 1870-74," *Historical Journal* 25 (1982) and in *Democracy and Religion: Gladstone and the Liberal Party, 1867-1875* (Cambridge, 1986). Agatha Ramm has stressed the overloading of the government's legislative program in "The Parliamentary Context of Cabinet Government, 1868-1874," *English Historical Review* 99 (1984). Her edition of the Gladstone-Granville correspondence (see section 1) is a major primary source for this administration, as is *A Journal of Events during the Gladstone Ministry, 1868-1874*, edited by Ethel Drus, Camden Miscellany 21 (London, 1958), an edition of Lord Kimberley's political diary.

Gladstone's own *Chapter of Autobiography* (London, 1868) recounts his movement toward Irish disestablishment. That measure is discussed by P. M. H. Bell in *Disestablishment in Ireland and Wales* (London, 1969), by D. H. Akenson in *The Church of Ireland: Ecclesiastical Reform and Revolution, 1800-85* (New Haven, Conn., 1971), and by G. I. T. Machin in *Politics and the Churches in Great Britain, 1869 to 1921* (Oxford, 1987). The Irish Land Act is covered in E. D. Steele's authoritative *Irish Land and British Politics: Tenant Right and Nationality, 1865-1870* (Cambridge, 1974). Steele takes a broader view in "Gladstone and Ireland," *Irish Historical Studies* 17 (1970). J. S. Hurt sets the education issue in a larger context in *Elementary Schooling and the Working Classes, 1860-1918* (London, 1979). D. W. R. Bahlman discusses ecclesiastical appointments in "The Queen, Mr Gladstone and Church Patronage," *Victorian Studies* 3 (1960). On the ballot question, see B. L. Kinzer's "The Un-

Englishness of the Secret Ballot," *Albion* 10 (1978); on the licensing issue, see Brian Harrison, *Drink and the Victorians: The Temperance Question in England, 1815-1872* (London, 1971); and on Irish universities, see T. W. Moody, "The Irish University Question in the Nineteenth Century," *History* 43 (1958).

9. GLADSTONE AND NATIONALITY, 1868-1898

Many of the general works on overseas relations listed in section 6 are also instructive with respect to the later period. The broad context is analyzed by P. M. Kennedy in *The Rise of the Anglo-German Antagonism, 1860-1914* (London, 1980) and in *The Realities behind Diplomacy* (London, 1981). C. J. Lowe provides further detail in his two-volume work *The Reluctant Imperialists: British Foreign Policy, 1878-1902* (London, 1967). There is much relating to foreign policy in the Gladstone-Granville correspondence (see section 1). The editor of the two-volume collection of correspondence, Agatha Ramm, gives an estimate of Granville in *British Foreign Secretaries and Foreign Policy,* edited by K. M. Wilson (London, 1987). Gordon Martel deals with overseas relations during the third and fourth administrations in *Imperial Diplomacy: Rosebery and the Failure of Foreign Policy* (Kingston, Ont., 1986). A. J. P. Taylor includes a chapter on Gladstonian foreign policy in *The Trouble Makers* (London, 1957). D. M. Schreuder assesses Taylor's thesis in "Gladstone as 'Trouble Maker': Liberal Foreign Policy and the German Annexation of Alsace-Lorraine, 1870-1871," *Journal of British Studies* 17 (1978). Schreuder's *Gladstone and Kruger: Liberal Government and Colonial "Home Rule," 1880-85* (London, 1969) is a thorough case study of dealings with the Boer republics in southern Africa. The foreign policy of the second administration is carefully dissected in the introduction to volume 10 of *The Gladstone Diaries.*

The classic study of Gladstone's response to the Eastern Question is R. T. Shannon's *Gladstone and the Bulgarian Agitation, 1876* (London, 1963). H. C. G. Matthew reveals fresh dimensions in "Gladstone, Vaticanism and the Question of the East," in *Religious Motivation: Biographical and Sociological Problems for the Church Historian*, edited by Derek Baker, Studies in Church History, vol. 15 (Oxford, 1978). Gladstone's own statement of the principles of foreign policy is contained in *Political Speeches in Scotland, November and December 1879* (London, 1879), reprinted as *Midlothian Speeches, 1879* (Leicester, 1971). They are discussed by Robert Kelley in "Midlothian: A Study in Politics and Ideas," *Victorian Studies* 4 (1960), and by R. T. Shannon in "Midlothian: One Hundred Years After," in *Gladstone, Politics and Religion*, edited by P. J. Jagger (London, 1985).

10. GLADSTONE AND PARTY, 1874-1894

H. J. Hanham presents an authoritative analysis of the political system in the wake of the 1867 Reform Act in *Elections and Party Management: Politics in the Time of Gladstone and Disraeli* (London, 1959). D. A. Hamer lays bare the divisions of the party and Gladstone's remedies in *Liberal Politics in the Age of Gladstone and Rosebery* (Oxford, 1972). His thesis is modified by T. A. Jenkins, who stresses the continuing vitality of the Whigs in "Gladstone, the Whigs and the Leadership of the Liberal Party, 1879-1880," *Historical Journal* 27 (1984) and in *Gladstone, Whiggery and the Liberal Party, 1874-1886* (Oxford, 1988). W. C. Lubenow argues for a greater degree of shared ideology within Liberalism in *Parliamentary Politics and the Home Rule Crisis: The British House of Commons in 1886* (Oxford, 1988). For studies of the leading Radical in the party, see Peter Fraser's *Joseph Chamberlain: Radicalism and Empire, 1868-1914* (London, 1966) and Richard Jay's *Joseph Chamberlain: A Political Study* (Oxford, 1981). For a consideration of the Nonconformists, see my essay "Gladstone and the Nonconformists: A Religious Affinity in Politics," in *Church, Society and Politics*, edited by Derek Baker, Studies in Church History, vol. 12 (Oxford, 1975) and my book *The Nonconformist Conscience: Chapel and Politics, 1870-1914*

(London, 1982). Wales and Scotland are dealt with, respectively, in K. O. Morgan's *Wales in British Politics, 1868-1922*, 3d ed. (Cardiff, 1980) and I. G. C. Hutchison's *A Political History of Scotland, 1832-1922* (Edinburgh, 1986). The labor section of Liberalism and its issues are the subjects of Royden Harrison's *Before the Socialists: Studies in Labour and Politics, 1861-1881* (London, 1965), Michael Barker's *Gladstone and Radicalism: The Reconstruction of Liberal Policy in Britain, 1885-94* (Hassocks, Sussex, 1975), and David Powell's "The Liberal Ministries and Labour, 1892-1985," *History* 68 (1983). The genuine popularity of Gladstonian Liberalism with the ordinary people is underscored by a number of essays in *Currents of Radicalism: Popular Radicalism, Organised Labour and Party Politics in Britain, 1850-1914*, edited by E. F. Biagini and A. J. Reid (Cambridge, 1991).

Two major domestic issues of the second administration are examined by W. L. Arnstein in *The Bradlaugh Case*, 2d ed. (Columbia, Mo., 1983) and by Andrew Jones in *The Politics of Reform, 1884* (Cambridge, 1972). The ministry is thoroughly covered in the introduction to volume 10 of *The Gladstone Diaries*, which, with volume 11, contains much primary material. Apart from the Gladstone-Granville correspondence (see section 1), there is a fine source for the second administration in the two-volume *Diary of Sir Edward Walter Hamilton, 1880-85*, edited by D. W. R. Bahlman (Oxford, 1972). The third administration is recorded in detail, though from a highly distinctive viewpoint, by A. B. Cooke and J. R. Vincent in *The Governing Passion: Cabinet Government and Party Politics in Britain, 1885-86* (Brighton, 1974): Gladstone is represented as a power-seeking opportunist. Concerning the fourth administration, the best study remains unpublished: D. R. Brooks's "Gladstone's Fourth Ministry, 1892-94: Policies and Personalities" (Ph.D. thesis, University of Cambridge, 1975). The final issue of Gladstone's premiership is examined by Sue Brown in "One Last Campaign from the G.O.M.: Gladstone and the House of Lords in 1894," in *The Gladstonian Turn of Mind*, edited by B. L. Kinzer (Toronto, 1985). H. C. G. Matthew offers a study of Gladstone's oratory in "Rhetoric and Politics in Great Britain, 1860-1950," in *Politics and Social Change in Modern Britain: Essays Presented to A. F. Thompson*, edited by P. J. Waller (Brighton, 1987). The statesman's late political views emerge in L. A. Tollemache's *Talks with Mr Gladstone* (London, 1898), which has been reprinted as *Gladstone's Boswell: Late Victorian Conversations*, edited by Asa Briggs (Brighton, 1984). Christopher Harvie points out some less familiar contours of his thought in "Gladstonianism, Provincialism and Popular Culture, 1860-1906," in *Victorian Liberalism: Nineteenth-Century Political Thought and Practice*, edited by Richard Bellamy (London, 1990).

11. GLADSTONE AND IRISH POLICY, 1880-1894

The Irish question has recently elicited some penetrating literature, including F. S. L. Lyons's *Ireland since the Famine* (London, 1971), Paul Bew's *Land and the National Question in Ireland, 1858-1882* (Dublin, 1978), and K. T. Hoppen's *Elections, Politics and Society in Ireland, 1832-1885* (Oxford, 1984). J. L. Hammond is too uncritical of Gladstone in *Gladstone and the Irish Nation* (London, 1938), but John Vincent recoils from Hammond to a hypercritical stance in "Gladstone and Ireland," *Proceedings of the British Academy* 63 (1977). In *Gladstone, Home Rule and the Ulster Question, 1882-93* (Dublin, 1986), James Loughlin points to some of the weaknesses in Gladstone's assessment of the Irish situation. Allen Warren provides the most convincing account of the evolution of his policies in "Gladstone, Land and Social Reconstruction in Ireland, 1881-87," *Parliamentary History* 2 (1983), edited by Eveline Cruickshanks, and in "W. E. Forster, the Liberals and New Directions in Irish Policy, 1880-82," *Parliamentary History* 6 (1987). Colin Matthew casts fresh light on the evolution of Home Rule in his introduction to volume 10 of *The Gladstone Diaries*. Gladstone's speech on the introduction of the first Home Rule Bill in 1886 is reprinted in *English Historical Documents, 1874-1914*, edited by W. D. Handcock (London,

1977). The subsequent campaign for Home Rule is examined by D. A. Hamer in "The Irish Question and Liberal Politics, 1886-1894," *Historical Journal* 12 (1969).

12. GLADSTONE AND VICTORIAN CHRISTIANITY

Gladstone's broadening religious sympathies are brought out in Colin Matthew's introduction to volume 9 of *The Gladstone Diaries*. His theological work is summarized in an essay by Malcolm MacColl in *The Life of William Ewart Gladstone*, edited by Sir Wemyss Reid (London, 1899). For discussions of the controversy surrounding the Public Worship Regulation Act, see P. T. Marsh's "The Primate and the Prime Minister: Archbishop Tait, Gladstone and the National Church," *Victorian Studies* 9 (1965) and James Bentley's *Ritualism and Politics in Victorian Britain* (Oxford, 1978). On the Vaticanism controversy, see J. L. Altholz's "The Vatican Decrees Controversy, 1874-1875," *Catholic Historical Review* 57 (1971-72) and Damian McElrath's *The Syllabus of Pius IX: Some Reactions in England*, Bibliothèque de la Revue d'Histoire Ecclésiastique Fasc. 39 (Louvain, 1964). Several essays in the second volume of *Religion in Victorian Britain*, edited by Gerald Parsons (Manchester, 1988) introduce aspects of the Victorian crisis of faith. A. W. Brown's *The Metaphysical Society* (New York, 1947) is a useful study. Gladstone's intellectual reliance on Lord Acton in his last years is brought out by Owen Chadwick in *Acton and Gladstone*, Creighton Lecture in History, 1975 (London, 1976). A significant article by Gladstone not reprinted in his *Later Gleanings* (London, 1898) is "Universitas Hominum; or, The Unity of History," *North American Review* 145 (1887). Gladstone's apologetic for the Bible is contained in *The Impregnable Rock of Holy Scripture* (London, 1890). His work in this area culminated in his edition of *The Works of Joseph Butler, D.C.L.*, 2 vols. (Oxford, 1897) and his *Studies Subsidiary to the Works of Bishop Butler* (Oxford, 1896).

The starting point for the study of Gladstone's personality is John Morley's chapter "Characteristics," in book 2 of the first volume of his *Life of William Ewart Gladstone* (London, 1903). Brief memoirs by members of his close circle are illuminating, including three by private secretaries: Sir Edward W. Hamilton's *Mr Gladstone: A Monograph* (London, 1898), *Reminiscences of Lord Kilbracken, G.C.B.* (London, 1931), and Sir George Leveson Gower's *Some Memories of Gladstone* (N.p., 1938). Two works by Nonconformist journalists reveal as much about Gladstone's popular image as about the man himself: J. E. Ritchie's *The Real Gladstone: An Anecdotal Biography* (London, 1898) and W. T. Stead's *Gladstone, 1809-1898: A Character Sketch* (London, [1898]). Even more reverent are [Hulda Friedrichs's], *In the Evening of his Days: A Study of Mr Gladstone in Retirement, with Some Account of St Deiniol's Library and Hostel* (London, 1896) and *The Passing of Gladstone: His Life, Death, and Burial* (London, 1898). The verse in chapter 12 is taken from *Poetical Tributes to the Memory of the Rt Hon. W. E. Gladstone,* edited by Samuel Jacob and C. F. Forshaw (London, 1898). The abiding impression made by the statesman is illustrated by an extraordinary book designed to raise morale during the Second World War — Peter Esslemont's *To the Fifth Generation: A Hundred Minutes with Gladstone* (Aberdeen, 1941).

Index

INDEX